Basic Camera Directions

- **Angle on:** This shot suggests another view of a previous shot.

- **Close-up:** A *close-up* is a shot that emphasizes a detail in a scene. It's often abbreviated to CU.

- **Continuation:** When a scene or a speech is interrupted by a page break, type MORE in parentheses at the end of the last line on the first page, and then type CONT'D after the character's name on the next page.

- **Cut to:** This term was used to cut quickly between scenes, but it's rarely used anymore. It appears at the bottom of a scene, to the right-hand side.

- **Dissolve to:** This direction is used in place of the CUT TO when you want to suggest a slow transition from one scene to the next. You may dissolve to suggest the passage of time between one shot and another, or because you want the effect of one image fading into the next.

- **Fade in:** Every screenplay begins with these words. They suggest the movement from darkness to an image on the screen. They're typed in all caps at the left-hand margin followed by a double space and the first slug line.

- **Fade out:** These words end a screenplay. They're typed to the right-hand margin and followed by six spaces and the words THE END typed in the center of the page.

- **Insert:** A writer uses this direction when he or she wants to highlight an object in the scene or include a detail that's outside the scene but important to it. To complete an insert, do one of three things: Return to the dialogue, switch locations with a new slug line, or type BACK TO SCENE at the end.

- **Intercut:** This direction indicates that two scenes are occurring simultaneously in separate locations. This term appears in all caps as the slug line or in the description.

- **Montage:** A *montage* is the dissolving of two or more shots into each other to create a desired effect, usually an association of ideas. These shots need not include the main character, and they don't have a beginning, middle, and end.

- **O.S.:** Shorthand for off-screen, this abbreviation is used when a character speaks outside the camera's view, or when the audience hears a sound but doesn't see where it's coming from.

- **POV:** Shorthand for *point of view,* this direction implies that the scene is being viewed from another character's perspective. You must identify whose point of view it is and what exactly he sees. If the POV alternates within a scene, employ the term REVERSE POV.

- **Series of shots:** This technique serves as a way to abridge action sequences into a number of short moments involving the main character, usually without dialogue. A series of shots has a distinct beginning, middle and end, and is often used to dramatize a passage of time.

- **Split screen:** This shot indicates two subjects in different locations on-screen simultaneously. The split scene shot conveys a distinct film style and is rarely used.

- **Super:** Shorthand for *superimpose,* this term is used if another element is being superimposed over the action of a scene. A super is often used to show dates, locations, or translation texts.

- **V.O.:** V.O. is shorthand for voice-over. This direction is used when the audience hears a character speak who's not in the scene. It's often used to underscore a scene with narration.

Screenwriting For Dummies®

Conquering Writer's Block

Here are a few things that you may want to try when writer's block strikes:

- **Do something else.** Sometimes, you just need a break from the computer or from your notebook, even if it's just for a hour. Trick your mind into thinking that you just don't care about that script. Answers often arrive when you least expect them.

- **Switch projects.** Doing so keeps your mind off the creative impasse and keeps you writing at the same time. Also, what you learn on one project may clarify a problem in another.

- **Outline the script.** You probably outlined your script before you began writing, but it never hurts to do it again. Outline what you've already written first, and then move on to what you intend to include later. If your story has changed, the outline will show you how. Tracing the steps leading to the block may lead to the next scene.

- **Read, read, read.** Other artists provide technique, dramatic examples, and inspiration. You needn't limit yourself to screenplays; read literature, poetry, and non-fiction, too. Read newspapers or old letters. Read anything that ropes you into a world other than your own or the one that you're creating.

- **Return to research.** Visit museums, collect photographs, listen to music, eavesdrop on conversations, and record what you hear. You've written part of the story, so your imagination knows what to look for now. You may discover details that you missed the first time around.

- **Try alternate forms of writing.** By "alternate," I mean try writing something other than a screenplay. Write a letter, send an email, start a diary, or give yourself an assignment and write for an hour. Like switching projects, this strategy also redirects your concentration while keeping your imagination alert.

- **Sleep on it.** If you've been tackling a block for a while, you're probably tense and exhausted. Go to bed. Your mind still works while your body sleeps. You'll definitely wake up refreshed. You may even wake up with an answer.

A Character Checklist

The following checklist can help clarify and enhance your characters as you write. Does your character have . . .

- A very distinct and detailed physical form?
- A job or way to earn a living?
- A place to return to at the end of the day?
- A safe place to relax?
- Locations they love, loathe, and fear?
- Concrete, positive goals?
- Opinions, beliefs, and world views?
- Friends and/or confidants?
- A strong external antagonist?
- Equally strong internal obstacles?
- Talents and the opportunity to express them?
- Unique and age-old routines?

For Dummies: Bestselling Book Series for Beginners

Screenwriting
FOR
DUMMIES®

Screenwriting FOR DUMMIES®

by Laura Schellhardt

Foreword by John Logan

WILEY

Wiley Publishing, Inc.

Screenwriting For Dummies®

Published by
Wiley Publishing, Inc.
909 Third Avenue
New York, NY 10022
www.wiley.com

Copyright © 2003 by Wiley Publishing, Inc., Indianapolis, Indiana

Published by Wiley Publishing, Inc., Indianapolis, Indiana

Published simultaneously in Canada

For general information on our other products and services or to obtain technical support, please contact our Customer Care Department within the U.S. at 800-762-2974, outside the U.S. at 317-572-3993, or fax 317-572-4002.

Wiley also publishes its books in a variety of electronic formats. Some content that appears in print may not be available in electronic books.

Library of Congress Cataloging-in-Publication Data:

Library of Congress Control Number: 2002114819

1B/RW/QR/QT/IN

ISBN: 0-7645-5486-7

Manufactured in the United States of America

10 9 8 7 6 5

About the Author

Laura Schellhardt is an Adjunct Professor at Northwestern University in Chicago where she is head of the Playwriting Program. She has assisted in the development of new works at both the Goodman and Steppenwolf Theatre, two of the nation's premiere performance spaces. While at the Goodman, Ms. Schellhardt worked with renowned writer/actress Regina Taylor in crafting the world premiere of "Oo-Bla-Dee." Her play "Electra Rising" won the Agnes Nixon Playwriting Festival in 1996. Since that time, she has overseen the adjudication and direction of the festival itself. Ms. Schellhardt holds degrees in screenwriting, playwriting, and poetry. She has studied writing with the likes of Maria Irene Fornes and has taught with Oscar nominated John Logan of *Gladiator* and *Time Machine* fame. She is currently working along side Paula Vogel and Oskar Eustis at Trinity Repertory Theatre in Providence, Rhode Island and teaching workshops across the country.

Dedication

To John Logan — for a beginning

Author's Acknowledgments

The author would like to acknowledge . . .

The fearless Schellhardt crew: Mary Kate, Eliza, and Stephen — for your love, your example, and your laughter.

Mom — for your much exploited editorial services, for your support, silent and otherwise, and for your guidance

Dad — for your much exploited advice, for your support, postmarked and otherwise, and for your guidance

Laura Bancroft Powell — for your stories and your name

The rest of my family — you know who you are

Natasha Graf — for your friendship and for the opportunity

Tim Gallan — for your patience and efforts

The extended support committee for the inspiration and the will —
John Logan, Mary Poole,

Lynn Baber, Paula Vogel, Joseph Epstein, Sharon Lanza, Jon Hoenig, Ross Martens, Sally Oswald, Emily O'Dell, Jordan Harrison, Deborah Stein, Quiara Hudes, Mr. Meyers, Patricia Palermo,

Anna Marie Baskin & Uncle Mark

And to Jonathan Becker — for all of the above and for getting me through it

Publisher's Acknowledgments

We're proud of this book; please send us your comments through our Dummies online registration form located at www.dummies.com/register/.

Some of the people who helped bring this book to market include the following:

Acquisitions, Editorial, and Media Development

Senior Project Editor: Tim Gallan

Acquisitions Editor: Natasha Graf

Copy Editor: Chrissy Guthrie

Acquisitions Coordinator: Holly Grimes

Technical Editor: Bryan Michael Stoller

Editorial Manager: Christine Meloy Beck

Editorial Assistant: Melissa Bennett

Cartoons: Rich Tennant, www.the5thwave.com

Production

Project Coordinatora: Kristie Rees, Dale White

Layout and Graphics: Carrie Foster, Stephanie D. Jumper, Tiffany Muth, Scott Tullis, Jeremey Unger

Proofreaders: John Greenough TECHBOOKS Production Services

Indexer: TECHBOOKS Production Services

Publishing and Editorial for Consumer Dummies

>   **Diane Graves Steele,** Vice President and Publisher, Consumer Dummies

>   **Joyce Pepple,** Acquisitions Director, Consumer Dummies

>   **Kristin A. Cocks,** Product Development Director, Consumer Dummies

>   **Michael Spring,** Vice President and Publisher, Travel

>   **Brice Gosnell,** Publishing Director, Travel

>   **Suzanne Jannetta,** Editorial Director, Travel

Publishing for Technology Dummies

>   **Andy Cummings,** Vice President and Publisher, Dummies Technology/General User

Composition Services

>   **Gerry Fahey,** Vice President of Production Services

>   **Debbie Stailey,** Director of Composition Services

Contents at a Glance

Table of Contents

Chapter 13: Surviving Writer's Block 181

Chapter 14: Formatting Your Screenplay 191

Chapter 15: Putting It Together: Structuring Your First Draft 213

Foreword

So, you want to write a movie. Where do you start?

My personal advice to aspiring screenwriters is always the same: If you want to write, read. Start with Shakespeare. He will teach you everything you need to know about drama. Read everything. Read slowly and carefully. Read aloud and open yourself to emotion. Hamlet and Falstaff and Iago and Cleopatra and Rosalind will teach you about dramatizing character and conflict. Shakespeare's glorious combination of prose and verse will teach you about language. *King Lear* teaches you tragedy. *As You Like It* teaches you comedy. *Antony and Cleopatra* and the *Henry IV* plays teach you both.

Then go back and read Aristotle's *Poetics*. Then you might treat yourself to Ibsen and Chekhov. If you're feeling really madcap you might then move on to Sophocles, Euripides, Shaw, Pinter, Beckett, and O'Neill.

And then read *Hamlet* again.

My point is you must be a *dramatist*, a theatrical storyteller, first and foremost. The structural concerns of the ideal three act movie structure or perfectly timed "inciting incident" must be entirely secondary to your passionate desire to tell the story honestly. Be an artist first, then a technician.

My dear friend Laura Schellhardt, the author of the book you are holding, offers some valuable advice on ways to approach writing a movie. She presents any number of provocative and clever ways to understand the screenwriting process. Used wisely, this book can help you hew your way through the very dark forest of screenplay construction.

I leave a final bit of advice from my frequent colleague, director Ridley Scott. After I delivered a particularly mammoth draft of *Gladiator,* Ridley turned to me with a wry smile and said, "John, write less words."

So, I guess that covers it. Read lots of words, and write less of them.

—John Logan

John Logan's film works includes *Gladiator, Any Given Sunday, Star Trek: Nemesis, The Time Machine, RKO 281,* and *The Last Samurai.*

Introduction

● ●

Screenwriting For Dummies? If this book wasn't part of the *For Dummies* series, I might've thought twice about writing it. After all, the last thing the world needs is another dumb screenplay. But rest assured that by "Dummies," I don't mean you. This book isn't for dummies — quite the opposite, in fact. Writing is challenging work. First of all, you have to decide who and what to write about. Second, you have to figure out how to expand your chosen characters and subject into a story — a 110-page story at that. To do that, you need some basic information and a newly organized daily routine. Finally, when you finish your script, you have to come up with a way to introduce it to Hollywood. To do that, you need some industry tips and marketing strategies. That's a lot of information.

So I repeat, this book isn't for dummies. This book is for writers — beginners, advanced, and anyone in between. This book is for both teachers and students — of cinema, of theatre, of life. This book is for film-lovers and filmgoers and for dreamers of all sorts. If you have an active imagination, curiosity, and a sense of adventure, welcome. This book just may be for you.

About This Book

To say that I enjoy writing would be an understatement. I *love* writing, and I *love* films, and I fervently believe that screenwriting is a craft worth pursuing. I also believe that it's a demanding craft with many facets to consider. Most screenwriting books cover one of those facets in detail — how to write a first draft, how to find an agent, how to sell your script to the industry, to name a few popular topics. There's nothing wrong with focusing on one portion of this complicated art form, but if you have the space, why not tackle it all? This book has the space. From finding an idea to spacing it on the page to marketing it in Hollywood — in this book, you can find out about the screen-writing process from A to Z (or Action to Zoom in film lingo).

Also, no two writers are alike in what they're after, and this book is designed with just that thought in mind. Read it cover to cover or jump around. Worried about writer's block? See Chapter 13. Want to protect your work? Flip to Chapter 18. Not sure where to begin? This book has two, count 'em *two,* tables of contents. The Contents at a Glance gives you a basic overall picture of what you can find in this book. Skim through it and see what ropes you in. Or simply close your eyes and point. When you find a topic that interests you, you can go straight to that chapter or use the detailed table of contents to get even more specifics of what to expect. Every chapter stands on its own, so take your pick and feel free to skip around at will.

Everything in this book is relevant. But some pieces of information are more essential than others. Once in a while, you may see a *Jargon Alert* icon or section of text that's shaded gray. A *Jargon Alert* icon suggests a definition for some film or writing term. I include these terms because you may run across them later in writing courses or seminars with industry professionals. Those gray boxes of text are sidebars. They're interesting pieces of information — true-life examples or historical anecdotes, usually — that provide examples of the subject at hand or a fun piece of trivia. Read through the *Jargon Alerts* and the sidebars if you're curious, but don't worry if you skip past them. Doing so won't hamper your understanding of the material. These paragraphs are supplemental, so just think of them as bonus bits of info.

Conventions Used in This Book

This book isn't heavy on special conventions. But it does have a few, and here they are:

- ✔ I reference a lot of films, plays, and television shows in this book, and to help you locate them in the text, the titles are in bold italics. For example, ***Gone with the Wind*** would look like this in the text.

- ✔ In this book, I also reference several novels because screenwriters often adapt novels for the screen. These titles appear in regular italics; for example, *The Cider House Rules*

- ✔ Short stories and poems appear in quotes; for example, "The Lottery."

- ✔ Web sites and e-mail addresses appear in `monofont`.

- ✔ Important words to know also appear in *italics*.

Foolish Assumptions

You know what they say about assuming, but sometimes, it just has to be done. Although this book is for a wide variety of people, I did assume the following about you when writing it:

- ✔ You enjoy writing or think that you might.

- ✔ You've written a script before or are looking to start one.

- ✔ You've been to at least one movie and enjoyed yourself.

- ✔ You believe that good stories can change the world.

How This Book Is Organized

Screenwriting is an art, a craft, and a business. Each aspect contains a lot of information. For your convenience and sanity, I've divided this book into five parts, each dedicated to one facet (there's that word again) of the process.

Part 1: So You Want to Write for Pictures

In this section, I introduce you to . . . well, to yourself — to your screenwriting self, that is. Artists sense the world in a slightly different way than people in other professions do, and screenwriters are no exception. These chapters focus on developing a writer's "eye" for detail, a knack for finding ideas, and the ability to organize a busy calendar around the expansion of that idea. If you've ever wondered how it "feels" to be a writer, turn to Part I and find out.

Part 11: Breaking Down the Elements of a Story

This section tackles all the building blocks of a story — the sequence of events, the characters, the conflict, and how the whole thing sounds when you toss those elements together. It also touches upon the writer's responsibility to all those movie-goers who eventually journey through that story with you.

Part 111: Turning Your Story into a Script

Part III involves the nuts and bolts of turning your story into something you can sell to Hollywood. From outlines to format to revisions, these chapters detail how your film should look both on the page and in the mind's eye of your reader. I also discuss how to adapt other mediums — poetry, fiction, theater — to the screen. And if you're writing with a partner? Flip to the final chapter in this part (Chapter 17) for some tips on collaboration.

Part IV: Selling Your Script to Show Business

Part IV involves switching hats from artist/creator to business person. You have a product to sell — actually, you have two. You want to market your script, yes, but more importantly, you want to market yourself as a writer.

This section helps you narrow your market and package your work accordingly. It then guides you through the crazy world known as show business — step by star-studded step.

Part V: The Part of Tens

I toss around a lot of examples in this final part. Want to know who's made a successful living as a screenwriter? Here are a few examples. Want to know who's "one-to-watch?" Here are a few examples. Want some scripts worth reading or a heads up on some screenwriting myths that you may want to avoid? That's right, here are a few examples.

Icons Used in This Book

In order to highlight some important and/or interesting information on the screenwriting profession, I've used the following icons throughout the book.

This icon does one of two things: It either suggests a theory or example worth bearing in mind as you read the ensuing text, or it reiterates advice from a previous passage that may be pertinent again.

Keep a lookout for this icon. It signals some time-saving suggestions and/or tricks of the trade.

This icon references a screenwriting term or some showbiz jargon and gives a plain-English definition. If you're really in a hurry, you can skip over these Jargon Alert paragraphs and still understand the chapter. But you may find the definitions to be helpful.

This icon alerts you to a theory or practice that may actually be detrimental to your writing routine or to your career. Don't skip these paragraphs; you'll regret it later!

Many chapters contains a sidebar, flagged with this icon, that presents an exercise for you. These exercises are totally optional, but you may find that they can help you develop your screenwriting skills.

Where to Go from Here

You can go anywhere you want in this book! Read it according to your personal needs as a writer or a writer-to-be. If you want to start at Chapter 1 and read the book cover to cover, great! (After all, I worked really hard on this book!) If not, that's fine, too — you won't hurt my feelings. The information in this book is accessible and relevant regardless of your path to it.

Outside the realm of this book, though, I suggest that you start your artistic journey by taking a walk, visiting a museum, or people watching at your local cafe or train depot. Purchase a notebook and a box of your favorite pens. Don't have a favorite pen yet? Don't worry, you will. Purchase a few and experiment. Oh, and may I suggest going to see a movie? These activities get your creative juices flowing and prepare you for the arduous but thoroughly rewarding process of screenwriting. Now, get going!

Part I
So You Want to Write for Pictures

The 5th Wave   By Rich Tennant

"It's Mr. Tarzan. He's got another screenplay. It's sort of a 'Breakfast at Tiffany's' meets 'The Philadelphia Story' meets 'When Animals Attack'."

In this part . . .

*I*t all begins with an idea. You're driving through the city (or waiting in traffic as the case may be) and all of a sudden a childhood memory flashes before your eyes. This would make a great film. You're reading a newspaper and a third page article sparks an array of images. This would make a great film. You're minding your own business in some public forum when you overhear a startling conversation and — you guessed it — this would make a great film. This part of the book is about the all important idea, finding it, nurturing it, imagining it on the screen. Because you know what? It probably would make a great film, and if you don't write it, who will?

Chapter 1

An Introduction to the Art of Screenwriting

In This Chapter

▶ Getting an overview of the screenwriting process

▶ Putting your ideas on paper

▶ Revising your work

▶ Selling your script

*S*o how do you know if this book is for you? Well, you don't — not yet. But I have an inkling that it may be for you if one, or all, of the following things are true:

- You've never written a screenplay before.

- You've written a few screenplays.

- You're an established screenwriter.

- You're a movie buff.

- You're a film, creative writing, or theater student.

- You're a film, creative writing, or theater teacher.

- You're wondering if screenwriting is the profession for you.

- You're interested in the business of film.

- You're a *For Dummies* fanatic.

That may seem like a fairly large audience, but that's sort of the point. Screenwriting is a craft, and like any craft worth pursuing, you can never know too much about it. You wouldn't tell a doctor to stop scrutinizing advances in medicine, would you? Can a teacher ever learn enough about education? The same principles are true of art. If you've never written anything — you have a lot to discover. If you're a professional writer — you can find projects within these pages for inspiration and practice. And if you're interested in the business, you can find info on that topic here, too. This chapter provides a glimpse of that information and where in the book you can go to find it. Consider it your preview of coming attractions.

Thinking Visually

Quick — in what book does a character require green glasses to enter a city gate? If you answered *The Wizard of Oz,* you're absolutely right. Dorothy needs green glasses to enter the Emerald City. So what does that question have to do with screenwriting? It's a question of vision — what do you need in order to see where you're going? Screenwriting also requires a unique vision, eyes trained to scan the world with particular acuity. It seems silly to say that screenwriters look at the world with a visual eye — of course they do, doesn't everybody? After all, *looking* is a visual act. And yet, there's a distinct difference between what screenwriters see and what people in other occupations see. Screenwriters break the world down into small visual clips or soundless images — in other words, into moving pictures. And they see with more than their eyes. Consider for a second that it's possible to see moving pictures while

- ✔ Observing the world around you
- ✔ Reading a novel, a play, or a poem
- ✔ Reading the newspaper
- ✔ Listening to music
- ✔ Listening to a story

Screenwriters look for moving pictures in everything, though some sources yield more than others. Want to know how your vision stacks up? Find a public place, sit down for a while, and record what you notice. Then, flip to Chapter 2 and find out how visual your eye really is.

Developing the Writer's Mind

Imagine a storage facility, with aisles and aisles of file cabinets, some overflowing and some empty but for one scrap of paper. Or imagine a playground full of, well, children, yes, but other people as well, people you wouldn't expect to see. Maybe two construction workers are playing basketball, or a few CEOs are eating cookies on the lawn; students and couples and blue-collar employees are all in the same space. Or imagine a long hallway full of doors. Occasionally, people emerge, have an exchange of some sort, and return behind those doors. Now, imagine a blank canvas. Paints and brushes sit nearby, but they remain, as of yet, unused. Any one of these spaces could resemble the mind of a writer.

Writers collect and store tons of details. They collect images, pieces of conversation, intriguing characters, sounds, expressions, slang, and more. They also costume what they find, envisioning different outcomes. Add some boots, some dust, and a gun — *voilà.* You're in a western. Dim the lights, strip away the color, and give everyone a cigar — presto. You have the black and white, suspense-filled world of a film noir. Introduce a spaceship or a time machine, and suddenly, the world becomes science fiction. This is how writers spend much of their time — not exactly a dull profession. So, I suppose that the question here is, What does *your* mind look like? If you want to find out, turn to Chapter 3.

Approaching Screenwriting as a Craft

Writers take their vocation very seriously. They'll do almost anything to inspire that muse, and I do mean anything. Rumor has it that

- Alexander Dumas color coordinated his paper with the type of fiction that he was writing. Blue paper was for novels, yellow paper was for poetry, and rose-colored pages were reserved for nonfiction.
- Mark Twain and Truman Capote had to write lying down.
- Ernest Hemingway sharpened dozens of pencils before he wrote.
- Willa Cather read the Bible before writing each day.
- Poet John Donne liked to lie in an open coffin before picking up a pen. Now, there's a story for you.

I'm not implying that to take up the craft of writing you have to become an eccentric, but that might happen of its own accord. Writing is both fun and frustrating; it requires flights of whimsy as well as hard work. It's equal parts imagination and preparation. Striking a balance between the two worlds is a constant challenge. Catching the muse is one thing, but keeping her with you is another — that's where the tools of the trade come in handy. If you want a glimpse of some of those tools, turn to Chapter 4 where I discuss the craft of screenwriting. You'll find advice on how to flex your imagination, how to channel it onto the page, and how to maintain the writing schedule necessary to do both. If you want divine inspiration, well — you'll develop your own methods as you practice this new-found craft. (I hear that lying in coffins really helps.)

Finding Your Screenplay's Story

So how do writers find material? It depends on the writer, of course, but in their ongoing quests for stories, writers resemble any or all of the following:

- Archaeologists
- Detectives
- Gardeners (plant a seed and it will grow)
- Reporters
- Research analysts
- Scavengers
- Secret agents
- Voyeurs

Great stories abound; you just have to know how to catch them, or hunt them down, as the case may be. You should also know what details attract you to a story. Are you a people person? Do locations draw you in? Are you compelled by certain kinds of events? You want to consider these questions now, before your story search begins. Chapter 5 is dedicated to helping you find the perfect story and discover which material you naturally gravitate toward.

Working through the Writing Process

As soon as you get an idea, you have to develop that idea. The development process isn't unlike chaperoning several restless children across the country in a small car. You're likely to hear the following questions over and over, and over and over:

- How does the whole thing start?
- What happens next?
- Who are these people?
- What happens next?
- What's the problem?
- Does that make sense?
- What happens next?
- Can we go any faster?

- ✔ Are we there yet?
- ✔ Why, why, why, why, why?

The whole journey will drive you nuts without a good road map, and in screenwriting terms, that map is known as *plot*. I consider plot to be so important that I dedicate three chapters to it — Chapters 6, 7, and 8. After all, every story has a beginning, middle, and an ending, and the same questions apply to each part. There's a whole other set of questions for character building in Chapter 9 and yet another chapter (you guessed it — Chapter 10) dedicated to orchestrating vibrant language for those characters once you know who they are. As you might suspect, without a navigation panel, you're in for a long, bumpy ride. So if you want to pacify that back-seat yammering, turn to Part II and start reading. Otherwise, you're liable to pull the car over and walk home.

Formatting Your Screenplay

Here are a few things that I've figured out about the screenwriting trade:

- ✔ Always look before you leap.
- ✔ People *do* judge a book by its cover.
- ✔ Actions speak louder than words.
- ✔ Brevity is the soul of wit (and most films, I might add).
- ✔ Try to make a long story short.
- ✔ You never get another chance to make a first impression.

You don't have much control over most aspects of the screenwriting profession. Ideas often arrive unbidden, characters sometimes dictate what they want to say, the ending of your story may change several times, and you may even find yourself in a different genre. And when you're talking about Hollywood, forget it. The business is always in flux. One day, they're looking for war films, and the next day, they want candy and roses. They may be searching for a script with the word "wedding" in the title; you just never know.

One of the only things a writer has complete control over is the script's appearance, and in this industry, appearance is everything (at least at the beginning). So how wide should your margins be? How do you introduce a scene? Where do you insert special effects? And how long is too long? Getting readers to flip past the cover is half the battle, and correct formatting may ensure that they do so. (For more on formatting your script, flip to Chapter 14.)

Constructing Your First Draft

By the time you sit down to write your first draft, you'll be armed and dangerous. Among other things, your arsenal will include the following:

- ✔ Strong characters
- ✔ Equally strong conflicts
- ✔ Character goals and dreams
- ✔ Locations
- ✔ A series of events
- ✔ Remedies for writer's block
- ✔ Outlines of the action
- ✔ A solid writing routine

So, now that you're considering a first draft, how good are you at puzzles — or at weaving, matching, or redecorating? Screenwriting requires all these skills. Crafting a draft is really a matter of arranging your arsenal of information into some desired form and then linking those moments together.

In screenwriting terms, your *catalyst* propels the action into the big event, which then shuttles the story towards a *midpoint* after which it rises to a *climax* followed by a *resolution* of some sort. Make sense? If not, don't fear; just read Chapter 15.

Rewriting Your Script

So, what do you have in common with Plato, Ernest Hemingway, Katherine Anne Porter, and screenwriter John Logan? Before trying to answer, consider the following facts:

- ✔ Plato revised *The Republic* 50 times.
- ✔ Hemingway rewrote the last page of *A Farewell to Arms* 39 times
- ✔ Katherine Anne Porter took 20 years to finish *Ship of Fools.*
- ✔ John Logan spent more than ten years rewriting his play *Never the Sinner,* during which time he removed a dozen characters.

So where do you fit in? All these anecdotes involve revision, and if you're serious about completing a script, you're going to encounter that process as well. Have you heard the phrase "If at first you don't succeed, try, try again"?

Well, in screenwriting, success arrives in stages, and you almost always have to try, try again. After you outline the action and throw the story onto the page, you'll probably want to try, try again. First drafts are generally dynamic, but they're also unruly, which is why many writers believe that the real writing occurs in revisions. Your first draft is written for the story and for you. Your internal editor isn't invited. But in the revision stage, the editor emerges in full form, sizing up each moment and weighing how it affects the whole. And will your revisions take you 20 years to complete? I hope not, but if you're worried that they might, flip to Chapter 16 for extensive advice on revisions.

Adapting Your Screenplay from an Outside Source

Have you ever read a story or watched a play and thought, "This would make a great film!"? If so, you've experienced the first step in the adaptation process — identifying a source. You can adapt all kinds of material for the screen. *Memento* began as a short story written by the director's brother, *Marvin's Room* was originally a play, and virtually every Merchant-Ivory film (the duo that brought you *Howard's End* and *Remains of the Day*) was adapted from a novel. Strong primary source material abounds.

Adaptations are challenging for many of the same reasons that writers are drawn to them. They provide instant character recipes, events, and themes that seem perfect for the screen. Somehow, a writer must find a way to make an original piece out of what he or she is given. Separating from the primary source is a difficult but necessary endeavor. In a way, adapting is like getting two pieces of art for the price of one. So if you're interested in adapting a work into a screenplay, flip to Chapter 17 for a few tips on the process.

Selling Your Screenplay to Show Business

With all the creative work that you're doing, you can easily forget that film-making is a business as well as a craft. When you're through with revisions, you become the CEO of your own private company. That company is you. Selling your work is an entirely different part of the process; therefore, it requires a new arsenal: determination, confidence (even if it's feigned), a positive attitude, a marketing strategy, a creative network, and a knowledge of the business and its players

Hollywood has so many paths that lead into it that you almost need a map to know where to begin. Should you approach an agent first, and if so, how? Should you send your script to producers, and if so, how? Should you be seeking out studios or independents, contests or festivals, television or film? And how, oh how, do you protect yourself and your work in the process? The last part of this book is dedicated to strategy, both personal and professional. Consider these chapters (Chapters 18 and 19) your map.

Just for fun

Are you a movie buff? Here's a little project to test your movie-trivia expertise. Know nothing about films but interested nonetheless? Consider this a project to launch your movie-trivia expertise. After all, you can never know too much about your craft of choice.

In the left-hand column, I've included famous film quotations. In the right-hand column, I've included the films that brought them to us. How many lines can you trace to their source?

1. "I gave her my heart; she gave me a pen."

2. "Marriage, fun? Fiddle-dee-dee. Fun for men, you mean."

3. "If you build it, he will come."

4. "I see dead people."

5. "I do wish we could chat longer, but I'm having an old friend for dinner."

6. "When you realize you want to spend the rest of your life with someone, you want the rest of your life to start right now."

7. "My name is Inigo Montoya. You killed my father, prepare to die."

8. "Roads? Where we're going, you don't need roads."

9. "Life moves pretty fast. If you don't stop to look once in a while, you could miss it."

10. "It's not the years, honey, it's the mileage."

11. "You're gonna need a bigger boat."

12. "You can't handle the truth."

a. *Back To The Future*

b. *The Princess Bride*

c. *Raiders Of The Lost Ark*

d. *Say Anything*

e. *Ferris Bueller's Day Off*

f. *Jaws*

g. *A Few Good Men*

h. *Field of Dreams*

i. *Silence of the Lambs*

j. *When Harry Met Sally*

k. *Gone with the Wind*

l. *The Sixth Sense*

Answers: 1-d, 2-k, 3-h, 4-l, 5-i, 6-j, 7-b, 8-a, 9-e, 10-c, 11-f, 12-g

Chapter 2

Preparing to Think Visually

● ●

In This Chapter

▶ Distinguishing screenwriting from other art forms

▶ Using visual art to sharpen your screenwriting sensibility

▶ Looking at the world with a screenwriter's eye

▶ Organizing images to create the desired effect

▶ Projects to get you started

● ●

So you want to write for pictures, huh? Are you sure? Of course you're sure, you scoff. You love movies. You have ideas for movies all the time. You want to write one of your own. Yes, I say again, but are you sure that it's a movie you want to write? Is your idea best suited to the cinema, or would it be better served as a novel, as a stage play, or as a television drama? Perhaps you're envisioning several images that could well be grounds for a poem. For beginning writers, the line between those mediums may blur, but they're nevertheless different forms that require different sensibilities. Screenwriting, in particular, is a visual art. It demands that a writer look at the world with new eyes, swiftly condensing action and physical detail into moving pictures. Do you have those eyes?

If you've written screenplays before, skip ahead to the visual portion of this chapter; you know a movie idea when you find one. If you're writing for the first time, or if you're just plain curious, read on. This chapter dives into various literary forms, noting their similarities and their differences in an attempt to help you view the world with the eyes and mind of a screenwriter.

Exploring Other Mediums

When people talk about movies, they're generally referring to films that they've seen, rarely to films that they've read. When they want a good read, they pick up a novel, a short story, or a magazine. A select few pick up a collection of poetry, but rarely does anyone reach for a movie script, despite their availability. For this reason, the public (beginning writers included) is more comfortable with other forms of writing than they are with screenplays, so when a creative idea strikes, that idea is much more likely to lend itself to a medium other than film. The jump to cinematic thinking isn't such a grand one, however, and the transfer from one mind-set to the other begins with a quick glance through those other literary forms. If you've struck upon a story already, you may want to peruse the following lists with that story in mind. Try to imagine it in each form. Doing so can help you clarify what aspects of the story lend themselves to cinema, and what aspects match other venues.

Fiction

Fiction makes up more than 80 percent of what people read these days. Unfortunately, it has little in common with screenwriting. Although the forms share an attention to detail and a tendency towards multiple characters and locales, fiction writers spend pages telling readers what they need to know, while screenwriters show it fairly quickly in action. In fiction, the mind of each character becomes a landscape. More time is spent exploring thoughts, emotions, and memories than is spent depicting action or crafting dialogue. In film, the opposite is true. A screenwriter must fashion images or active moments that reveal those thoughts as they arise. In other words, screenwriters present moments that fiction writers explain. Finally, in fiction, the author tends to emerge in the form of a clear narrative voice, while screenwriters strive to fade into the background.

So basically, you know that your idea may be better served as a work of fiction if

- ✔ It has copious characters, plotlines, and locations.
- ✔ The action moves between the physical and psychological worlds of each character with ease.
- ✔ The characters' internal conflicts are as important as their physical actions.
- ✔ The story requires more than 200 pages to be explored fully.
- ✔ A clear narrative voice (or several clear narrative voices) guides the action.
- ✔ Many events are described in detail, but few are shown in action.
- ✔ Symbols and foreshadowing abound.

If you discover that your idea lends itself more readily to fiction, never fear. Virtually every story has cinematic possibilities; the trick is to discover them before you start to write.

Stage plays

Though theater is growing more physical in nature, stage plays have tradi-tionally relied on language to convey action, character, and theme. As I write this text, several exceptions pop to mind; however, as a general rule, plays depict in dialogue what films depict in physical action. Unlike screenplays and novels, which bounce from locale to locale, introducing character after character, stage plays generally limit themselves in cast size and number of settings. Plays with large casts often ask actors to take on multiples roles, and plays with many locations tend to utilize lights, sound cues, and props to suggest leaps therein. Plays rarely try to re-create public locations as realistically as film does. (To do so wouldn't be financially or artistically wise.)

To break it down, your story idea may work better as a play if

- ✔ You can tell the story in 90 pages or fewer.
- ✔ The story concentrates on a handful of characters in a handful of places.
- ✔ Characters reveal themselves through dialogue more often than through physical action.
- ✔ The story benefits from interaction with a live audience.
- ✔ The action suggests a heightened reality or is surreal/absurd in nature.

The line between a theatrical idea and a cinematic one is often vague. If you're unsure whether you've dreamt up a play or a film, try to imagine your story as a series of pictures. If those pictures keep talking to you, you probably have a play. If your mind jumps from image to image, and if every image is full of physical action, you may just be ready to write a film script.

Poetry and studio arts

These mediums share several elements in common with cinema. They rely on quick clips of words or images, often sensual in nature, which encapsulate an event or a tone. Film also relies on the organization of pictures to convey plot and emotion. Poetry employs metaphor, allegory, and rhyme, while visual art uses color, light, and the strategic manipulation of an image to communicate its central design. These forms generally aren't substantial enough to support a lengthy text; they instead hint at a larger story or provide a limited portion of it. Their subjects are better served in a few well-crafted stanzas or in one print altogether. In a way, a screenplay continues where the poem or visual piece leaves off. It tells the "before and after." It expands the subject into an idea that can sustain a dramatic through-line.

Your idea may work best as a poem or a visual art piece if

- ✔ The subject appears in a flash of color or light, or as a single image.
- ✔ The subject feels stationary in nature.
- ✔ The story lends itself to metaphor and rhyme.
- ✔ The story requires a verbal chorus to set it off.
- ✔ You imagine the image as a photograph or a portrait.

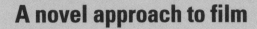

A novel approach to film

The fastest way to understand the differences in artistic mediums is to move between them yourself. The following selection is from *A Tale of Two Cities* by Charles Dickens, a novel that has been made into a film on several occasions. This particular scene takes place in court.

> It happened, that the action turned his face to that side of the court which was on his left. About on a level with his eyes, there sat, in that corner of the Judge's bench, two persons upon whom his look immediately rested; so immediately, and so much to the changing of his aspect, that all the eyes that were turned upon him, turned to them.
>
> The spectators saw two figures, a young lady of little more than twenty, and a gentleman who was evidently her father, a man of very remarkable appearance in respect of the absolute whiteness of his hair, and a certain indescribable intensity of face. His daughter had one of her hands drawn through his arm, as she sat by him, and the other pressed upon it. She had drawn close to him, in her dread of the scene, and in her pity of the prisoner. This had been so very noticeable, so very powerfully and naturally shown, that starers who had had no pity for him were touched by her; and the whisper went about, "Who are they?"
>
> "Witnesses." "For which side?" "Against." "Against what side?"
>
> "The prisoner's."'
>
> The Judge, whose eyes had gone in the general direction, recalled them, leaned back into his seat, and looked steadily at the man whose life was in his hand, as Mr. Attorney-General rose to spin the rope, grind the axe, and hammer the nails into the scaffold.

After you read through the selection several times, try to envision it as one image — a photograph or a painting perhaps. Will you portray the woman, the woman and her father, or the entire court? If you have a lyrical bent, try your hand at a poem or a scene from a stage play. Finally, distill the scene into five images, and try envisioning it as a film.

Poems and visual art pieces aren't often transformed into film, but they can easily become the inspiration for one. If you see your piece as a series of photographs, imagine them moving. Imagine all the photographs that go in between and then ask yourself how you might get from one image to the next. You may discover a film idea after all.

Screenplays

For clarity, here's a list of elements that are particular to screenwriting.

Your idea may be a screenplay if

✔ Events reveal themselves in action.

✔ The story contains a clear beginning, middle, and end.

✔ It suggests moments of intricate detail.

✔ It has a *hook,* an aspect of the idea that will grab attention immediately.

✔ It wants to be told in 100 to 120 pages.

✔ The story suggests the possibility of an equally compelling subplot.

Screenplays subsist on the visual details of every scene, and you may be surprised by how many details you find when you know how to look. Consider this example: Harold comes home from work early, hears a noise upstairs, creeps up to investigate, and discovers that he's being robbed.

Look at each portion of that scene closely. How would you break the action up? A novel would describe every nuance of the action, as well as Harold's heart beginning to race and the little voice inside his head screaming to run away. It might even flash to a memory from Harold's childhood of older brothers jumping out to scare him from behind closed doors. In a stage play, audiences might hear Harold's car in the driveway moments before keys jingle in the lock and Harold enters the room. After the sound effect, seemingly from above, Harold slowly climbs the stairs. You may see what happens next or just hear the next bit as it unfolds offstage. Want to distill it even further? How about condensing the experience into one photograph or portrait? Perhaps a shot of a man ascending a staircase into a darkened hall, or a shot of his hand on the doorknob upstairs. All these forms are possible visual representations of the fear involved.

A screenwriter, however, breaks that scene into a handful of pivotal moments and then hunts for visual details in between. She envisions Harold's blue Chevy pulling into the drive, and then his feet crossing the front lawn. He stops to grab the mail; then, his keys jingle in the lock. The door opens to reveal his face when he hears the noise from upstairs. Perhaps his eyes narrow at the sound; perhaps he hesitates before one hand grips the banister and slides steadily up the rail. Remember that a camera can go anywhere; the visual possibilities are endless. Individually, no one piece makes sense, but organized in a particular way, the pieces paint a very vivid and silent story. Dialogue may be layered on as necessary, but in screenwriting, the situation exists first.

The Visual Life of a Screenplay

If your script becomes a film, a director and a cinematographer will eventually haggle over the composition of each shot and the overall look of your piece. Among other things, they'll discuss the following elements:

✔ **Color:** What colors pop out or highlight the shot, and what is the overall look? Is the moment realistic or surreal in nature? Compare the look of a Clint Eastwood western to a David Lynch film and you see how important color choices can be.

- ✔ **Light:** Questions to answer here include: What time of day is it? What season and weather conditions are at work? Is a specific lighting source suggested, and if so, what is it? The shots in *Ice Storm* are bleak and overcast, in stark contrast to overly bright films like Hal Hartley's *Flirt.*

- ✔ **Movement:** This element refers to the quality of movement both within each image and between shots. Do your pictures dart about in a dangerous fashion as in *Reservoir Dogs,* or are they languid and expansive as in *Gosford Park?*

- ✔ **Organization:** The order of details in an image is as important as the image itself. In other words, what portion of the moment do you reveal and when? *E.T.* has a shot in which the little alien hides himself among stuffed animals in the daughter's closet. That moment is successful because when the mother opens the door, the camera moves slowly from left to right, moving past a stationary E.T. just as the mother does. The audience doesn't know where he is until that moment, either.

- ✔ **Sound:** Each moment in a screenplay exists in a three-dimensional world. What sounds fill out that location? Do any of them conflict with the emotional content of the image itself? If the shot is of a child lost in an amusement park, don't forget to imagine the music and the laughter of the park itself. Those sounds further isolate her.

- ✔ **Location:** In life, you can't always choose where important moments occur. In screenplays, you can. The location of each shot should be a specific choice on the part of the writer. It underscores the content of the scene. It's no accident that the most tragic scene in *Dead Poets Society* takes place in a gorgeous New England landscape during a particularly beautiful winter's day.

- ✔ **Contrasting elements:** Some moments benefit from pitting opposing energies against each other. In many romantic comedies, one person walks the streets alone, surrounded by happy couples. In *The Untouchables,* one man is brutally murdered while another man enjoys an opera. The two moments are linked by the situation but also by the music. The intended emotion of a scene is often magnified by the addition of its opposite form.

- ✔ **Symbol and/or metaphor:** Depending on how it's shot, an image can simply help establish a scene or provide a metaphor for the entire piece. In *Titanic,* the image of the necklace disappearing into the ocean takes on much greater significance after watching the ship go down and the protagonist's love interest disappear beneath the water as well.

Great, you say, so a director and a cinematographer will eventually discuss these elements. What does that have to do with me? At the beginning stages of the screenwriting process, it has everything to do with you. In your hunt for images, you become both director and cinematographer for the piece, and although all these visual details won't make it into your script, the reason won't be because you haven't thought them through.

From something to nothing

Now, I'll give you a full image and let you strip it down. Take away one sentence at a time.

Image: The sound of sirens. Red and yellow lights flash through the space, illuminating the scene of an accident. It is nighttime in the city and raining. Doors open up in a hall down the way, and teenagers flock outside. It is apparent that a school dance has just let out. Swing music filters through the streets. Some of the kids notice the accident and linger a bit to watch. Others hurry home or take off hand in hand down the street. A hubcap spins off the car, rolls for a bit, then clatters on the ground.

You decide how you want to eliminate details. If a detail wants to hang in for a while, take the others away and save it for last. Try reversing the order in which you eliminate them. Which order feels right? In this way, you find out how the image works and which portions of it you're particularly attached to.

The key to understanding the visual world of a screenplay is the key to understanding any medium. You want to view the world as that kind of an artist. How do you do that? In this case, read screenplays, see movies, and practice looking at the world with an eye towards detail and image. Eventually, the ability to break life into a series of pictures becomes second nature.

From the outside in

In this first method, you concentrate on one element off the list and begin to create a visual moment with that element in mind. After you can picture that element clearly, choose another element and layer that choice in, and so on. Your goal is to imagine a moment or an image that satisfies all the senses. For example, say that you've chosen the element of light. You decide that the light in your image comes from a single candle. Next, you choose location and decide that the image takes place in an abandoned warehouse. You might choose sound next and layer in the dripping of water in the distance, or the scuttling of rats off in the corners of the room. You get the picture. By the time you're done, you have a complete image in your mind's eye. That image may suggest a scene or a situation; it might not. In any case, you're training your imagination to create something from nothing.

From the inside out

In the second method, you begin with a preconceived image. This method is particularly helpful after you've settled on a story idea and have a few moments devised within it. Now, you begin what I call the "bolstering and breaking away" process.

First, go down the list and make sure that you've included each element in the image. Challenge yourself to make specific choices. You may know that it takes place at dusk, but do you know what color dusk is in your image? Dusk in the woods of Colorado is distinctly different from dusk in Manhattan. After you've gone down the list once, start stripping the elements away. One by one, those portions of the moment disappear until you're left with what? Which is the last element remaining? This process may help to suggest the most important aspects of each image as well as the movement within it.

From nothing to something

Following the guidelines listed in the section "From the outside in," try to create an image from the ground up. This project may help you detail a previously conceived story, or it may simply help strengthen your imagination.

Beside each visual element, I include the first decision. Use this detail as a launching point into eight grander images, layering on each element as you go. When you're done, circle any image that intrigues you and disregard the rest.

   Color: Red and white

Light: Several flashlights clicking on in succession

Movement: Frantic and clipped

Organization: From the porch, to the yard, to the beach, to the boathouse, to the ocean

Sound: The chopping of wood

Location: An attic

Contrasting elements: Laughter and tears

Symbol and metaphor: Footprints on the sand

Chapter 3

Diving Into the Screenwriter's Mind

With the incredible variety of movies that come out each year, you may think that the only thing screenwriters share in common is their profession. Like most artists, screenwriters have different modes of finding an idea and developing a story. Some ransack the local libraries, writing between ever-growing stacks of books. Some haunt coffeehouses, waiting for the next great conversation to pick up nearby. Some writers interview, and some adapt. Were you to question a small handful of writers (and I have — trust me it's rough), your head would soon whirl with differing opinions, approaches, advice, and techniques. So where does an aspiring writer begin?

For starters, take a closer look. You may notice a glazed or faraway glint in their eyes; their heads may tilt to one side as if listening for something behind them; their speech may clip along as if irritated. Overall, you may feel that they're really somewhere else. And why not? After all, they're working. They're not sitting in front of a notepad or a computer, but they're still working.

A screenwriter's sensibility resembles that of a conscientious parent who has children romping upstairs. He or she never knows when something more important may call him or her out of the room. A screenwriter moves through the world with a heightened awareness — a writer's awareness. Can you develop this sensibility? Sure. It just takes practice and a few friends who are willing to put up with the new, perhaps improved, you.

Learning from Other Writers

The first step in approaching any artistic medium is to surround yourself with examples of the art form. If you want to paint, you go to a museum. If you want to compose, you buy scores of music or frequent concert halls. If you want to write movies, you do two things: First, you study the impact of films firsthand by going to the cinema and by supporting the local video store. Second, you discover much about writing movies by reading screenplays — lots of screenplays. The time you dedicate to reading, even if minimal, can reap great rewards. Here are just a few of the many things you'll garner from other writers:

- **Multiple points of view:** The most compelling stories are told again and again. They continue to be written because each writer has a unique approach. Reading other writers forces you to consider similar stories from not-so-similar angles.

- **Clarity of opinions and ethics:** The best screenplays ask difficult questions. Considering those questions as you read can help clarify your own set of beliefs.

- **A sense of language:** Strong writers possess a large vocabulary and an understanding of grammar. Different writers use different words in different ways. Learn from them.

- **An understanding of format:** Many new writers know what they want to say but are unsure of how to lay it out on the page. Reading other screenplays familiarizes you with the format.

- **An enjoyable way to spend a few hours:** Screenplays are fun, fast reads. Reading one is like traveling without standing in line or spending more than ten dollars on airfare.

I encourage you to examine failure as well as success. In addition to watching great movies and reading well-constructed scripts, study some box-office disappointments and scripts that failed to tell a compelling story (the two are not always mutually exclusive). If you can identify what components of the story caused it to fail, you may be able to avoid the same fate in the future.

All in all, reading screenplays provides a familiarity with the craft itself. You're learning through osmosis — the gradual, often unconscious absorption of details. Reading screenplays regularly can prepare you, and often encourage you, to sit down to write with confidence.

Reading for dramatic intent

After reading a screenplay once through for the general story, you may try scanning it again to concentrate on one portion of the development. Among the items to track are

   ✔ How the writer develops characters

   ✔ How the writer structures crucial events

   ✔ What images the writer repeats and why

   ✔ What techniques the writer employs to move from scene to scene

   ✔ The writer's dramatic intent

The first four items on the list tackle how and when the writer gives the audience relevant information. Detailing the people in the script, revealing key secrets, and manipulating images are all part of character and plot development, which I discuss further in Part II. For now, let me just concentrate on the final item on the list — dramatic intent.

Dramatic intent refers to the screenplay's specific purpose or design. It alludes to the main question the screenplay asks or the thought a writer attempts to communicate through story.

What's the writer trying to say? What does the writer want to know? Keep these two questions in mind as you read for dramatic intent. The strongest, most complex scripts are written out of a great need: the need to understand life and human interaction or the need to test on the page something the writer has learned. This need determines the screenplay's subject. So when you're looking for dramatic intent, keep an eye out for three things:

   ✔ **Point of view:** Who or what does the writer want you to root for? To condemn? Does the writer have an opinion on the events you're watching, and how do you know? If you can answer these questions, you've probably located the writer's point of view.

   ✔ **Theory:** Does the script present a hypothesis that the action then tries to prove? Look at the movie *Kids,* a raw portrayal of city kids engaged in destructive behavior. Each scene proves that the lack of discipline and guidance has destroyed their chances for a decent life.

   ✔ **Questions:** What questions keep you reading? Which ones crop up again and again? Every scene in the movie *When Harry Met Sally* asks the question, Can best friends sustain a romantic relationship? Generally, the characters' answers to the question may suggest the story's conclusion.

The most compelling screenplays engage the audience with the inquiries or opinions at hand. If you answer the main question in the first few frames, people have no reason to continue watching your film. If you ask the question in a variety of ways, people can form their own answers. Present several arguments, and they may even change their answers once or twice. In other words, you give them the ability to participate in your story rather than simply observe it.

Why read for dramatic intent? Screenwriters write in part because they have something to communicate. No doubt you have something to say and are, therefore, pursuing the craft. If you can locate another writer's intent, you may discover how to craft scenes that present your own. Look at scripts you admire. What questions do they pose? What about them keeps audiences guessing, or on the edge of their seats, or both? If you can locate the thematic questions of other films, you'll quickly discover what themes sustain an entire draft, and which fall short.

Recognizing a screenplay's genre

Take a walk through your local video store and jot down the categories videos are shelved under. These categories outline each movie's genre.

A film's *genre* refers to the artistic category it belongs to. The genre is generally determined by a distinctive style, form, or content. It sometimes alludes to the way writers approach their subject. Comedies and dramas, for instance, often approach the same subject in very different ways.

The most common genres include

- **Comedy:** Comedies approach subjects with humor (of course). *Dark comedies* and *romantic comedies* fall within this genre. Dark comedies tackle heartbreaking or frightening material in a comic way, and romantic comedies explore that crazy thing called love.

- **Drama:** Dramas tend to be true-to-life stories of a serious nature. They may contain humorous moments, but the overall effect is poignant and sometimes tragic.

- **Sci-Fi and Fantasy:** These movies take audiences to a future time frame or an imaginary world. The characters may or may not be human beings, and the locations may or may not resemble ours. The ***Star Trek*** films are successful examples of such a genre.

- **Action and Adventure:** These films portray characters tackling dangerous events in an atmosphere of excitement and suspense. The characters may be on a quest, as in the ***Indiana Jones*** series, or they may be in physical combat against a formidable enemy, as in ***Rambo.*** Generally, they encounter both — they're on a quest and must defeat the foe before they can complete it.

- **Family:** If you can take your children to see a film, it probably belongs in this genre. Family movies generally lack cursing, sexual content, and graphic violence. This genre may include some animation. ***Monster's, Inc.*** and ***E.T.*** are some successful examples of this genre.

- **Horror and Suspense:** These are two different genres that attack the same subject. *Horror films* tend to be more graphic in their violence, such as the ***Friday the 13th*** series or ***Scream,*** while *suspense films* generally depict a steadily unfolding mystery. Virtually every Alfred Hitchcock film falls within the suspense genre. When deftly executed, both genres make you want to lock all the doors and turn on the lights.

✔ **Art House and Independent:** These often low-budget films don't hail from large production companies. *The Blair Witch Project* and *Welcome to the Dollhouse* are some successful examples. These films generally allow more creative freedom, which may account for their acute sense of style.

Many of the strongest scripts combine genres, thereby appealing to a broader audience. *Star Wars,* one of the most successful movies of all time, is both a sci-fi film and an action/adventure. *E.T.,* another blockbuster hit, is a sci-fi and a family film with elements of adventure. *The Pink Panther,* with Peter Sellers, is a very funny suspense story. If you can identify the genre (or genres) of any movie you see, you can quickly pick up the rhythms and events associated with it. Although you can't follow a specific formula for writing a particular genre, an intimate knowledge of the categories can help you identify your own.

Developing an Artistic Sensibility

You've probably heard the saying "Imitation is the oldest form of flattery." I'm not suggesting that you copy the stories or even the style of other writers, but you may want to try moving through the world as they do.

In the old stereotype, writers don all black and scowl at the world while scribbling furiously in a notebook or subsist on coffee and cigarettes while scribbling furiously in a notebook or drink heavily while scribbling furiously — well, you get the picture. Although you can certainly offset your creative anxiety in healthier ways, that stereotype does contain a small grain of truth — writers are always scribbling, whether armed with a notebook or not. Their senses are story-ready, carefully selecting details from their environment and sequestering them away somewhere for the next great script. Some writers are born with this awareness, but most hone their skills with every new project. To develop this sensibility in yourself, you need to take a closer look at which details writers collect and how they select among them.

What a writer sees

Imagine that you attend a school reunion. You see all the usual trappings: a welcoming committee equipped with name tags, tables piled with food, a beverage bar, party decorations, and perhaps a band. Most people find old friends, socialize a bit, and call it a night. Most people do, but not most writers.

A screenwriter notices the tight smiles on everyone's faces, their quizzical look before they remember someone's name, the one-time school football star drinking too much in the corner, the former sweethearts who exchanged glances then left arm in arm, and so much more. The writer can also recreate the scene in such a way that those images are evident to a casual observer. Under a writer's piercing gaze, these moments flourish and may quickly become the next scene in a script.

The writer's process here is no different from any type of physical training. You're preparing your eyes to catch certain details — in particular, details that personalize the scene. Some of those details include

- **The scene's overall layout:** Screenwriting consists of visual images constructed in a telling way, by which I mean with choice details in mind. When you enter a space, test how quickly you can assess it, close your eyes, and then recreate it. How would you write it down so that someone else imagines the same space?

- **Anything out of the ordinary:** Scan the scene for unusual details. What about it seems out of place or ill at ease? The man in the suit wearing the lovely woman's wristwatch or the table of sports enthusiasts drinking hot cocoa — many stories rise out of something curious.

- **Telling looks or exchanged glances:** If someone looks at another person for any length of time, generally, something's going on. He may be recalling a past visit, trying to catch her eye, or checking up on her for someone — any number of musings are possible. If two people exchange glances, a silent conversation's underway. Watch and see if you can translate what's being said.

- **Loaded gestures:** Many conversations take place in a single gesture. A father puts his hand on his son's shoulder — this movement may be menacing, commanding, or supportive depending on how it's executed. The gestures of any given moment become a silent score of what's going on beneath the conversation. If you can track the gestures, you can recreate them later.

- **Personality quirks:** Someone's eccentricities, physical and emotional, immediately distinguish that person from others. Twin brothers may look, walk, and talk alike, but one of them may dress with care while the other seems to own a single sloppy outfit. If you watch the world long enough, you soon acquire a list of personality traits ready to enhance any character you create.

Looking at the world this way eventually becomes a habit. Your eyes automatically adjust to the process. When that occurs, you may be ready to retrain the next sense — your sense of sound.

What a writer hears

Imagine the school reunion again. Interesting visual images crop up all over the place now, but what sets them off? Is it the overly loud dance music, the constant whispering behind you, the clinking of glasses in toast, or the flash and click of numerous cameras? Screenwriters pick up on all sorts of sounds that enhance a scene. Try locating the following in your own surroundings:

✔ **Noises that suggest the event:** Many scenarios come equipped with their own soundscapes. You'd be quick to distinguish a christening from an accident site, even with your eyes closed. Whether your scene takes place outside in a field or inside a prison cell, the surrounding noises immediately provide an atmosphere for your piece.

✔ **Noises that punctuate the scene:** Occasionally, you may notice a sound that enhances the moment. If you're watching a man cry softly to himself, the laughter of two lovers nearby may enhance the man's loneliness somehow. In the film *In the Bedroom,* Sissy Spacek smashes a dish on the counter the moment she gives way to her anger. The sound of shattered glass mimics her emotional state.

✔ **The rhythms of conversation:** Every conversation has its own unique sound. The pace of the voices, the repetition of phrases, the moments of silence — a screenwriter listens to all these things. Listening to the rhythms of conversation helps you compose your own dialogue and provides aural examples of human communication.

✔ **Slang and jargon:** These terms refer to words and phrases that suggest a culture, a socio-economic background, or a profession. They suggest character immediately, sometimes even location. Filmmaker Spike Lee often utilizes street slang to differentiate between cultures, gangs, and prejudices. Television shows like *E.R.* rely on hospital jargon to give them a believable edge.

TRY IT

Journaling your environment

This project may help jumpstart your newfound artistic sensibility.

Carry a notebook with you for the next few days, a small one not likely to attract attention. After you find a comfortable place to observe your surroundings, begin composing two lists. In the first list, include any visual details or images that you see. The list doesn't need to be in any particular order. Just record whatever your eye lands on as it moves across the space. In the second list, keep track of any and all sounds you hear around you. Depending on your location, you may be able to close your eyes. See how specific you can be, from the conversation behind you to the fans buzzing overhead. When you've done it in one location, try it in the next. Eventually, a pattern may emerge.

Want to take the project a step further? Select two details from each list and combine them in a new scenario. How may the images be connected? How can the sounds help set that relationship off?

You're not responsible for including all the sounds that you discover in the body of your script. However, if you can close your eyes and hear a scene, you'll be far better able to write it. Sound is often a more intimate way of understanding your story. Because the noise represents the world of your characters, this process may also help you understand their internal dilemmas as well as the external ones.

What a writer remembers and what a writer forgets

Enhancing your perceptive skills can be a full-time job. When you consider the volume of compelling images around you, it's a wonder that most screenplays aren't four hours long. After your senses adapt to this new process of viewing the world, finding and recording those details is the easy part. Like spring-cleaning, the difficulty comes in selecting which few you may keep and letting the rest go.

Of course, which exact details a writer cherishes and which he forgets will vary according to personality. However, if you're stumped as to what you may hold on to, consider the following information.

It may be important to remember

- ✔ **Details that create a compelling image:** By a "compelling image," I mean one that is full — full of tension, full of emotion, full of potential movement, full of life. As a screenwriter, your job is to grab an audience's attention through such images. Remember anything that catches your eye in this way.

- ✔ **Details that raise a question:** Questions are the key to strong writing. Personal questions fuel the desire to write and find answers; the characters' questions determine the choices they make throughout your story. Any detail that forces a question is worth remembering.

- ✔ **Details that tug at your moral or ethical code:** Hopefully, every script you write will serve some purpose — to inspire, to spark debate, to inquire, and so on. In order to communicate clearly, a writer needs to know what she stands for and why. Any details that refute or support your own views may come in handy later.

- ✔ **Details that establish a debate:** Many films rely on ongoing arguments to bolster the momentum. Whether the argument exists between characters or audience members, if your script sparks a debate, it successfully engaged someone. Watch for the moments in real life that elicit arguments of various kinds.

- ✔ **Details that help you understand the human condition:** Most art strives to understand life and its injustice, its irony, its savage nature, and its glory. Once in a while, you encounter a moment that provides a piece of the puzzle. Keep those moments close above all.

If the detail in question doesn't fit into one of these categories, it may be worth abandoning. Remember that you're constructing every image with an aim in mind. If the details you include distract from or compete with that aim, getting rid of them isn't only a good idea — it's your job.

Consider this example: I'm constructing a scene from the school reunion, and I want the audience to focus on one girl hovering by the buffet table stuffing food into her purse. If her eyes dart over the crowd, if she has the hollow look of a woman who hasn't eaten in a while — these are details to preserve. They strengthen the tension of the moment. The fabric of her purse, the size of the table, the number of brownies she takes — these details are unimportant. They distract from the scene's primary focus — the action of a person quietly stealing food.

This process also becomes second nature as you orchestrate your own scenes. The screenwriter's job is to tilt the audience's head towards the most dynamic portion of each scene and let that portion jump into the next. Eventually, the story will become so clear that it demands the necessary information and refuses the rest for you.

Recognizing a Story When You See One

If your curiosity's intact, many situations will command your attention. Sometimes, you may feel as though the more events you discover, the more ideas you have to investigate. By the time you're 15 years old, you probably have enough material to generate numerous screenplays. Yet only a few of those ideas will become stories that become scripts, and many will slip away.

Why is this the case? Often, just because a story interests you doesn't mean that it's film-worthy. It may only interest you for a few days, you may not have the experience to truly understand it, or it may generate an opening image and little else. Chasing every idea that comes your way is exhausting and often futile. Knowing how to recognize a story when it appears saves you time and ensures you a greater chance at cinematic success.

Identifying the call to write

Take a second and think about the stories you remember from your childhood. Recall the events that happened to you as well as those moments that someone else relayed. What is it about these moments that remains with you? Can you pinpoint why they may have lasted in your memory?

The call to write generally emerges after some stories have already suggested themselves to you. If you've come to this book with an idea in mind — one that's been pestering you for a long time or one you'd feel ashamed to ignore — your idea probably has lasting value. Simply phrased, that means that if you dedicate the time and energy to it, your story will get told.

If you've come to this book curious about the craft, with a pocketful of ideas all equally compelling in some way, you may want to sit with them for a while until one calls to you louder than the rest. Take a second to look at the reasons you may be called to write:

- ✔ You write because you have something to say and only you can say it.
- ✔ You write to immortalize an event you've discovered or lived through.
- ✔ You write to immortalize an important human being.
- ✔ You write to better understand life or the human spirit.

The four items on the list are purposefully grandiose in scale. You may also be called to write as an outlet, because it's a fun way to let off steam, so to speak. That kind of writing is important for your emotional well-being, but it won't necessarily elicit a palpable story. These four reasons will.

You'll know that you've been called to write because the idea will plague you off and on. Other stories may whisper to you and float away, but some will tug at your arm a while, growing stronger by the day. If you've been imagining people and locations for your tale, if scenes present themselves to you on a regular basis, the time's probably come to answer the call and start writing.

The four important P's of story

After you've selected one story to focus on (or after the story's selected you, as the case may be), you need to piece it together. A screenplay takes form as you begin envisioning the four basic components of storytelling:

- ✔ **People:** Who's in your story? Imagine everyone for now, from the waitress in the diner to the love interest; you can always trim the cast list down later.
- ✔ **Place:** Where does your story occur? Does it span a concentrated amount of time in one location, or do you envision jumping between numerous time frames and locales?
- ✔ **Picture:** What do you see when you think about the story? What images, colors, textures, movement, and so on? What does your story look like?
- ✔ **Plot:** What are your story's pivotal events? In its most basic sense, plot refers to what comes next. (I speak about plot in greater detail in Chapter 7.)

TRY IT

Crafting a scene from a single image

You've developed several clear images, and you'd like to construct something more. Here's a technique that I call "the Great What If" that may help you generate some more material, using what you already have.

The Great What If refers to a set of hypothetical situations that you layer on top of your chosen image that spur it into action. The What If could alter or enhance any portion of the image itself. The trick is to pay close attention to what happens *after* you pose the hypothetical.

For instance, suppose that I settle on the image of a child playing jacks on his front porch. Here are some "what if" scenarios that I may layer on:

✔ What if it's midnight, and he's been playing for days?

✔ What if the ball slips out of his hands and falls between the floorboards?

✔ What if someone interrupts the game by stepping on the jacks and kicking the ball off the porch?

✔ What if someone starts whispering in his ear?

✔ What if every bounce of the ball causes the earth to shake?

Each one of these hypothetical situations forces a change, thereby nudging the image into action. The possibilities for change are endless. You may come up with several opening moments for your script by utilizing this technique. Write them all down. Eventually, one moment will emerge victorious.

If your idea is a strong one, envisioning these components won't be difficult. Sometimes, a story survives even if you only have one piece to the whole puzzle. But you need to see one piece fairly clearly for any type of script to evolve. Remember, you're just imagining the details now. You'll write them all out later, after lots of research and dream time.

Finding an opening image

The beginning of any story is magical. You may feel as if, after stumbling around in the dark, you come across one image from which anything is possible. If you've identified the four P's of your story, you'll have several sets of images to choose from:

✔ **Person:** If you start with a person, who is it, and what is he or she doing? The movie *Guess Who's Coming to Dinner* revolves around race relations and prejudice in the 1960s. It, therefore, begins by following an interracial couple off their airplane flight and into a cab, laughing together the entire way.

✔ **Place:** If you start with a location, where is it, and how does an audience discover it? Many movies that take place in a major city fly over the ocean before finally landing on the skyline in question. This technique keeps the audience guessing for a few moments before landing somewhere concrete.

✔ **Picture:** Perhaps another type of image begins your piece. The image of a smoking gun lying on the sidewalk certainly pulls an audience in and suggests a conflict that we've yet to discover.

✔ **Plot:** If your story centers around a few major events, beginning the story in the middle of one of them may be a good idea. The movie *Rookie* begins with a ball game in a run-down field decades earlier. That field later becomes an important baseball diamond for the entire town.

If you know what you want to say, you'll know which image to begin with. After you've settled on one, you need to spur that image into action and, eventually, into a scene.

Chapter 4

Approaching Screenwriting as a Craft

1 begin writing workshops by posing the question, "Do you think that some-one can teach you how to write?" Though most people attend workshops expecting to be taught something related to writing, the response to this question is nevertheless mixed. A theory has been floating around for years that implies that artists are born, not made; and many people fear that they lack the natural abilities of a writer. This fear is often so great that it prevents them from putting pen to paper at all.

To this theory I offer a resounding "Pshaw!" A skilled writer must possess three qualities: the desire to tell stories, the experience to round those sto-ries out, and the stamina to see them through to completion. You may come into the world with these qualities or discover them later on in life. Most new writers possess the desire and some experience, but few possess the endurance necessary to finish a work. They have a storyteller's imagination, but they lack a sense of craft. Without that sense, their stories remain ideas forever or meander around on the page until the writers lose interest or give up. This chapter takes a closer look at natural talent and offers advice on how to further your own. It then outlines initial techniques designed to funnel that talent onto a page. In short, it's a chapter on screenwriting first as an art and then as a craft.

In a way, this chapter is about elusive words — words like *talent, imagination,* and *craft.* The essential ingredients for an artist all elude concrete definition. It seems only appropriate then that I begin with the most maddeningly intangible word of them all — *creativity*. In a way, the fact that creativity has no concrete definition is rather fitting. As soon as you concoct one, some creative individual will no doubt arrive to question its validity and suggest an alternative. So rather than try to define the indefinable, I just concentrate on what seems to be involved.

A Look at the Creative Process

At first glance, creativity involves problem solving — or, in other words, questioning validity and suggesting alternatives. I don't mean to imply, however, that creative people sit around waiting for problems to solve; they don't. Creative people are inherently curious. They pose questions that no one else has thought or dared to ask. In this way, creative people seek out problems *and* attempt solutions. Writers are no different. The most common problems that a writer faces are Which story do I tell? and How do I tell it?

In recent years, scientists and sociologists from all over the world have taken an interest in the process of creative problem solving. They believe that many people encounter the same five phenomena on the journey toward a solution. They have labeled these five stages as

- **First insight:** The stage in which an idea or a question suggests itself. This is the moment that a writer discovers a story or the seeds of one.

- **Saturation or the "input" stage:** The period of study or investigation that ensues. Any research a writer does — interviews, peoplewatching, reading, studying other films, daydreaming, and so on — falls under the category of saturation.

- **Incubation:** A period of reflection to process the new information. For a writer, this time generally involves working through the idea on a page, sharing the idea with friends, and good old-fashioned waiting for inspiration.

- **Illumination:** A moment of inspiration when a possible solution suggests itself. When writers talk about "the muse," they really mean the moment of illumination.

- **The verification or evaluation stage:** The testing period, during which the individual, in this case the writer, determines whether his solution really works.

None of these stages has any set length of time, although most writers experience illumination as a brief, often unexpected flash. Some writers spend years researching a story; some only a few days. Some find inspiration right away, but for others, the incubation time is endless. In any case, though no two writers arrive at a story in the same way, they tend to share these five stages. So the next time you're tearing out your hair because a story eludes you, never fear. It's part of the process.

Imagination: Your Creative Arsenal

Aspiring and established artists alike often spend years fretting over the notion of talent. Chiefly, what is it, and do they possess it? My general reply to writers who inquire, "Do I have talent?" is, "I don't know. Tell me a story."

Without definition, the notion of talent is so grandiose that it seems to belong in a mystical realm of its own. Talent — it's something you're born with; talent — it means that you're skilled in some area; talent — it allows certain blessed individuals to channel words onto the page while others nearly go crazy waiting for inspiration. All these statements are true. They're also vague and of little help to writers struggling to better their dramatic abilities. Yet, substitute the word *imagination* for talent, and the question of whether you possess it may become clear. You probably do.

Writing talent is generally a mixture of life experience and the ability to imagine beyond it. You have, in however many years, constructed a creative arsenal comprised of the following:

- ✔ Anecdotes
- ✔ Beliefs
- ✔ Dreams
- ✔ Emotions
- ✔ Fears
- ✔ Images
- ✔ Legends
- ✔ Opinions
- ✔ Past events
- ✔ Questions

This arsenal is, in a sense, your talent pool. It informs your choices as a human being and a writer, and it cannot be taught. Your ability to access that arsenal and convert it into stories, however, is an acquired skill that begins with the writer's strongest muscle: the imagination. When flexed on a regular basis — through artistic exercise and constant writing practice — the imagination will generate material for you. So your best bet is to prepare that muscle now.

Flexing the imagination

It's important to separate talent from craft. Talent is something you have, and craft is something you garner. Each element is controlled by a different mode of thought. For a better explanation, take a look at Table 4-1. It illustrates how each mode looks at the world.

Table 4-1	Talent versus Craft
Talent notices	*Craft records*
Interesting conversations	Specific words and phrases that make the conversations unique
Dynamic stories	Potential beginnings, middles, and ends
Compelling people	Details of personality and appearance that make that person stand out
Inspirational environments	The color, scope, light, and textural components of those environments
Grand emotions	Situations leading to and away from those emotions; words and actions that reveal them
Eye-catching images	The physical construction of images, possible scenarios surrounding them, and metaphors associated with them

Notice a pattern? Talent, or imagination, selects the material while craft searches for ways to translate it onto the page. Your first job as a writer, then, is to surround the imagination with as many options as possible. The more you learn and the more you see and hear, the more ideas you have to choose from later on. Here are a few simple, inexpensive ways to begin flexing the imagination:

- Attempt a crossword puzzle.
- Cook a meal for at least four guests.
- Do something that scares you.
- Exercise (any physical activity will do).
- Frequent public spaces.
- Listen to music.
- Look through scrapbooks.
- Read and/or watch the news.

- Read, read, read.
- Rewrite an age-old story.
- Take up photography.
- Travel someplace new.
- Visit a museum.
- Write a letter to someone you know.
- Write a letter to someone you don't know.

Your goals when flexing the imagination are simple: Stimulate the senses, learn as much as you can, and document what you find.

This part of the writing process should be fun. If nothing on this list interests you, find something equally stimulating that does.

Putting the imagination to work

The imagination's first official job is to hunt for a story. And because the imagination can only hunt in fields that the artist has explored, a writer should strive to be "multitentacled," as John Logan of *Gladiator* fame puts it. This means having a hand in as many pockets of knowledge as possible. You never know where a story resides.

First off, make a list — mental or actual — of areas you know little about. Try to record at least three people or events from any or all of the following categories that you want to investigate:

- Athletes and athletics
- Current events
- Economics
- Education and social reform
- Environmental and agricultural concerns
- Historical eras and/or events
- Legends and myths
- Other artistic mediums
- Other artists
- Other cultures
- Politics past and present

✔ Religion and faith

✔ Science and/or scientific discoveries

The list isn't meant to overwhelm you, though it might. Nor is it meant to make you feel ignorant in any one area. Its purpose is to challenge you to search beyond what you already know. Researching any one of these fields grants a writer unending possibilities, it broadens his talent pool, and it forces the imagination to question "What if?". What if you wrote about the Berlin wall? What if you set your story in England after the plague? What if you wrote about your mother's first glimpse of America? Which angle would you take? Which story would you choose? Remember that everything you learn informs your work.

If an idea still eludes you, consider the following four arenas. Most stories spring from one of these sources:

✔ **Current events:** Glance through the paper, listen to public radio, or watch the evening news. You find yourself besieged with story possibilities. Seek out unlikely sources as well. The obituaries and the classified ads suggest both quirky characters and lives worth celebrating. The hit movie *Jaws* was based on a brief headline concerning a great white shark. *Desperately Seeking Susan* began with a series of intriguing messages sent via the personals.

✔ **Fiction:** These stories emerge almost entirely from the writer's imagination. They may materialize as original human adventures like *All About Eve* or *The Royal Tenenbaums,* or they may take on some new world altogether as in *Star Wars, Star Trek,* and *Lord of the Rings.* In this type of film, the characters and structures in place may be loosely based on the human experience, but details of location and culture remain unique.

✔ **Historical accounts:** History provides some of the most compelling stories. The events are generally documented in some form and may suggest characters and pivotal events right away. A quick glance through articles, criticism, personal letters, journal entries, literature, and art of the time may also suggest language and images that will be crucial to your piece. Such movies as *Gone with the Wind, Braveheart, Apollo 13, Gladiator,* and many others capitalize on historical sources.

✔ **Personal experience:** Here's where the old adage "Write what you know" comes in. Situations that you've lived through or that have been handed down to you are often easy to envision and already hold personal meaning. The characters, usually based on people you have an intimate knowledge of, tend to emerge quickly as well. The challenge is to extend the event's significance beyond your own experience and create characters that may differ from the real people. *Erin Brockovich* is based on one woman's life. Neil Simon and Woody Allen are also notorious for writing comedies based in large part on their lives.

TRY IT

The imagination project

I find newspaper headlines useful in many ways — from story suggestions, to plot twists, to revision work. They're also grand for strengthening the imagination.

I list five unrelated headlines below. Choose the one that catches your attention first. Don't think too hard in making your decision; the first choice is usually the instinctual favorite and, therefore, the place to start. After you've settled on a headline, let your imagination twist it into one solid image, not unlike the cafe example above. Who or what is in the image, where are they, and what might be going on?

✔ "A Pardon For Walter Burnett"

✔ "Dinosaurs Flock To The Field"

✔ "Ice Cream Social Gets the Cold Shoulder"

✔ "10 Saved, Three Still Missing"

✔ "Diamonds Missing From Local Ballpark"

Created an image? Great. Now imagine an audience in a darkened theatre. You're about to show them this image. How will you do it? Concoct at least three versions of this moment, bearing in mind the elements of style: color, texture, the order of details and the pace between them, light and shadows, and the proximity to the subject. Record each version and compare. Which one do you like best? Though predominantly a project for your imagination, you may also discover something about your writing voice in the process.

Fictional stories require a writer to concoct the details from scratch and, therefore, require a slightly different approach. I refer to original plot development in later chapters. The other three sources, though — historical accounts, current events, and personal experience — involve actual happenings, so your approach to those stories may be similar. Start by asking the following questions:

✔ **What exactly do I know about the account?** Record as many details as you can recall. Where did it take place and during what period of time? How did it start and end? Who was directly involved and/or affected? What is your sense of the account — was it funny, tragic, foreboding, awe-inspiring, intimate, or epic? The more you can record now, the easier it will be to assess what kind of research or dream work you'll need to do later on.

✔ **How reliable are my sources?** Historical documentation is often recorded from a point of view. The plantation owner's account of slavery, for instance, would be far different from that of a slave. Family stories are similar in this regard. Most people only remember events as they were personally affected by them. Finally, these days the media often choose sensation over strict fact when composing a report. Check your sources, and check their particular bias. If you can only locate one side to the story, imagine another.

- ✔ **What don't I know?** Even after extensive research, your story will undoubtedly have holes. Consider this dilemma to your advantage as you can dream up some action to fill those gaps. The most compelling scripts often emerge from events you know little about. Why is this? Because unanswered questions are the heart of drama. They create mystery, and they demand that the writer dream up some answers.

- ✔ **What interests me most about the event?** The answer to this question will keep you writing long after the novelty of the idea has worn off. Often, the most intriguing portions of an idea are those that you know the least about or those that elicit some strong emotion — fear, confusion, anger, awe, and so on. This is your angle on the story and, therefore, is what makes it unique.

- ✔ **What interests me least?** This question will help you edit or pare down your script. Taking on an entire event is difficult, and doing so often weakens the effect of any one storyline. *E.T.,* for example, is a film about the personal relationship between one family and an alien. It is *not* about other planets, the details of E.T.'s planet, or a scientific explanation of the event. After you know what details interest you least, find a way to suggest them in your script, or imagine how the story shifts without them.

Creating a script based on real events is a common but nonetheless challenging process. A precarious balance exists between preserving the essence of a situation and crafting an original version of the story. You want to maintain the integrity of a historical moment while raising it above the facts and into the heightened realm of drama. The artist's right to dramatize and shape real events around a specific purpose is known as *artistic license.* When employing artistic license, you're using real events as a blueprint for a largely fictional work.

When tackling real events, you should consider the following at all times:

- ✔ Your emotional distance from the event
- ✔ Your personal judgment of the proceedings

A strong, emotional involvement with a subject may enhance or destroy your script. It often impairs a writer's clarity and, therefore, the clarity of the final product. Here's the test: Can you imagine changing key elements of these people — their opinions, their fates, their genders — if necessary? If you can't imagine changing them, don't write them yet. You should be able to see the people in your script as characters that you can alter to fit your ultimate design. Also, don't judge the characters in advance or you unwittingly delegate an audience to the role of passive observer rather than active participant. In other words, don't create good or evil characters; create human beings that perform good or evil actions. Let audiences judge for themselves.

Identifying your writing voice

The term *writing voice* is often used interchangeably with the word *style,* yet they differ in one small regard. Your writing voice determines what catches your attention and, therefore, what you want to communicate. Style refers to the techniques and language you choose to communicate with. Your voice stems from imagination; style stems from knowledge of craft.

You already possess an artistic voice. It's the result of your life experiences thus far, and it will alter as you experience more. Unsure of what that voice sounds like? Try answering the following questions. The answers may suggest your unique way of viewing the world.

- ✔ What subjects are you drawn to and why?

- ✔ What kind of stories do you pursue? Comic or tragic? Supernatural? Realistic or surreal? Romantic?

- ✔ What is the scope of the stories you're drawn to? Intimate, Epic, Familial?

- ✔ How do your stories reveal themselves? Through character, dialogue, image, or an equal mixture of the three?

- ✔ What kind of language do you use when expressing yourself? Poetic, terse, lengthy, mysterious?

- ✔ How do you move from one image to the next? Chronologically or out of sequence? Quickly or in slow motion? Do images blend together or cut back and forth?

- ✔ What patterns, if any, exist in your previous works? Consider works of any kind; don't limit yourself to writing works.

Every writer experiences and, therefore, expresses a subject in a unique way. The result? Many different films about roughly the same subject. Consider this scenario: A woman is sitting at a window table in a coffeeshop. She's reading a book and drinking espresso. She twirls a pen in her right hand between sips and occasionally glances up to scan the street before retreating back to her book.

Hand this image to three screenwriters and you'll end up with three diverse scenes. One writer begins with the image of the hand twirling the pen, then slowly moves up the arm to the eyes staring out at the street. Another writer pays close attention to the book itself, zipping from the blue cover to the title to the first page, keeping the woman's face in shadow. The third writer reveals the whole scene at once, allowing the audience to guess the situation. All approaches stem from one image, yet they differ in several distinct ways:

    ✔ The order in which details are revealed

    ✔ Color

    ✔ Texture

    ✔ Light and shadow

    ✔ Pace between details

    ✔ The proximity to the subject

These are the initial components of style, and it doesn't hurt to begin tracing them through your own story ideas now. How would you have revealed this image? A note of caution, though: Voice and style are not something to lose sleep over. If you continue to test your imagination, if you continue to read and reflect and question, they'll take care of themselves.

Craft: A Vehicle for Your Imagination

So you've defined talent and discovered how to access it. Congratulations, the more difficult work can now begin.

As I suggest earlier in this chapter, there is a difference between a talented individual and a writer. That difference is known as *craft.* Craft acts as a shuttle between the idea and the finished screenplay; it's how you get from one part of the process to the other. I may harbor many imaginative ideas on how to build the perfect car, but I wouldn't try until I'd taken Automotives 101. The same is true of writing. Ideas do not a screenplay make. You need a sense of craft.

So what is craft exactly? Or rather, what does it involve? On a general level, it can be broken down into three elements: *form, technique,* and *discipline.*

Form

Form refers first to the dramatic structure of the work you're creating. Films generally require a clear beginning, middle, and end — though they're not always revealed in that order. ***Memento,*** for example, follows two trajectories: the main character's chronological attempt to piece together his identity and the story of his life to this point, which moves backward in time. The movie ***Intersection*** takes place in the time span of one car crash. The main character's life flashes before his eyes split seconds before the crash occurs. However, the three parts of the story still exist in these exceptions, they just exist in a different order.

Form also refers to the script's technical format. Novels exist in chapters or lengthy portions separated by jumps in time or narrator. Plays exist in scenes or vignettes arranged in a particular way on the page. Screenplays are generally divided into three acts with particular attention to font type, page layout, and length. Having a concrete knowledge of both dramatic structure and screenwriting format is important. You may eventually choose to stray from traditional forms, but learn the basics first. They tend to work. I talk more about both parts of form in Part II.

Technique

Even without a definition for craft, you probably know a well-crafted film when you see one. In such scripts, the writer demonstrates an ease with any or all of the following elements:

- Action
- Character depiction and growth
- Choice of location
- Conflict
- Description
- Dialogue
- The manipulation of theme
- The use of time

Technique refers to the "how" of all these elements. There are as many ways to reveal any one of them as there are types of films. For instance, if your story's main event involves a murder in high society, will you underplay its effects in favor of character development a la *Gosford Park?* Will you use it to generate the comic suspicion and overall chaos of a murder mystery like *Clue?* Or will you write another *Presumed Innocent* and spend your time piecing together a crime to absolve an innocent man of blame?

How you tell your story is infinitely more important than what's being told. In the hands of a less skilled writer, the quiet family drama *You Can Count On Me* would hold little impact. As it stands, the characters' ordinary dreams are portrayed in such extraordinary ways that the story feels as important as any epic. It's all in how a writer conveys information. I detail each of the listed story elements individually in Chapters 6 through 10.

However, I should detail three elements of technique now. They are the foundations of clear writing — dramatic and otherwise — and they affect all elements of a story. They are

- ✓ Vocabulary
- ✓ Grammar
- ✓ Organization

Consider these items your assets, your "big guns" so to speak. Strive to master each, if for no other reason than this: They help you control your stories. Have a clear idea but no clear thought on how to express it? A knowledge of the these three items can help.

Vocabulary

As a writer, a limited vocabulary thwarts your ability to travel. Think about it. Want to travel to Britain for your film about the bourgeoisie? How will you craft the characters without a sense of language? If a lord opens his mouth in the first scene and says, "Hey guys, like, what's going on?" you're sunk. Look at verbal masters like Spike Lee. He realistically conveys multiple ethnicities and educational backgrounds through the vocabularies of his main characters alone.

It never hurts to have a running list of writers and the words they brandish. I encourage you to sift through writers of all types when compiling your own collection. If you're looking for words with a poetic lilt and a Southern bent, Tennessee Williams is your man. Want your language terse and intense? Looking for socially minded vulgarity? Read David Mamet. And for one- and two-syllable words that resound together with ten times their individual worth, read Robert Frost. This list acts as a reference guide should you need a quick lesson in one vocabulary or another. That way, if you do write a film on the British bourgeois society, you'll know to read Charles Dickens.

Learn to love words — words like baggage, scrumptious, contrivance, wicked, daft, okey-doke, crackers, keen, wily, and winsome, to name a few of my favorites. Each one packs a different wallop (another great word.) Respect their differences, respect what they do, and accrue as many as you can. This doesn't mean that you should dress up your language at every opportunity; it means know your options. The more you know, the more places you can go.

Grammar

Ah, the dreaded grammar. For many people, it conjures up visions of high school, pop quizzes, and extended hours in front of a chalkboard. If this is you, don't worry. Does it help to have a comprehensive understanding of our language and its structure? Yes. Should you bolster your grammatical skill? Probably. Can you write scripts even if you scraped through high school English? Yes. You just need to know the basics. Because books on grammar abound, I'll just offer you a few beginning tips.

Character voices

Few people speak in grammatically correct English, and it's a good thing. You'd be bored to tears if they did. Your characters will speak in different ways, with different grammatical structures. Write them as you hear them; don't get hung up on grammar. You are, however, also responsible for description — of location, of character, and of action. You want that portion of your script to be clear, efficient, and effective. This is where the grammar lessons come in handy.

Sentence structure

Do you need to write in complete sentences? No. You should, however, at least know how to construct a complete sentence, which requires a knowledge of nouns and verbs, and you should be consistent with whatever sentence structure you choose. If your description begins in phrases, stick with phrases: "Enter Allen. Goes to door. Checks outside. Closes it again and hurries upstairs." If you prefer full sentences, "Allen enters the room. He goes to the door and checks outside. Satisfied, he hurries upstairs," then maintain this choice throughout.

The royal "we"

Many writers use the royal "we" in description, alerting the reader to certain details in the scene. For example, "Sam enters. We see that he's concealing something under his jacket." I usually caution against relying on this technique too frequently. Drawing attention to the reader distances him or her from the story; your screenplay suddenly becomes a script with an audience and not a world of its own. Also, if you simply write what happens as it happens, the reader will see it. You might write "Sam enters. He is concealing something under his jacket." I see it, you needn't tell me that I do. Reserve the royal "we" for details in the scene meant only for the audience and the camera. If in the middle of a party, for instance, the image of a car appears out the window, you might say, "In the window, we see a car approach." We see it; the characters don't.

Adjectives and adverbs

The resounding rule here is when in doubt, cut them out. You can't avoid all descriptive words, if the wallpaper is stained and peeling, you may just have to tell me that. However, the addition of a few lines of dialogue often alleviates the need for adjectives. You needn't tell me the mountains are beautiful if a character says, "They're more beautiful than I'd imagined." If the day is hot, let it affect the characters in scene. Discovering a detail is much more effective than being handed one. You can exchange most adverbs for a strategically chosen verb. Why not replace "She walks quietly upstairs" with "She tiptoes upstairs"? Or "The castle is heavily guarded" with "Hundreds of soldiers guard the castle"? Verbs are powerful words. Trust them. Let them work for you.

Passive voice

Your high school teacher and I may share one thing in common — our opinion of passive voice. It probably irritated her, and it irritates me. Active voice means that the subject of the sentence does something: for example, "Molly washed the car," "Harold sweeps the floor," "Margaret plays the piano." Passive voice means that something is done to the subject of your sentence: "The car was washed by Molly," "The floor is swept by Harold," "The piano is played by Margaret." Feel the difference? The first sentences are accessible; they have energy and life. Passive voice tempers that energy, making the sentences safe. Screenplays are about action, so write them with active strokes.

As with all rules, after you've mastered the basics, you can branch past them should the need arise. The aforementioned rules are intended as guides toward more effective writing. What you do after you absorb them is up to you.

Organization

If art is in the details, the writer's voice is most often in the organization of details. Organization asks two questions:

- What do I want to reveal?
- How do I want to reveal it?"

It asks these questions of every portion of the screenplay, from the overall plot structure to the dialogue in-scene to every sentence of description. You're writing for an audience; you want to lead them somewhere. Strong organization clarifies what information that audience receives first, toward the middle, and what the writer's saving for last. This is not unlike the previous example of a woman reading in a cafe. Do you want my eyes to travel from her hands to the book she's reading then to her face? If so, your first line of description may read: "Manicured fingers wrap around a book. It's a copy of *War and Peace*. The reader turns a page, and the book tilts for a second, revealing a brunette of startling beauty." If she turns her head to reveal a scar on her cheek, even better. Now, there's a reason for organizing your sentence in this way. Want an example of organization at its best? The opening sequence of *The Big Chill* jumps between various people receiving bad news and clips of one man getting dressed. In the final shot, the man's sleeves are cuff-linked. Both his wrists have been cut and stitched over. In this way, the writer waits until the last moment to reveal that the man being dressed is dead. Your organization is important. It tells a reader, a director, the camera, and, therefore, an audience how to watch your film.

Discipline

Imagine that you're the high-powered CEO of company, or that you own and run a small business. Imagine, for that matter, that you're a butcher, a baker, or a candlestick maker. It wouldn't occur to you not to show up to work one day. People are counting on you, there's money to be made, and the job requires your presence. Now, imagine that you're a screenwriter. It shouldn't occur to you not to show up to work. The same principles apply.

Discipline is what separates a writer from someone who likes to write. It may be the most important element of craft. Why? There are hundreds of reasons *not* to write: You have children to look after; you have meetings to attend; you travel constantly; you have phone calls to make or errands to run or letters to mail; basically, you just have no time. I'll tell you something, none of that is going to change. If you're a writer, you have to find time to write.

If you want to churn out a 120-page script, if you want to churn out more than one, you have to consider writing your job. I repeat: It's not a luxury, it's your job. So first things first — you need a place to work, and you need a working schedule.

Creating your workspace

In theory, a writer only requires two things of a workspace: It should be yours, and it should have a door that closes. In order to concoct cinematic worlds on the page, you need to shut out the one outside. That said, you need a few other accoutrements as well. The following lists outline both necessities and possible additions to any writer's office.

You *will* need:

- A computer and a working printer
- Extra ink cartridges and printing paper
- Pads of paper
- A stash of pens and pencils
- 1½-inch to 2-inch brass brads for binding
- A three-hole puncher
- A quality dictionary and thesaurus
- A hard disk to back up your writing files

You *may* need:

- A bulletin board for images and other research
- A cassette or CD player nearby (some writers require music)
- A timer for timed writing projects

There are also items that you will *not* need in a writing space. Televisions, telephones, and video games all hinder writers from completing a project in peace. If you must have a telephone in the space, make sure that you can turn it off or unplug it as necessary. Seek privacy at all costs. After all, this is your job we're talking about.

Managing your time wisely

The most prolific writers write habitually. They punch in every day, and they get the job done. Or perhaps I should say, they get the job done *because* they punch in every day. Think about it. Of the numerous things you do with your life, which of them are routine? Brushing your teeth, walking the dog, business lunches, exercise, carpools, phone calls and, oh yes, writing. If you want to make it into that workspace every day, writing has to be part of that routine.

Think that's impossible? Think again. Try revising your schedule with the following rules in mind:

- ✔ **Prioritize the time.** Your writing time has to be as important, if not more important, than all the other things you have to do during the day. Alert your friends and family of your schedule to avoid unnecessary interruptions. Place it high on your list of priorities.

- ✔ **Plan ahead.** Don't wait to see how much time each day allows you; plan your work time in advance. Set up a weekly schedule, if not a monthly routine. This is important. Chisel out the time.

- ✔ **Show up.** The "muse" is just another word for the imagination, which, if you remember, is a muscle. If you tell yourself that you're going to write, that muscle prepares to do so. If you don't show up, you confuse that muscle and therefore the process, and it will be that much harder to write the next time.

People often ask me, "Do I have to write at the same time every day?" Ideally, yes, because it makes the process easier. If you write at the same time every day, your mind eventually shifts into writing mode at that time. You find yourself prepared to write before you even sit down. However, schedules these days are fierce and often don't permit continuity. If this is the case, choose another scheduling goal. Do you have a few hours? Promise yourself that you'll write for two hours regardless of when they occur. Setting a page requirement is another option. Promise yourself five to ten pages a day, and fill those pages when you can. It may take some doing, but with these tips in mind, you'll be off and running, or should I say, and *writing*.

Part II
Breaking Down the Elements of a Story

The 5th Wave   By Rich Tennant

"If you must know, the reason you're not in any of my screenplays is that you're not a believable character."

In this part . . .

An idea does not a story make, not necessarily anyway. But a strong story might result in a solid first draft, so this section is dedicated to developing a story strong enough to transfer easily onto the page. Where does the story start? Who's involved? What's the conflict and why do we care? These are a few of the questions facing every writer with a premise. The following chapters provide examples, techniques, and projects to guide you toward some answers.

Chapter 5

Unpacking Your Idea

So, you have an idea for a screenplay. It interests you; you've mentioned it to your friends, and it interests them. You're convinced that it might even interest people other than your co-workers and immediate family. Fantastic — now what?

An idea is really just a glimpse at the whole story. Your imagination sparks, and for a moment, an entire chain of events presents itself. Unfortunately, unless you have a sense of how to pin those thoughts to a page, they may disappear again. Your next step involves fanning that initial spark into a flame and then into a fire. Thus, an idea becomes a story; a story becomes a script.

I Have This Great Idea. Now What?

Can you identify which part of your idea excites you most? Do you know why it may excite someone else? Any idea of what type of script you have and what keeps the action moving forward? Not sure? These next few paragraphs highlight what steps the screenwriter must take before beginning the writing process.

Extending an idea into a story possibility

If you're interested, I've included a project here to motivate your imagination and generate story options. Find something or someone to observe. When you notice a change in the behavior, in the environment, or in the image, come up with three possible reasons for the change to have occurred.

For example: You observe a girl on a park bench. Periodically, she pulls her hair in front of her face, as if hiding. Here are three possible reasons she does that:

✔ She's concealing a scar she received as a child.

✔ She's avoiding an old flame who just walked into the park.

✔ Her behavior is a secret sign between her and another person in the park.

Those are just three possible motivations that may lead to a story idea. Now, you try it.

Pinpointing your interest in the idea

Before you tackle writing an entire draft, think about why and how you discovered the idea in the first place.

Picture it: You're enjoying a night on the town with friends when suddenly, an attractive somebody catches your eye. Your heart skips a beat, and your mind begins to race; in other words, you're hooked. You must get to know this unique somebody new.

Freeze. Before pursuing this mysterious stranger, ask yourself two questions: Why this person, and why now?

What attracts us to another individual is generally clear: his blue eyes, her contagious laugh, the way he tilts his head when he smiles. The journey toward a story isn't so dissimilar from the scenario just depicted. You'll be excited by your first idea. Your heart may race; your breath may catch; you may want to run out and alert the media. Flirting with an idea is a wonderful feeling, but it's also temporary. Just like forging a relationship, completing an entire script takes effort and determination — not to mention hours of time spent at a computer or notepad. You're about to commit yourself to that effort, so pinpoint *why* your story's great while it's still fresh in your mind.

While trying to locate your interest in the idea, ask yourself these questions: Was my idea sparked by

✔ **An event?** If your idea came to you because of an event, how did you discover that event? Was it a story that you read in a newspaper, or did you witness the incident firsthand? Sometimes, a story relayed by friends will ignite your imagination. Recreating the scene helps keep your initial excitement alive. Also, be as specific as you can in what you remember. For example, you're at a football game when it starts to snow. The crowd begins to leave, but you notice one fan in the front row cheering the team on despite those walking past him. This incident alone may spark an idea for a story, but look carefully. Is it that general image you're intrigued by, or the fact that he cheers louder the harder it snows, or is it the way he refuses to take his eyes off the field? Finding the details may provide information that you'll need later.

✔ **A person?** If a person caught your eye, your imagination may be creating a character. Try to recall the person in question. If you read about her in a book, you may be able to find out more through historical research. If it's someone you know, you may be able to watch her more closely, interview her perhaps. If it's someone you glimpsed in passing — a woman feeding pigeons on the Cathedral steps, for example — you'll need to think carefully about why that person grabbed your attention. Was it her physical appearance — how her hair matched the matted feathers of the birds? Her vocal tone in calling them to her? Or was it something that she did? Eventually you'll be creating characters for your own script, so practice recreating the people you observe now.

✔ **A conversation?** Sometimes, you can grab an idea from something you overheard. Whether you're eavesdropping or debating a point with a friend, conversation sparks very vivid images. Why? Generally, the conversations that I remember are those told with great conviction. They're already interesting, which alleviates the need for me to make them so. Also, it's easy to get a sense of people by what they choose to say and how they say it. An overheard conversation could well become a scene in your script or suggest several characters, so try to remember what you heard and how it was said. (I detail more exact ways to document those pieces of information in the next section.)

✔ **An image or location?** You may find yourself inspired by an isolated image or an environment. Again, ask yourself what specifically draws your attention here. David Mamet's play (later a film) *Glengarry Glen Ross* was inspired by time spent in a real estate office. The details of that location — the fluorescent lights, the peeling wallpaper, the cigarette stains on the chairs — all informed the final product. The result is a very honest and powerful script. Memorize the details of your image, from the placement of objects to the sounds and smells of a locale. They may color your eventual story.

✔ **Another art source?** Perhaps other artistic mediums provoke you: photographs, paintings, literature, other plays, or films. Scan each selection you find. What fascinates you about it? The use of shadow, the texture of paint, a fleeting moment with a character? Your work may begin where another artist's ends. The Oscar-winning script *Shakespeare in Love* was the result of a number of Shakespeare's plays and several imaginative writers.

Documenting your interest in the idea

After you've narrowed down the origins of your idea, document them in some way. You're not unlike a detective in this sense; you've found clues to your story, you'll want to refer to them later on. Here are a few suggestions on how to document your idea:

- ✔ **Write it down.** The sooner you capture the moment, the more details you'll recall later. Write down everything that occurs to you — the time of day, where you were (or are, if you're that fast), what you noticed first, and so on. If you're an artist, sketch the image if you like. Memories tend to fade, so write quickly.

- ✔ **Record it.** If you're lucky enough to have a video camera or a tape recorder when an idea hits you, by all means, use it. Obviously, you don't want to invade another person's privacy, but if you're privy to an interesting conversation, it's always better to capture it firsthand. Some people carry a small tape recorder around with them so that, should something strike them as funny or appropriate to the piece they're writing, they simple speak it into the recorder and write it down later

- ✔ **Take a picture.** Having a camera ready is never a bad idea. Like scribbling in your notebook, snapping photographs of what catches your attention may become second nature. Because photography is a visual medium, it may also help you to see the world as a filmmaker might.

- ✔ **Acquire the source.** Pocketing part of the moment may also help jog your memory. For instance, if you're out walking and you notice a ring lying on the sidewalk, let your imagination go. Thousands of stories may come to mind: a lover's quarrel, a lost family heirloom, and an attempted proposal to name a few. You might keep the ring to remind you of those story ideas later on.

When you've become adept at pinpointing where your idea began and documenting the source, you may notice a pattern in the subjects you're drawn to. People may interest you; locations may not. Sounds may capture your attention. Perhaps you find yourself collecting paintings of children, workmen, or landscapes. That pattern may suggest where your strengths lie as a writer or what kind of stories you're drawn to right now. For the time being, be diligent and remember that knowing what drew you to your story in the first place will keep you writing long after the initial excitement over the idea wears off.

Getting to Know Your Audience

Screenwriters write for an audience. Sometimes, that audience is small and defined; sometimes, it's a general age group; sometimes, it's your Aunt Betty or people like her. Whoever it may be, that audience and your awareness of it keeps your writing clear, efficient, and honest. Writing is a form of communication, so it's important to determine who you're talking to and why they might want to listen.

Matching the story to the audience

Even if your goal is to write a script that delights audiences of all types and ages, you may want to consider who it will realistically reach. If your story involves violence, it probably isn't for children. Similarly, certain kinds of audiences are statistically proven to frequent certain films. It may be advantageous to know who you'll probably sell the most tickets to when it comes time for your movie to be released.

Here are some questions to ask yourself when identifying your audience:

What do you like about your story?

Generally speaking, if you're excited about an event you've witnessed, someone else will share your enthusiasm. The more passionately you can recount that event, the larger your audience will be. I know very little about the stock market, but the whirlwind energy of the trading-room floor makes me wish that I did. The movie **Wall Street** transformed that energy into a box-office hit.

Using the information you've collected on your story so far, clearly define three things that you love about your idea. I call them "those three things." Those three things keep cropping up when you talk about your idea and never fail to put a smile on your face. Does your story take place in Italy, a location that enchants you? Is your main character a brooding young man with a secret profession? It may be something as vast as the landscape or as minute as the image of children running across a beach — if it excites you, write it down. You will return to those three things later for inspiration, scene ideas, and tone. They will also help define your audience.

Who shares your taste?

The quickest way to discover your audience may be through a quick scan of your social circles. Who among them holds similar views on entertainment, politics, or personal relationships? Who might share your interest in those three exciting things that you've discovered in your idea? The people you identify and people like them will undoubtedly make up a large portion of your audience. If those people vary in age, gender, and social make-up, your story may have a universal or mass appeal. If they all resemble you in form as well as opinion, you may be writing for a target audience.

A *target audience* is a film industry's best guess as to who might spend money on your film. This statistic is generally compiled through surveys and test audiences, and by comparing your script to others of similar subject or genre. Remember that films are marketed in a variety of ways. The audience you attract determines that marketing approach.

Who might your target audience be?

Identifying your target audience is really a matter of understanding what kind of people like your kind of film. Take a look at this list for some ways that you might approach finding out:

- ✔ **Compare your idea to existing stories.** It's never a bad idea to know what films are similar to yours in subject and what kind of interest they generated. If you're writing a story about a man-eating crocodile, you may find it helpful to know who liked the movie *Jaws.*

- ✔ **Know which category of film your idea fits into.** Take a walk through your local video store and jot down the categories around you. Assuming that your story becomes a movie, which becomes a video, would it eventually be shelved under Comedy or Romantic Comedy? Drama or Suspense? Adventure or Sci-Fi? Those categories come equipped with their own audiences.

- ✔ **Pitch your idea to different types of people and record their response.** Mention your idea to people you don't know very well, and a pattern may emerge in their responses. If the same type of people — all women, all teenagers, all children — respond in a positive way, they may be your target audience.

A *pitch* is a brief summation of your movie concept that emphasizes its exciting and novel qualities. Pitching an idea isn't unlike selling a product; it requires a dynamic presentation and a solid knowledge of your story's strong points, such as its tone, genre, and what existing films it resembles. It may also include what actors you envision for the roles and who your audience will be. I discuss the pitch in greater detail in Chapter 16.

Connecting with your audience

Certain story elements are almost always appealing to large audiences, and many of them date back thousands of years. Here are some sure-fire ways to connect with an audience. See if they exist in your own idea.

Passion

People go to the movies to see life painted in bold strokes. I don't go to a movie to see stories that are less interesting than my own; I go to lose myself in worlds of greater adventure, comedy, and truth than my own. One of the resounding differences between art and life is the depth of passion art allows us to tackle. Look at the following list of passions and see whether they exist in your story idea.

Universal Passions:

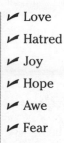

- ✔ Love
- ✔ Hatred
- ✔ Joy
- ✔ Hope
- ✔ Awe
- ✔ Fear
- ✔ Betrayal
- ✔ Revenge
- ✔ Triumph

Other passions exist, but many of them fit into one of these categories. Love, for instance may be broken down into infatuation, lust, and obsession. Fear may be divided into confusion, distrust, and panic.

Notice that I'm *not* choosing words with a vague or gray connotation but rather, strong words that suggest action. A crush isn't nearly as interesting as an obsession, nor is a spat as exciting as a battle over one's honor. Choose words that suggest something is at risk in your story. Search for words that raise the stakes.

Raising the stakes is a term that alludes to those elements of your story that are at risk and worth fighting for. The people in your script must want something desperately, to the point at which they feel that they'll die if they don't get it. By raising the stakes, you're making it that much more important that they achieve their goals. In the movie *E.T.,* the children at first help E.T. get back home because that's where he belongs. The writer later raises the stakes by making it clear that he will, in fact, die if he doesn't reach the spaceship in time.

Mystery

Great stories ask great questions, or they present situations in which questions abound. Look at your idea. What questions do you have? Does your story's mystery lie in an event, a person, or both? If I witness two characters whispering to each other, I'll at least wait to see what was said. If a character behaves in a way that seems out of the ordinary, I'll want to know why. Questions give you somewhere to go, which, in screenwriting terms, means another scene to write. The more questions your idea raises, the easier it will be to transform it into a full draft.

Creating scenes full of mystery keeps an audience leaning forward in their seats. Omitting information that may be necessary to understand your general story will confuse and frustrate your audience. Mystery occurs when you've set the scene but left out the reasoning behind an action or a conversation. Remember that mystery occurs when you know generally what is going on but want to know the details.

The pros and cons of focusing on audience

Locating your target audience may help clarify your story, but it may also hinder your creative freedom. The following two lists suggest possible arguments in each direction.

Pros:

Your target audience may help you market your script. Think of audiences as customers. If you know who your customers are, you may know how to reach them when it's time to sell your product. If children are your target audience, you may advertise during Saturday morning cartoons; if avid sports fans are your target audience, you'll advertise during the Super Bowl.

Your target audience may suggest research possibilities. Target audiences enjoy similar things. If you know what they like to see, you'll know where to look for existing inspiration. If children are your target audience, you'll have an assortment of literature, cartoons, films, video games, and reference books to research while gathering ideas for your own script.

Your target audience may help answer questions on tone, conversation, and subject matter. You're bound to find a handful of films out there that resemble yours in some way. Watching them may provide examples and inspiration on how to approach writing yours.

Cons:

Your target audience may distract you from your original story. Investigating stories similar to yours, cinematic or otherwise, may be detrimental to your storytelling. You may doubt the power of your story in comparison to others. You may also find other writers influencing what you come up with.

Your target audience may cause you to stereotype your characters. Discovering what types of people target audiences are drawn to isn't difficult. If you become too eager to please an audience, you may fall back on writing stereotypes and clichés instead of people.

Your target audience may affect the depth of your dialogue. Target audiences see similar films, and similar films often sound alike. In trying to please your audience, your choice of language may lose its unique edge by catering to what they're used to hearing.

Bear in mind that films with the same audience as yours may be radically different in story and, therefore, not at all threatening to your process. You may see your story so clearly that researching someone else's film couldn't possibly alter it, or you may think it best to write this first draft without distraction. In any case, the main difference between your script and everyone else's is that *you* are writing it, and eventually, *you* will decide how much an audience will affect your writing choices.

Spectacular events

Thousands of people in the United States flock to fireworks displays every Fourth of July. Why? In part, they attend to foster a sense of community, but they also go because they're drawn to the enormous demonstration of beauty that fireworks provide. Audiences like to be thrilled, shocked, and dazzled, and screenwriters are in a perfect spot to capitalize on that request. From the helicopter chase in *Outbreak,* to the UFO landing in *E.T.,* films continually rope us in with their own version of visual fireworks. Your spectacular event may be as large as a volcano eruption or as small as a red balloon disappearing into the sky. Both scenes command an audience's attention, and an audience that gasps together, stays together (at least until the credits roll).

Knowing What Happened Before Your Story Began: Creating the Backstory

Most writers dream a little before they tackle writing their scripts. Actually, they dream a lot. Before you craft an environment, you want to know its history, its geographical location, and its condition. Before you write a scene between parents, you want to know what attracted them to each other, how long they've been together, how many children they have, and the like. Before your characters go to war, you have to know what moments in political history led them to that battlefield.

The ability to write complex events inhabited by complex people comes from knowing everything you can about why those events occurred and who those people are. The details you unearth may not all make it into your final draft, but they will add color and depth to the eventual script. Compiling your information now will also allow you to write with fewer interruptions later because you will have answered many questions in advance.

Backstory refers to everything that occurred in your story's past. A character's backstory may include family background, job history, psychological condition, and any memories you create for that person from childhood on. The backstory of a situation includes events that led up to it and a suggestion of why that situation's occurring now.

Elements of the backstory

You may find it helpful to invent your script's history one section at a time. Just as detectives follow a certain line of questioning, so will you subject your story to an inquisition of sorts. Here's a list of categories that you may want to consider in your search for a backstory.

- ✔ **Convictions and beliefs:** What are your character's political, social, and economic views? Does your character have any theories on life in general or in detail? How did he or she come to feel that way?

- ✔ **Education:** Consider both formal education and acquired education in this category. Where your character went to high school may be as important as the three months he spent on the streets learning to play the drums.

- ✔ **Family background:** Invent your character's family history, including the uncle she was named after but never sees. Friends are included in this category.

- ✔ **Geographic location:** Detail any environment that helped shape your character's present circumstances. Create everything from the climate to the socio-economic make-up of the community to the carefully manicured lawns.

- ✔ **Key past events:** Virtually every main event in your story will be possible because of something that's occurred in the past. What events led up to those in your story, and why did they occur?

- ✔ **Past successes and failures:** People are shaped in part by their best and worst memories. Knowing what your character's track record is may be helpful in certain situations that arise in the script itself.

- ✔ **Phobias:** Your characters' fears dictate what they avoid in life and in some cases, what's pushing them to succeed. Think specific and general; a fear of rose thorns may be just as compelling as a fear of commitment. The film *Arachnophobia* was fueled by the main character's fear of spiders.

- ✔ **Profession:** How do your characters make a living? Do they enjoy working at the library, or are they biding their time? How did they get where they are?

- ✔ **Quirks:** What makes them unique, physically and psychologically? In *Forrest Gump,* the main character is compiled of odd characteristics, one of which is how fast he can run. The film *A Beautiful Mind* tackles one man's battle with schizophrenia. A character's quirks may propel your story forward.

- ✔ **System of values:** People differ in where they draw the line between right and wrong. What do your characters value most in themselves? In a lover? In a child? What types of behavior would make them ill?

- ✔ **Talents:** What has your character always been good at? Does he utilize that talent, or has it gone by the wayside? Perhaps your story starts on the day an opportunity arises for that talent to emerge.

- ✔ **Time period:** What part of history are you tackling? Whose history will you portray? Is yours a Civil War story or that of a future age? If you plan to flash between moments in your character's life, how many moments and what were they?

Each of these categories suggests its own series of questions that you might answer about your story. Jot those questions down as they occur to you; you'll undoubtedly return to them with each new person and environment you create. Although it's impossible to highlight upon all that you discover in a single script, much of your story may come from the information you invent now.

Developing a screenplay through backstory

Imagine that you're a tourist in a foreign country — you don't speak the language, the people aren't familiar, and anything might happen to you next. This experience isn't unlike that of most movie-goers. They need someone to guide them through their journey and a guidebook to understand the importance of what they see along the way. You are their guide; the backstory is their guidebook.

A detailed backstory may be your greatest source of support as a screenwriter. It renders your characters unique and colorful, which will inform how they speak and behave throughout your story. It helps establish a clear world for your characters to explore and, therefore, provides the fuel for most — if not all — of the future scenes in your script.

Consider the information that you have: You've created a time period, an environment, and some character biographies. You may also have envisioned several situations leading up to your story's main events. Your next step involves conveying those details to an audience that knows next to nothing about your story.

You can easily convey time periods and locations through costume, dialect, a lingering description of the landscape, or a caption alerting your audience that the story takes place in Paris, 1763. Past events and character traits are often more elusive. Although there's no single formula for using this type of backstory to generate scenes, you may want to consider the following process as a way to begin:

1. **Identify the detail that you want to develop.** It might be an event, a trait, a location, a family member, or a friendship. Choose one element.

   For example, I've decided that my main character moved around constantly as a child and is, therefore, unable to settle down as an adult. That unsettled sensibility is the detail in question.

2. **Visualize three ways the detail manifested itself in the past.** In particular, concentrate on what moments might reveal the detail to a stranger.

   For example, I envision my character as a child. She's kept her bedroom decidedly blank, anticipating the next move. She fidgets constantly in school, often upsetting her classmates. She travels with an imaginary friend — the only constant in an ever-fluctuating environment.

3. **Visualize three ways the detail manifests itself in the present.** Every character exists in at least three roles during the course of a day. Your main character might be at once a mother, a neighbor, and a renowned biologist. Decide how the detail affects your character in several venues.

   For example, I imagine that my character is a marathon dater, unable to settle on any person for a length of time. She juggles three jobs at once, constantly dashing from one end of town to another. Although she's lived in an apartment for a year, she has yet to completely unpack.

4. **Decide which scenes might exist in your screenplay.** Flag any scenario you visualized that will help an audience understand the story you want to write. If more occur to you along the way, jot those down, too. You'll return to those scenes later when you begin piecing your screenplay together.

Not every piece of information you come up with will find its way into your screenplay. If I'm telling a Civil War story, I may concentrate on my character's political history and ignore his family background. On the other hand, if my Civil War story centers on Abraham Lincoln, his upbringing might be important. The type of story you're telling will dictate which details you reveal from the past. But remember, whether you focus on it or not, everything you imagine will enhance and strengthen your script.

Identifying the Tone of Your Piece

It's important to distinguish a film's genre from its tone. In Chapter 4, I outline the most common movie genres. They include comedy, drama, action and adventure, family, sci-fi, fantasy, horror, and suspense. You can generally determine a movie's genre by the story's content and the audience that it might appeal to. So if the genre of a film refers to *what* a writer is depicting, the film's tone refers to *how* the writer depicts it.

A movie's *tone* indicates a certain quality, mood, or atmosphere that the writer establishes through the careful manipulation of the pace, texture, and selected images. Tone can often be understood as the way a movie makes you feel as you watch it. A comedy may feel dark and slightly twisted (*War of the Roses*) or frivolous and light (*Legally Blonde*) depending on its tone.

In creating a tone for your own screenplay, try exploring three pivotal story elements:

✔ **Pace:** The speed with which your story is told. The pace is determined by the length of your scenes, how fast your action moves, and how quickly you provide your audience with information.

- **Texture:** The colors, sounds, and other sensory details that you include throughout. How intimately you depict each scene determines the film's texture

- **Tension:** The mental, emotional, or psychological thread between characters. Tension comes in all different forms — angry, uneasy, frightened, and sexual — to name a few. The thread becomes strained as the tension mounts.

You might regard the genre as a kind of spectrum housing various types of comedy, drama, suspense, and so on. You're trying to decipher where your film lies on that spectrum. For example, the comedy genre includes anything from the fast-paced chaotic nature of *Noises Off* to the slapstick humor of Laurel and Hardy. Still unsure? You might also ask yourself this question: What words would I use to describe the overall feel of my story? Is it secretive or raucous, whimsical or ominous? Any of these descriptions may be your tone.

Why do you even need to know the tone of your script? Sometimes, you don't. Sometimes, a tone will suggest itself as you're writing, and you can enhance it then. Sometimes, you'll complete a draft and realize that you've unconsciously selected a tone. However, knowing the rhythm and texture of your piece in advance may help you decide which details to select as you write.

Deciding When to Start Your Story

Why start your story now? is a two-part question. It really asks, Why should you personally start writing now, and Why does your story begin when it does? The first portion of the question can be answered in the following ways:

- You'll forget the story if you don't start writing now.

- You'll lose your momentum if you don't start writing now.

- You've taken time to enhance the idea; the story is becoming clear.

- You've set aside time in your schedule to concentrate on a script.

- This is a story that needs to be written now.

- If you don't write it now, someone else may.

- You've put off writing long enough.

Writing isn't unlike a sport. If you practice every day on a set schedule, your muscles will remain supple and ready to work for you. If called to race a marathon, you could do it. Your imagination is also a muscle that will tire without regular exercise. You've invested time in an idea, and though the initial euphoria may have worn off, you now have an arsenal of creative paths to explore. If the initial excitement remains, better yet. Start writing soon.

Why does your story begin when it does? is one of the most important questions you have to answer before sitting down to write. There are as many different answers as there are types of stories. However, one thing is clear: Your story begins when it does because something unusual is about to happen. Lives are about to change.

Consider successful movies you know. In *E.T.,* the planet is about to be visited by an alien. *Gone with the Wind* begins on the brink of the Civil War. *Star Wars* thrusts us into a galaxy at odds. These stories also begin at the moment a change will occur for the main characters. Elliot in *E.T.* will find an unusual, much needed friend. Scarlett O'Hara will suffer poverty and heartbreak for the first time. Luke Skywalker will lose his aunt and uncle and discover that he's a Jedi knight. All these movies begin on the verge of a grand shift, and that shift propels the ensuing action.

Try to identify the biggest change that might occur in your own story. Is it a shift within

- ✔ The family?
- ✔ The workspace?
- ✔ The environment?
- ✔ The political, social, or economic scene?
- ✔ A character's romantic life?
- ✔ A character's emotional or physical well-being?

Generally, if the story is about to change in one realm, the other realms will shift around it. Should someone close to your main character die, for instance, that death might affect his work, his friendships, and perhaps his romantic attachments. Choose the grandest shift you can find and begin your story there.

Why start your story on the verge of something new? Because change is inherently dramatic. Change puts characters in a vulnerable state where they'll have to make choices for the first time. It forces them to rely on their baser instincts to succeed or, in some cases, survive. It allows the audience to learn along with the people they're watching.

Your beginning moment also suggests a time clock for your action. Even if your story is based on a famous person, you can't tackle his or her entire life; you simply don't have time. Nor would people find it interesting to see every moment dramatized. You'll want to concentrate on a small portion of that journey, and that portion will suggest it's own conclusion. As Luke Skywalker begins his quest yearning to avenge his family's murder, the audience will want to see if he's able to do so. Anything after that attempt is information for another film. Identify this shift in your own story, and you'll have your opening scene.

Getting to Know Aristotle: A Dramatist's Best Friend

Aristotle was a Greek philosopher who lived from 384 to 322 B.C. So what does he have to do with screenwriting? In some ways — everything. An author of many notable works, his doctrine entitled *Poetics* may be the first text devoted entirely to literary criticism, and the terms he employs within it have become the cornerstones of dramatic arts today. For a writer, Aristotle's six poetics are the building blocks of any well-crafted script.

Aristotle's Poetics are

- **Plot:** A plot can be defined as a series of actions, and an action can be defined as an event that causes something else to occur. A boy borrowing his father's car isn't necessarily an action. A boy borrowing his father's car after being told not to do so *might* be an action, as it will undoubtedly spark an argument later on. If the events in your story don't cause other events to occur, you don't have a plot. You simply have a series of events.

- **Character:** A character is any person or presence in your screenplay that performs an action or causes another character to do so. I say "a presence" to allow for the possibility that something other than a human being may be a character in your script. Ghosts, for example, cause people to act in certain ways, and the cast of characters in many family movies might include animals or make-believe creatures.

- **Thought:** The thought of your screenplay can be broken down in several ways. It refers to the initial thought that sparked your interest in the idea as well as the thought you put into the construction of a story. It refers to the thoughts that your characters express throughout your script, which may differ widely from your own. It also refers to the points of view that you may want to convey to an audience. In this sense, the thought of your script may also be its theme.

- **Diction:** The diction of your script refers to the types of words you choose to depict your action. Like fashion trends, words suggest a personality or type. The words you choose quickly denote a character's education, profession, sexual persuasion, political bent, age, ethnicity, and emotional or mental state. I talk about diction at greater length in Chapter 9.

- **Music:** Like thought, music has several definitions. It can refer to the actual music that you employ in your screenplay, be it the live band you're writing about or any music you hear underscoring your piece. It can refer to the general soundscape — sound effects that you highlight or silences between characters. It also refers to the sounds of the words themselves. If you could mute the meaning of each word and concentrate on the consonants and the vowels, you'd have the script's music.

✔ **Spectacle:** Spectacle has recently taken on a negative connotation, referring to any expensive, grandiose technical effect that a movie employs to dazzle an audience. Yet, in fact, it originally meant any moment that visually impressed an audience, be it small or grand in scale. The blazing city in *Gone with the Wind* might amaze an observer, but so might the first moment that Scarlett O'Hara walks on-screen in her enormous dress. Spectacle moments are often what makes the story film-worthy and unlike everyday life. Without them, the movies may seem very dull.

The *Poetics* provide a clear roadmap for any writer. Before you sit down to the page, you may find it helpful to glance through them individually to clarify story choices that you've already made. How do the categories work together? Where do they overlap? Have you been thorough in your research? They will help you later when you've completed a first draft and face the daunting task of rewriting. I have them pasted above my computer screen for just that moment. They remind me that I need only tackle one component at a time as I go back through with my red pen. Also, if your writing falters, it usually means that you don't know enough about one of these elements, and it's time to return to your backstory. When the *Poetics* are fully realized, your screenplay will sing.

What's It All About?: Writing a Nutshell Synopsis

The nutshell synopsis is one of the great ironies of screenwriting. You spend months, if not years, developing your idea, researching your backstory, embellishing your characters, and identifying a tone. Then, you're asked to condense all that information into five sentences or less. It sounds crazy, but it's an exercise that pinpoints the crucial moments in your story while preparing you for the demands of the Hollywood scene.

Turning Your Synopsis into a Movie Trailer

Here's a quick and fun way to vamp up your nutshell synopsis. Movie trailers are a film company's best bet for drawing an audience into the theater. They generally employ a combination of vibrant music, quick flashes of action, and a dynamic announcer to rope people in. Imagine that your film is about to be released, and you're in charge of marketing it. Using your synopsis as a guide, construct a movie trailer that will dazzle the public and send them to the box office with money in hand.

A *synopsis* is a short description of your screenplay that highlights the main characters and the journey they go on, with particular attention to conflict and resolution. A *nutshell synopsis* is a shorter version of the same, generally running from three to five sentences in length.

The ability to tell a story effectively in a short amount of time is a skill that most successful screenwriters have turned into an art form. In Hollywood, time is money, so you won't be given enough time to say everything that you know about your script. If you've done your job, it would take hours to tell, and you're probably going to get 5 minutes. So start thinking now about what details you would keep.

It might help to break the idea down into five concrete sentences. I've included some examples of opening phrases to get you started. The element you're trying to emphasize is in boldface at the start of each phrase.

- ✔ **Character:** My story is about a (insert character type here) in (insert location here).

- ✔ **Goal:** S/he wants more than anything to find (insert hope/ dream/ passion here).

- ✔ **Journey:** Her/His journey begins when (initial event here) and s/he decides to (character action here).

- ✔ **Conflict:** S/he runs into trouble when/with (insert conflict or conflicts here), which s/he tackles by (character action here).

- ✔ **Resolution:** The story ends when (insert event here) and s/he discovers that (insert conclusion here).

You can alter and rearrange these sentences in many different ways to suit your particular screenplay. You may abandon the sentence structure altogether and come up with phrases of your own. However, the elements that I'm choosing to emphasize create the spine of most stories, and you'll probably want to include them in any synopsis you construct.

After you've devised a paragraph of five sentences, try telling your story in three. Now try one. It may seem impossible, but when you're through, you'll know exactly what your script is about.

Chapter 6

Plot Part I: Beginnings

● ●

In This Chapter

▶ Making your opening images great

▶ Planting your story's conflict

▶ Structuring your first moments

▶ Glancing through successful film openings

▶ Projects to get you started

● ●

*P*lot and character are the pillars of all great stories. Without a solid plot, nothing happens in your screenplay; without compelling characters, things happen, but no one cares. So which pillar do you construct first?

Well, consider that most people approach stories by inquiring, "What's that story about?" Then consider the question that you'll be asked most often by friends, family, future agents, and producers when they discover that you're writing a script: "What's your story about?" Finally, consider the question that you'll ask yourself when you reach a stumbling point and can't seem to generate any pages: "What's my story about?"

Yes, it's the same question, but, more importantly, it's the *first* question you're likely to encounter at every stage of a new draft. Sure, people will inquire *who* you're writing about, but they'll probably do so *after* you've supplied a synopsis. And if you look toward the five minutes you get to convince the Hollywood heavyweights of your script's worth, you'd better have a dynamic plot ready to rope them in quickly. And how do you construct such a plot? It's a challenging process that begins . . . well, with your beginning. This chapter concentrates on crafting an opening for your story that will entice readers and audiences alike to remain in their seats.

Enhancing Your Opening Images

Close your eyes. You're sitting in a darkened theater, staring at the screen. At first, nothing happens. Perhaps some images dart past as the credits role.

Finally, the screen flickers to life. You're about to watch the opening sequence of your film. What do you see?

The first ten minutes of every movie determine what an audience expects from the remaining two hours. A story's setup determines, in large part, how your story will unfold. And if it doesn't suggest the movie to come, it should. Here are a few things a strong opening should do:

- ✔ Introduce your main character(s)
- ✔ Establish a routine or pattern of life
- ✔ Suggest a conflict that may break that routine or pattern
- ✔ Introduce your subplots and suggest their conflicts
- ✔ Set the tone and style of the piece
- ✔ Suggest a villain or opposing force in the story
- ✔ Suggest something important at risk
- ✔ Raise a compelling question

These eight components comprise "the rules" of your screenplay. By "rules," I mean that these components provide the boundaries or structure within which your action occurs. If the movie starts as a horror flick, it shouldn't switch to a light comedy halfway through; if I spend the first 20 minutes getting to know one young man, I'll watch for him throughout the remainder of the film. You may want to think of these rules as the game plan upon which your audience forms expectations of the ensuing action. You will fulfill or thwart those expectations as you go, and quite often, you'll do both. So you've got a lot riding on those first moments. How do you construct them to speak volumes in an efficient way? Much like a three-dimensional puzzle, you build it piece by moving piece.

Person, place, or thing: What do you want to present first?

You can't establish all eight components at once, it's too confusing. However, you can determine the primary element of your opening, in other words, where your audience should look first. You'll probably want to know who's on the screen, where they are, and how each scene looks when the film starts to roll, so consider the following elements in advance.

The people

Movies are always about people. Even if you focus on a historical event, you'll be tracking how that event affected a person or group of people.

For instance, the movie *Titanic* — though centered around a great historical tragedy — primarily depicts one couple's budding romance. The audience witnesses the fear, horror, and hope of the event through them.

Unless you're constructing a documentary, which relies more on facts than fiction, you'll know in advance from whose eyes your audience will experience the story. So decide whether your script revolves around

- ✓ One person.
- ✓ A small group of people.
- ✓ A community or nation.
- ✓ Several communities or nations.

Because your film probably consists of a plot and a subplot (if not two subplots), you'll want to determine the subject(s) of each.

A *subplot* is a smaller storyline that supports the film's main plot. It comes equipped with its own set of characters, conflicts, and actions. The characters in a subplot may or may not be moving towards the same objective(s).

By determining your film's subject, you soon pinpoint its scope, be it an epic adventure of warring nations (*Lord of the Rings*), an intimate family affair (*You Can Count On Me*), or something in between (*Malcolm X*). You choose initial images that suggest that scope.

The location (s)

In a stage play, it's often beneficial to confine your story to a small number of locales — if not limiting it entirely to one. Movies, however, can lead audiences anywhere: from the office lobby to the city street to the cafe to the cafe's storeroom to a phone booth in the cafe's storeroom. A screenwriter has no limit to where he or she can go. So let me first distinguish between location and location. Sound crazy? It's not, I promise. You can define the word in two distinct ways:

- ✓ **Physical locations:** The site-specific locale of each scene, where every moment takes place
- ✓ **Esoteric locations:** The contrasting worlds your script unites — be it social/political spheres or the internal world of a character

The physical locations will take care of themselves as you write, and they may become overwhelming when considered in advance. Esoteric locations are more important and more manageable. They help both writer and audience understand the story's larger themes. They suggest locations that a writer might periodically return to, images that frame the action like posts in a fence. Consider this example:

The number of physical locations in Mel Gibson's ***Braveheart*** is staggering. The writer jumps from tavern to alley to glen to lake to dungeon to battlefield and back again. Yet the movie's core depicts two distinct worlds at war — the working-class Scotsmen and the controlling British aristocracy. More specifically, the film unites the main character's world with that of the English villain after he destroys Gibson's young wife in the opening sequence.

Your use of time

A script that spans several generations will begin very differently from a script that encompasses a few days. Most films handle time in one of two ways:

- **In one concentrated span of time.** Most great stories occur during one portion of someone's life or in one tight span of history, so you shouldn't be surprised that most screenwriters restrict their use of time. Films of this nature generally suggest early on what event the action is moving toward and push the audience toward it chronologically, scene by scene. The writer may track several characters simultaneously, but they usually exist in the same time frame and are moving towards similar conclusions. ***When Harry Met Sally,*** for example, tracks two couples simultaneously, but both couples are moving toward marriage.

- **By jumping between time periods.** Scripts of this nature also tend to move chronologically towards one goal, but they provide details from the past and the present and, perhaps, offer glimpses of the future along the way. These films often employ memories, dream sequences, and/or flashbacks to advance the action.

Your need to alert your audience early to the time choice you've made. How? If your movie propels the audience ever forward, without deviating from a realistic time span, the audience will assume that you'll continue that trend. If you plan to jump around, you may follow a scene set today with a scene set in 1945. You may allow a character to reference time travel or muse about the future. You can employ a flashback right away. You can solve the problem in numerous ways, but remember — an audience will assume that your plot will be current and chronological unless you tell it otherwise.

How do you suggest alternate time periods? If you're writing a period piece, you might let the costumes, a description of the city, and the type of vehicles present or absent orient your audience, or you may precede the action with a caption reading, "Italy, 1886." If you're inventing a time period, as the ***Star Wars*** trilogy does, find a way to alert the audience that it's about to enter a strange place and a strange time. ***Star Wars*** launches each movie with an informative prologue that scrolls through space. And whatever technique you employ in the first 10 to 20 pages you can use again later because the audience will be prepared.

The atmosphere

Layer in the atmosphere or tone of your story. Some films do this immediately. Five minutes into the movie *Jaws,* the audience knows that it's watching a horror film. *Waiting for Guffman* introduces its mock-umentary tone right away with interviews of highly exaggerated character types. Some films do this gradually. *Rear Window* begins pleasantly enough, but it soon becomes clear that the protagonist is witnessing a murder. From that point on, the suspense is palpable.

The stakes

The *stakes* of a story refer to what's at risk in any situation. If your story's about a bus full of people, nothing in that scenario is immediately intriguing. If you tell me that a bomb's on the bus, I'm interested. If you tell me that the bus driver has a wife and kids and three mothers are on the bus as well as a main character I relate to, I'm suddenly invested in their safety. Now, something's at stake. That storyline became the box office hit *Speed.* The stakes in a film can be anything the audience roots for or worries about. If the stakes prevent the audience from leaving until after the concluding scene — you've done your job.

Conflict: What's wrong with your story?

If your opening shots don't grab an audience's attention, you'll have an even harder time gaining their interest later. You don't have to shock or horrify the audience to do this; you might seduce, con, humor, or badger them into watching — but for heaven's sake, do something.

After the first five steps are in place, *conflict* becomes the key ingredient. Conflict sparks action. Conflict raises questions, and the audience's desire to answer those questions creates tension. Keep two things in mind: You have limited time, and you're writing about the most compelling time in your characters' lives. If they've experienced these conflicts before, they'll know how to behave, and your story is over. The encounter you're dramatizing is different; it will change lives. So most screenwriters start as close to that struggle as possible. Generally, the opening sequence does one of two things:

- ✔ **It provides a brief look at the story's platform.** Your characters, like most human beings, have a routine — a "normal" way of life. And what's crazy for you and me might be this character's average day. Even if she never does the same thing twice, that ability to not repeat herself becomes her routine or her platform. Movies that begin with a clear routine provide a suggestion of how the characters may act when that sense of normalcy is disturbed. Harry Potter begins his journey as an orphan being raised by hideous relatives. This is his routine until he receives a letter informing him that he's a wizard. *American Beauty* spends a full half an hour detailing the main character's rough family life and mundane job, so that the audience feels a sense of relief when that platform shifts.

✔ **It starts the story mid-conflict.** These movies plunge the audience into the action at the point of attack. Everything is questionable — who the script's about, what's just gone wrong, how it will affect everything else. Although this method is a great way to jumpstart your film, you still need to convey how life looked prior to the conflict, so the audience knows what's been lost. You simply give us that information later. *Lord of the Rings* and *Star Wars* are examples of this method. Both films begin with a narration that launches the audience into a new world on the brink of war.

The *platform* of a story refers to a generally safe and stable way of life that exists prior to a life-altering event. The platform may be comprised of habits, job schedules, points of view, everyday routines, political or international stability, and anything a character might take for granted as secure. The *point of attack* then refers to the event or the moment in the script where the platform falls apart.

Possible ways to begin your story

There is no one way to start your script. The opening will be determined by the subject matter you've chosen to convey and the genre you're working within. However there seem to be several trends in opening techniques, and one just may work for you. Many movies convey their choice of opening in one of four ways:

✔ **A long first scene.** These openings firmly establish the initial event, detailing it from various angles and, sometimes, points of view. *The Untouchables* is an example of such a beginning.

✔ **Fleeting moments.** These openings move through an average day or the initial conflict quickly, often concentrating on the more intimate details of each scene. They may also bounce between locales and characters. *The Big Chill* opens this way.

✔ **A narrator.** Here, a main character talks the audience through the opening sequence, pointing out key details or secrets, perhaps introducing characters along the way. *American Beauty* and *Ferris Bueller's Day Off* begin this way.

✔ **A montage.** A *montage* is a series of shots strung together in rapid succession, generally underscored with music and often without dialogue. The opening sequence of *Guess Who's Coming to Dinner* begins this way.

You'll discover other techniques as you watch and read screenplays, but most of them fall within one of these categories. Again, there is no one way to start a story, and I'd be the last person to suggest there was a formula to follow. Sometimes, the best technique is to visualize a scene, write it down quickly, and return to polish it later. I divide the opening components up in this way to make the process manageable and to provide examples of proven opening techniques. The subject of your first sequence, the location, the atmosphere, and time frames — these are simply categories waiting to be embellished with your details. Together, they help you provide a lot of information in an efficient manner and raise at least one question compelling enough to keep audience members in their seats.

Tracking Success: Five Compelling (and Contrasting) Movie Beginnings

Everyone's tastes in movies differ, so, frequently, the best way to discover how you want your script to look is to study the movies that compel or repel you. Now that you're aware of what a great opening should do, look at the movies you love. How do they set up the action? What information do they immediately transfer to the audience? What images do they use to present that information? Any movie that fails to pull you in, fails because the writer neglected one or more of those components. The successful beginnings pack as much as they can into a small amount of time.

With so many strong films to choose from, I had a hard time narrowing the focus down to five. However, five it is. I've chosen these scripts to give you a sense of different ways to launch equally enticing stories. All these screenplays can be obtained online or through the library, so you can track how the images look both on the screen and on the page.

I encourage you to read these scripts as well as see the films. Doing so will help you later when you envision the beginning you want but aren't sure how to lay it out on the page. I track some of these movies through Chapters 7 and 8 as well to give you a sense of how the writers keep the tension mounting and ultimately conclude each tale. For now, see what you can discover from their opening scenes.

The Untouchables

Brian DePalma's movie, written by David Mamet, is a perfect example of the mid-conflict beginning. The first three shots set up the villain, the conflict, and the unlikely hero in rapid succession. Here's how they look:

✔ Scene 1: Al Capone lounges in a barber's chair surrounded by the press and his staff who at once trim his nails, massage his neck, and shave his face. A short summary in the corner of the screen alerts the audience that the movie takes place in Chicago in the 1930s, mid-Prohibition. It further states that the city has been taken over by Capone and his gang-glord friends. When a reporter inquires about Capone's brutal tactics, Capone vehemently denies involvement in any violence whatsoever.

✔ Scene 2: A little girl walks into a bar and holds her pail up to the counter to be filled. A man next to her leaves his briefcase on the stool, clicking the top of it before he hurries out. The little girl grabs it and runs after him, calling that he's forgotten his briefcase. The case explodes in her hands, killing her and demolishing the bar and street outside.

✔ Scene 3: Elliot Ness from the Treasury Department reads of the damage in the local paper. His obviously pregnant wife reminds him of the time and tells him to make a good first impression. It's his first day as Special Agent.

In three scenes, Mamet introduces the main forces and the main conflict — the battle to clean up Chicago. He also alludes to the stakes. A child is killed in the second scene. This tugs at our heartstrings and establishes Capone as a ruthless murderer. Ness's wife is pregnant; the audience will root for him to survive.

American Beauty

This 1999 Oscar-winning film begins with a narrator and palpable tension.

✔ Scene 1: A young girl, partially clothed, glares into a hand-held camera complaining about her father whom she considers to be a royal embarrassment. When the man holding the camera asks if she'd like him to kill her father, she coyly replies, "Yeah, would you?"

✔ Scene 2: The voice of the narrator, Lester Burnham, introduces himself, and, in the same breath, he cautions that he'll be dead in less than a year. He then casually guides the audience through his morning. Scenes follow of him waking up and masturbating in the shower, of his wife in the garden, of the homosexual neighbors both named Jim, and of his cynical teenage daughter. His commentary throughout suggests a pervading disgust at his life, at himself, and at something he feels he's lost along the way. He ends this sequence by saying, "It's never too late to get it back."

Here, the writer sets up the entire story in two scenes. The story is about the final portion of Lester's life. His goal is to break the mundane routine he feels trapped in. The audience has met virtually every important character in ten minutes.

Jaws

Spielberg's breakaway hit offers one of the most satisfyingly horrific beginnings in film history. The scenes are shot realistically, without distracting technical effects, and capture the audience in less than five minutes.

- Scene 1: A group of teenagers are drinking and chatting around a campfire. One young man and one young woman exchange glances and hurry towards the ocean, tossing clothes off as they run. The woman plunges into the water, while the man struggles with his shoes, obviously quite drunk. The scene shifts below the water, as a shark watches the woman swim. Her feet and arms flail above the creature. Suddenly, she's tugged from below and then dragged, kicking and screaming, around in a circle. The man has fallen asleep on the beach and doesn't hear her continual screams for help. Eventually, she's pulled below. All is silent.

- Scene 2: The chief of police wakes up next to his wife and receives a call that someone has gone missing. He jumps into his truck and drives down a road past a billboard of a girl on a surfboard welcoming tourists to Amity Island.

- Scene 3: At the beach, the policeman and the boy from the previous night discover the girl's severed hand lying washed up on the sand.

As horrible as these opening moments are, I repeat that they're also highly satisfying. Although most filmmakers might have lunged immediately into the grotesque shots of her death, Spielberg waits a bit. He jumps between the woman's perspective at the surface, and the shark's view from below. The billboard suggests that the tourists will be coming soon — so the stakes are set. And we've met the opposing parties — man and beast.

Guess Who's Coming to Dinner

This movie was released in 1967 to a wave of controversy. It follows an interracial couple as they announce their impending wedding to both her upperclass Caucasian family and his working-class African American parents. In many ways, the fact that this movie was released at all is amazing. That it won an Oscar at that time is almost unthinkable.

Yet the script's strength is obvious from the onset. The film begins with a montage. The camera follows the young couple off their plane, through the airport, and into a cab. Their smiles and exchanged glances suggest that they're very much in love. When they finally begin speaking, the girl reveals that she hasn't prepared her mother for her fiancé's arrival, nor has she alerted her parents that she's even engaged. This revelation is the first moment of discord. These images, coupled with the movie's title, prepare an audience for all the action to come.

Construct two openings for the same story

You can approach this project in two ways. You may want to begin by jotting down a generic scenario to practice on, or you may want to revisit the synopsis of your own story and begin there. In either case, consider the opening moments with two methods in mind:

✔ **With a platform.** Construct three images that set up an average day for your main characters.

✔ **Mid-conflict.** Construct three images that suggest the first big change in your characters' everyday routines.

After you have those three images, put them in an order that raises the most questions in the audience. Do you think that this sequence could be a solid opening for a film? You can also try envisioning already released movies with different openings. Imagine how *Jaws* might look if the writers took the time to introduce the town prior to the first attack. One of these openings is bound to be a more compelling choice than the others.

The Big Chill

This movie's opening bounces between two trajectories, both of which culminate in the same event. The first scene in the series shows a man giving his young son a bath. His wife takes a phone call, and the look on her face says that she's received bad news. From that point, the audience sees two courses of action:

✔ **Course 1:** A man is being dressed. His pants are pulled up, his shirt buttoned, his shoes tied, his tie tightened, his hair brushed, and his cufflinks inserted.

✔ **Course 2:** Numerous people receive the same bad news. One is a graphic artist, one an executive, one a ballet dancer, one a celebrity, and one a pill-popper.

The final shot in Course 1 is of the man's arms. His wrists have been sewn up. It dawns on the audience that he's a corpse. The final shot of Course 2 unites the people together at the funeral. This opening relies on questions to pull an audience along. Who are these people? Where are they going? What have they learned? Who has died? All these questions arise in the opening frames of the film.

Chapter 7

Plot Part II: Middles

• •

• •

*T*he middle of a screenplay, otherwise known as the *second act,* is usually the most difficult and, therefore, the most daunting portion to write. It's the longest section, often three times the length of either the beginning or the end. Its aim is to test the main characters' fortitude, throwing obstacle after obstacle in their paths as they charge (and sometimes hobble) toward their destinations. Writers often feel emotionally drained at the end of this section and/or wretched for having put people they respect through so much turmoil. The middle also demands a writer juggle many tasks — increasing tensions and threats, revealing character secrets at opportune times, willing the audience to root for each success, and keeping them guessing as the writer barrels toward a conclusion.

Most moviegoers visit the restroom during the second act of a film, during a "lull" in the action. Don't let them! (Or at least make them worry that they'll miss something great while they're gone.) Writers anticipate every scene, selecting not what *might* come next, but what the story dictates *must* come next. Then they convince the audience that it's too important to miss. Sound daunting? Read on. This chapter offers advice on how to answer the anxiety-ridden question, "How do I know what happens next?" Because if you know it's worth sticking around for, there's bound to be a way to alert someone else.

Deciding What Comes Next

Bravo, you have an opening sequence, and it's perfect! You've introduced your main characters and established the world they live in. You may even have suggested what's wrong with the world they live in. You're ready for the next step, and the next step is . . . ? In part, that answer depends on you and your writing habits. There are three common approaches to structuring the remainder of your script, and the one you choose depends upon the level of organization you require to write. Here are the three methods:

- **Piecemeal:** This method is based on the theory that writers take a journey *with* the character and should, therefore, sense what happens next. Writers who construct plots this way generally research their stories inside and out, making it possible to intuit the next event and the ensuing character responses. You may want to select this method if you fear that an outline may limit your creativity. However, this method offers little comfort if you encounter writer's block.

- **Dot to dot:** In this method, a writer preselects three to five pivotal events and then constructs scenes that carry an audience from point to point. This technique works well for writers who both crave and fear the structure of an outline. The targets are chosen in advance, but the path to them remains unclear.

- **Full roadmap:** A writer who uses this approach spends more time planning his script than he does writing it. After constructing a thorough scene-by-scene outline, the writer tracks everything from character changes to secrets revealed to the growing threat (whatever or whomever it may be). Though the thought of extensive outlining may seem daunting, it keeps a writer focused and on track. It remains the preferred method of plot construction among screenwriters.

Again, the method you choose depends entirely on your writing habits. I say your *writing* habits and not your personal habits because the most unorganized people are sometimes the most meticulously prepared writers and vice versa. So how much research have you done? How well do you know your characters? If you feel that you have a thorough grasp on the story, if it's beginning to speak to you regularly, you may be able to piece it together scene by scene.

Screenplays are complex works made up of fleeting visual moments. You can easily become mired in details and lose sight of the whole entity. Perhaps the clearest way to choose between piecemeal and the other two methods is to ask, "What will you do when you forget where you're going?" If your answer is, "I'll look back through my research, reread my current scene, and find out," you may be able to choose the piecemeal method. If the situation worries you at all, you may want to start with an outline.

From Lights to Camera to . . . ACTION!

Any 6-year-old knows how to tell a story. Human beings are born equipped with curiosity and a strong desire to understand what goes on around them. If you present an audience with a short film, secretly removing a key frame in the middle, most people will connect the images in some coherent fashion, regardless of the gap. They'll assume that it's supposed to make sense, and they'll inherently concoct a plot that explains it until they tire of the effort.

You may be surprised, therefore, that many adults are afraid of the very idea of telling a story — suddenly unsure of their once-keen ability to do so. Yet with a few structural reminders, stories generate themselves. And the primary term to understand is *action*.

An *action* occurs when one event causes or allows another event to take place. Two events linked in a causal relationship comprise an action.

Screenplays subsist on action. They don't debate action or merely illustrate it; action is what holds them together. And one action is really two linked events. Consider this example: I run away from home. This event in itself isn't an action. If I run away from home *and, therefore,* my mother calls the police — those events together comprise an action. My mother calling the police (Event #1) can be the start of a new action if, for instance, it causes the police department to begin a nationwide search (Event #2).

Want a film example? In the movie *Jaws,* a girl is eaten by a shark in the first scene. Although it's obviously the kickoff event, on its own, it remains just "something that happens." It becomes an action when her body is found on the beach, and the town panic begins.

This distinction is especially important to make in film, where it would be quite simple to illustrate events without providing the information necessary to link them together. As a way to practice, try visualizing these events:

- A boy disappears.
- His mother passes away.
- His father leaves town.

These are three separate events. How might you link them to convert them into actions? I could rewrite them to read, "In despair over her only son's disappearance, a young mother dies weeping in her husband's arms. Unable to return daily to his now empty house, the boy's father quietly leaves town." I've now connected them through anguish, but there are many other possibilities. How would you do it?

So if an action is two causally linked events, what's all the other stuff that happens in a scene called?

Presenting both action and activity

Beginning writers often confuse action with anything and everything that a character does in a scene. Yet movies are exactly what they advertise to be — pictures in motion. Some of that movement is action and some is not. You need to construct scenes where people demonstrate hobbies, habits, professions, and idiosyncrasies. But these attributes don't all lead to action; in fact, most of them don't. You often watch a scene and ask, "What is that character doing?" and "What is she *doing?*" in the same breath. Generally, she's doing two distinctly different things. She may be cooking an omelet and planning the next corporate takeover in the same moment. Cooking omelets is an activity — it probably doesn't lead to anything other than a nice breakfast. Planning the next corporate takeover will probably force another event. It may even result in your next scene. So it's an action.

Really compelling scenes rely on *both* action and activities. Without action your scene won't go anywhere; without activities, it'll be fairly boring to watch. Here are a few ways activities embellish a scene:

- **They reveal character information: habits, hobbies, and idiosyncrasies.** Does your character roller blade, paint, harbor an insatiable desire for chocolate cookies? Does she brush her hair 20 times before bed or collect coins in her spare time? These activities add color, dimension, and an original sheen to your characters. They separate your romantic comedy from numerous others.

- **They quickly establish location or profession.** If your script takes place in a university during final exams, you may construct scenes in which students huddle together over books. If your character is a teacher, perhaps she's grading papers or preparing for class. Strategically chosen activities often provide crucial establishing information in an efficient manner.

- **They offset and/or counter the way an audience views an action.** Humans often behave in ways that contradict their actions — it's in part what makes them fun to observe. Think about it: The man who is compassionate and well liked and causes only positive things to occur won't interest an audience for long. But if that same man unwittingly causes his company's demise? I'll watch him then, and, moreover, I'll root for him to survive the disaster.

Constructing scenes in which the activities contradict the actions may be the key to dramatizing real life. In the film, *In the Line of Fire,* John Malkovich plays a presidential assassin. In one key scene, he fishes alongside two local townsmen. The activity creates a serene, oddly safe environment. However, he's also fashioning a wooden gun in the scene — a gun he intends to use to kill the President. The casual activity of fishing makes his action all the more frightening; for a second, it lulls the audience into seeing him as the average man next door.

If you recognize the difference between an action and an activity, you can coordinate them in your own structure. The activities embellish your plot; the actions propel it.

Establishing the story's time clock

If your average 6-year-old knows how to tell a story, he most certainly knows when the story is complete. And it's not generally complete just because he couldn't think of anything else to say or because his mouth grew tired. Every story moves to a fixed point. When the story reaches that point, it's over, or very nearly done. More importantly, every story has a problem the characters must struggle to solve. The story's time clock refers to the amount of time you give them in which to do so.

A film's *time clock* refers to the amount of time a writer allots for the main characters to achieve their ultimate goal. The time clock gives the story shape — the action must be completed in a certain amount of time or else. The time clock may be a measurable amount of time, or it may be based on some impending event.

Time clocks vary in type and specificity. They may be

- **Highly specific:** Time clocks in these films are set from the beginning and mentioned throughout. The main characters in *Speed* must keep the bus over 60 miles per hour to keep the bomb from going off, but the bus will eventually run out of gas. Their time clock is limited to that tank of fuel. In *Night Mother,* Sissy Spacek tells her mother that she's going to kill herself before the night is over. Her mother has roughly two hours to persuade her against it. Because the audience never forgets that time is running out, these films are packed with dramatic tension. You can almost hear the clock ticking away in each scene.

- **Historical:** These films feel like "slices of life." The writer makes it clear that she'll present a short period of time that's important for reasons yet to be disclosed. Those time frames may encompass portions of a true historical epoch as in *Age of Innocence* and *Braveheart,* or a stretch of time in someone's personal history a la *Stand By Me* and *The Green Mile.* Audiences remain in their seats because they want to see where the characters will go and because they think that they may learn something along the way.

✔ **Competitive:** Like glimpses of evolution, these films are fueled by a "survival of the fittest" regime. Here, opposing forces battle for final control, and the movie is over when one of them destroys the other one. It's always "just a matter of time" before something drastic occurs. Audiences don't know when that moment will be, but they know that it's coming. In **Lord of the Rings,** it's just a matter of time before the dark lord takes over Middle Earth. Frodo must destroy the ring before that happens. In **Jaws,** it's just a matter of time before the shark consumes (literally consumes) the town. The police chief must destroy it first.

As the story progresses, time generally begins to run out. This phenomenon is based on a theatrical mandate known as *rising action*. The mandate suggests that a story's intensity must escalate as it heads toward a conclusion. This means that generally halfway through your second act, the pace of your film picks up.

Rising action refers to an increased momentum of the film's action as it progresses toward the main objective. As a film reaches a resolution, its pace usually increases, and the time clock shortens.

Rising action affects both your main plot and your subplots simultaneously. Each storyline has it's own trajectory that bolsters the other ones. You may speed each plot along by using shorter scenes, by taking less time between important discoveries, or by making it more important that the characters achieve their goals. This last technique is called *raising the stakes*.

Raising the stakes refers to the increased amount of pressure that a writer puts on his characters to achieve their goals or solve a problem. The writer usually achieves this increased necessity by putting a human element at risk — a child, a family member, the main character's own life — and by shortening the time allotted to achieve success. When the stakes are raised, ultimate victory becomes a matter of life or death.

Remember two things as you determine your time clock. First, always start as close to the conflict as possible. Second, choose a time in your story that chronicles the most shocking, exciting, funny, or tragic portion of your characters' lives. In other words, choose a time of struggle, humorous, horrid, or a mixture of the two. When does that portion begin, and when does it end? Regardless of whether you've written a full outline or the action, you'll want a general idea of where you're ultimately headed. Without a sense of the time clock, there's no end to the events you might explore and, therefore, no clear end for your script.

Status: Where's the Upper Hand?

Audiences thrive on competition. Think about it: The most exciting sporting events are those where the score fluctuates, when control of the game continually changes hands. If you want an invigorating game, watch two equally assertive, equally adept teams vie for one winning spot. Crowds love it; it's in their blood. If the favored team spends the whole game crushing the competition, fans will leave pleased but uninvested. After all, they hardly exerted themselves on their team's behalf. Their players didn't need support; it was an easy victory. If the opposing team dominates the game, fans will leave furious. Not only were their heroes beaten and humiliated, they hardly put up a fight.

Keep this dynamic in mind as you construct the middle of your script. Exciting cinema closely resembles a great basketball game. Power changes hands, control over precious cargo is won and lost, wars are fought on both a small and grand scale over top billing. A writer heightens this struggle; she brings it to an audience's attention, and drama is born. So, identify your hero, identify your villain, and determine how closely they're matched. What you're tracking here is that crucial and often elusive ingredient known as *status*.

Status refers to control. The person who dominates a scene physically, sexually, professionally, intellectually, or in some other way is in a position of *high status*. He controls the action. Those people he dominates are in a *low status* position. Status is based on power and control, not necessarily on expected social rank or class structures.

Status roles affect every kind of relationship, and an alert writer discovers exactly how. Writers act as sociologists in this way, pinpointing the type of relationship between two characters, determining who controls that relationship, and making educated guesses on what would happen if that control increased or diminished. Those guesses eventually become scenes.

Study the relationships around you and assess where the power lies. Those associations generally fall into one of the following categories:

> ✔ **Social.** Every culture consists of social classes. Even those groups that profess otherwise have some system with which to rank each other. Is that system based on money, political power, physical appearance? Is it an intimate system, employed within one circle of friends, or a complex cultural structure? Often, each tier of a social system can be similarly divided into high and low power roles. Within a group of servants, for example, one is the head of affairs, and the others answer to her. The Oscar-nominated film ***Gosford Park*** capitalizes on shifts in social status within the classes.

- ✔ **Professional.** Unless your character is self-employed and works alone, she's part of a pecking order in her professional world. Each profession ranks employees according to their credentials and provides standards for further advancement. Because people spend entire lifetimes trying to get that promotion, status shifts in the professional world, especially when abrupt, are full of dramatic possibility. *Working Girl* is a classic example of such a film.

- ✔ **Sexual.** In seduction, one person generally pursues the other. Sexual relationships, from the initial spark to the courtship to the marriage (if they go that far), are all about status games played by both parties. Romantic comedies like *When Harry Met Sally* are structured around those games.

- ✔ **Intellectual.** Intelligence exists in many forms. Characters may survive through academic achievement, biting wit, or an intuitive intelligence that's sometimes called "street smarts." In films based on these relationships, the smartest people generally win, and if they don't, the audience wishes they had. *The Untouchables* works in this way.

- ✔ **Physical.** Here, the person in control is either the one with the most brute strength or the one holding the biggest gun. Action/adventure films rely on these relationships to proceed. *The Terminator, Rambo,* and *The Godfather Trilogy* are just a few of the many examples.

- ✔ **Personal.** This option refers to the relationship a character has with himself. He may be battling an individual trait, phobia, addiction, instinct, or, perhaps, a disability for control over his actions. The Oscar-winning drama *A Beautiful Mind* is a clear example of such a film.

The same characters may share several kinds of relationships in any given story. The bond between a king and a servant is one that's primarily defined by social rank. However, it may also become an intellectual relationship, or even a sexual one. A person plays many roles in any given day. For instance, a woman who's at once a professor, a mother, and a wife may have unfettered control over her classroom (high status role) but remain timid and withdrawn at home (low status role). A shift in her personal status at home may well affect her teaching dynamic.

So how does status affect the action of a film? Status shifts, no matter how slight, create tension between family and friends, community, or rivals. This tension, however palpable, propels action. Characters will fight to heighten or alleviate that tension, and, usually, the fight to regain stability drives the story forward. If you thrust someone who's unaccustomed to power into the spotlight, he'll either fight to maintain notoriety or fight to escape it. If you strip someone of power that they're used to wielding, that person will fight to get it back. This quest is, in part, what drives Al Capone to distraction in *The Untouchables.* Whether the characters shift toward or away from control, the change makes them active and, therefore, compelling to watch.

Writers also continually shift status between the audience and the characters. When characters have the upper hand, they know something that the audience doesn't. If this secret is alluded to or suggested, the audience will wait to discover what it is. They'll participate in the action by searching for clues to the undivulged information. When an audience gains the upper hand, it knows something that the character doesn't. The result is a tension known as *dramatic irony.*

Dramatic irony occurs when the audience knows more than the characters. It raises the audience to a position of advanced knowledge in which they'll wait for the character to discover what they know. It adds a level of dramatic tension to a scene that would otherwise not be present.

If the audience knows something that a character remains ignorant of, the audience will participate in that character's well-being, fearing for his safety or cheering him toward discovery. In **Jaws,** the audience is aware of the killer shark, but the crowds of tourists are not. The tension mounts as they plunge into the water unaware of the danger below. This tension is crucial in a horror film where the writer wants his audience to be glued to the action. It also exists in comedy. In **Gold Rush,** a starving man imagines that he sees a gigantic chicken in front of him. The audience knows that it's actually Charlie Chaplin and will wait to see what happens when he tries to eat him. In both cases, audiences wait for the moment of discovery when the character discovers what they already know. They're immediately invested in the action.

So, if the script is your sporting event, the audience is your referee. Shifts in status help an audience keep score. If your players are well crafted and the trophy worth attaining, everyone will stick around to see who the ultimate victor will be.

What's Your Problem? Introducing Conflicts and Obstacles

I've established that the dynamic of sporting events is comparable to that of films. So, too, are their structures. Generally, both venues consist of the following:

- ✔ A team or player to root for
- ✔ A team or player to heckle
- ✔ One ultimate goal that both teams are invested in
- ✔ Conditions under which players can achieve that goal

In stories, the player we cheer for is known as the *protagonist*. Anyone standing in her way (that person we jeer at or hiss) is the *antagonist*. The goal is what each character wants. It may be a grand, admirable goal, or it may be interesting to only your protagonist. It's only important that the characters feel that they won't survive without achieving it. The conditions under which the players achieve that goal are the previously mentioned "rules" of your film: where the struggle takes place, each character's moral code, the allotted time clock, and so on. The antagonist is the most important element on this list because she is generally the first obstacle you'll introduce.

An *obstacle* is anything that prevents your protagonist from achieving her goal or at least makes it difficult for her to do so. An obstacle results in tension, as the character struggles to overcome it. That tension is known as *conflict*.

Whereas a ballgame has one antagonist in the opposing player or team, movies employ all sorts of adversaries. A strong film antagonist may be any of the following:

- **One person (also known as the villain).** Darth Vader, for example, in the *Star Wars Trilogy*.

- **A community or nation.** Amity village, for example, in the first half of *Jaws*.

- **The environment or a force of nature.** The multiple cyclones, for example, in the movie *Twister*.

- **The protagonist him or herself.** For example, John Forbes Nash, Jr. in *A Beautiful Mind*.

Any one of these rivals, or perhaps a few in combination, can prohibit a protagonist from attaining his or her goal. The goal may be power, justice, love, or a seat on the stock exchange. What matters is how committed your characters are to attaining it. The more important the goal is to both the audience and the main character, the more terrifying the antagonist's power becomes. As a writer, the more power you give your antagonist, the more interesting the struggle becomes. The first three obstacles that I mention in the previous list are external, but when the protagonist is working against himself, as the final option in that list suggests, you're constructing an internal obstacle. Internal obstacles may be:

- A phobia

- An addiction

- A psychological or physical illness

- An overbearing or embarrassing personality trait

- A debilitating state of mind — depression, jealousy, defeat, anger, or indecision, for example.

The most compelling films employ both internal and external obstacles. In *Jaws,* the police chief battles a killer shark (external obstacle) despite the fact that he's afraid of the water (internal obstacle). The film *Arachnophobia* is a perfect example of this fusion; poisonous spiders attack the town, and what do you suppose the main character can't stand? You guessed it — spiders.

An easy victory or a quick defeat offers little satisfaction. Audiences want heroes to beat the odds, to win under seemingly impossible circumstances. Internal obstacles give your characters something to overcome in themselves while the physical action ensues. In a way, that's two conflicts for the price of one.

Keep in mind that obstacles are goal related; they prevent a character from achieving something he desperately wants to achieve. If your obstacle isn't strong enough to do so, if it's the heavy traffic or the rising temperature or the misplaced car keys, it may only be an annoyance or a bother. These irritations may color your action, but don't rely on them to propel it.

Exposition: From Clunky to Creative

It's sometimes easy to forget that your audiences begin this journey knowing virtually nothing about your plot. You've thoroughly researched the subject, and you've spent weeks (if not months) with the characters — you're a field expert here. But your audience? Sure, they've arrived at the theater for a reason; they may have seen a trailer or read a review. But trailers are 30 seconds long, and reviews are generally subjective. The likelihood is that they probably don't know much about your film at all. Audiences need *exposition* in order to understand the story that you already know so much about.

Exposition refers to information that the audience needs in order to understand the present story. The information may concern a character's relationship to others or historical details surrounding an event. One or all the characters generally already know this information. Exposition differs from backstory. Backstory encompasses everything that you've imagined about these characters and their pasts. An audience won't need all this information to follow the story. Exposition strictly refers to details of backstory without which an audience will be confused.

Exposition is often difficult to reveal in a natural manner. On first try, it tends to feel awkward or forced like a stutter in an otherwise fluent speech. It breaks the scene's momentum. Why does this difficulty arise? In large part, exposition is awkward to present because it rarely occurs in real life. Most of your characters will share a past, and when you share common experiences with people, you rarely have to retell the whole story to remember it correctly. You discuss those memories with the acquired shorthand that exists among friends, family, and partners in crime. However, stories are written for an audience. The audience didn't experience everything that took place in the backstory, so they'll need more explanation. The challenge lies in providing that information in a natural way.

There are two types of exposition:

- ✔ Information the audience needs but everyone else knows
- ✔ Information the audience needs but only a few characters know

Sharing info the characters know

The first kind of information presents a distinct problem. In most stories, characters already share information about each other, so writers must concoct reasons for them to reveal or relive it again. This important info may concern their relationships, past or present, with other characters or details of events that they were all a part of — in any case, it's old news for them. The world of the audience doesn't concern them, they aren't aware that it exists. So how do you construct scenes that smoke the details out into the open?

Many writers use their opening sequence to handle exposition. Scenes introducing main characters may visually suggest the types of relationships shared as well as present their professions, possible desires, and/or their goals. The first ten minutes may be a series of time jumps that guide an audience through key moments in the past before beginning the present action. In this way, the audience shares past experiences with the characters and begins on the same page (so to speak). You may use a narrator for the same purpose — to alert us to details we may otherwise miss, but that technique is often too easy to produce great drama. In any case, you can't possibly pack every piece of expository information into the first sequence, nor would you want to. Your opening would than be instructive instead of intriguing. So, in crafting your second act, keep in mind these pieces of information that you may need to clarify throughout:

- ✔ A character's past successes and failures
- ✔ A character's secret feelings or opinions of another character
- ✔ A character's secret feelings or opinions of an event
- ✔ A character's personal tendencies, including fantasies, addictions, hopes, fears, and regrets
- ✔ Past events that continue to haunt your characters
- ✔ Basic information about any new character you introduce.

Remember that any information you share should remain on a "need to know" basis. You may uncover details that, while fascinating, aren't necessary. Exposition is *relevant* information, without which an audience would be confused about the action. For this reason, you need to try to reveal the information at the moment that it's most helpful. In *Jaws,* for instance, I need to know right away that it's Fourth of July weekend in a town that survives on tourism in order to understand the fierce resistance the police chief faces when he suggests closing the beaches. I don't, however, need to know that the chief's afraid of water until later when the shark swims past his son, and he stands powerless to help. If you divulge too many details in advance, those details may distract me from pertinent action in the moment, and I may forget them well before they become important.

Sharing info the characters may not know

The second type of exposition is less difficult to maneuver because it suggests more dramatic possibilities. If one character knows something that the others don't, eventually, that character will confide in someone, and the audience will be privy to that conversation. The character may also have the job of presenting information as needed. In *Jaws,* Richard Dreyfuss plays a marine biologist and a shark expert. The writer lets Dreyfuss's character provide the data on what sort of a creature the town's up against. Both the other characters and the audience need this information because the remainder of the film takes place on the water in combat against the beast.

Study films with an eye toward exposition, and note how they convey necessary information. Does the writer alert an audience to pertinent facts through flashback scenes? Through character confessions? Or does the writer weave the information in gradually, explaining behavior and action as it seems necessary to do so instead of at the onset. Many screenwriters solve the problem in similar ways. The most successful films strive to do the following:

- ✔ Convey as much as possible through visual images rather than relying on dialogue
- ✔ Drop the information in a moment of extreme conflict or humor
- ✔ Only say what's necessary when necessary
- ✔ Avoid didactic speeches
- ✔ Force the characters to work for the information

A little information goes a long way. Extraneous details make for unimportant action.

Note also the difference between exposition and *dramatic secrets.* Secrets are details the writer intends for everyone to discover together, characters and audience alike. That withheld information isn't crucial to the audience's understanding of the script. It comes as a satisfying surprise; it may be something an audience waits for. But the audience would understand the drama without it. With exposition, you plant the information when the time is right and get back to the action as quickly as possible. If you're crafty, you can find a way for the information to fuel an event, thereby making it an action in itself.

Determining What to Write from What You've Already Written

Many writers, beginning and veteran alike, panic at the thought of generating 100 to 120 pages of compelling drama. Yet this dread often exists because they're constantly looking forward, straining to see what comes next and afraid that nothing will occur to them. However, much of the writing has been done for you after you craft your opening sequence. You just have to revisit it and see what you've already done.

Every portion of your screenplay will consist of a few moments that ring above the rest. By "ring" I mean that they seem to be prominent or important in the scene for a reason that may be unknown even to you as you write. As you begin the process, you may want to record a few scenes as you see them unfolding and return afterwards, noting anything out of the ordinary. You're looking for items known as *dramatic plants*. And though it sounds this way, I'm not talking about potted greens with a flair for theatrics.

A *plant* (in film lingo) is a piece of evidence or information that's strategically placed in a scene in order to be discovered later on. As the action progresses, the plant assumes new meaning and may then be reincorporated for greater effect in an ensuing scene. The moment of renewed discovery is called the *payoff*. A dramatic plant may be any of the following:

- A key image
- A line of dialogue
- A motion or a gesture
- An object
- A costume piece
- A song or intriguing sound effect

The key to every strong plant isn't necessarily what it *is,* but rather how you *reincorporate* it into the action later on. Suppose that I construct a scene in which a mother warns her children against playing near the china cabinet, pointing out one bowl in particular that's been in the family for generations. That bowl is the plant. You know what has to happen later don't you? That bowl has to break. Every time a child moves near it, the tension mounts. If it breaks in the next scene, I've robbed my audience of that tension. But if I construct a few scenes in which it nearly breaks, I'm reminding the audience periodically to watch for the impending disaster. And if the mother finally breaks it, I've found a surprising conclusion, but one that's perhaps satisfying in its irony.

You'll want to place distance between the plant and the payoff to ensure that the plant has time to acquire meaning. In *Good Will Hunting,* Robin Williams tells Matt Damon a story about missing the World Series to go on a date with his future wife. When Damon inquires what excuse he gave his friends for missing the event, Williams says, "I told them I had to go see about a girl." This line rings at the time because it's well constructed and because it ends the story. It doesn't show up again until the final moment of the film when Damon decides to leave town to track down his love interest. The note he leaves for Williams says the same thing. Throughout the story, numerous experts try to break through Damon's stubborn veneer and teach him something. Although this line is funny the first time an audience hears it, by the end, it stands as proof that Williams got through to him. He learned something.

Take a look at your opening sequence and circle anything that you might reincorporate later. If you've introduced more than one character, you'll probably want those characters to meet at some point. If you begin with a crucial image, perhaps you'll revisit it later; if danger lurks in your first moments, you'll want it to return in a different, perhaps stronger guise. If you repeat this process with every scene you write, future moments may suggest themselves to you. You'll worry less about what to write next and concentrate instead on how to get there. The next step is to craft plants from the start and place them in a scene with some advance sense of how you'll use them later.

Don't confuse *reincorporation* with *repetition,* though. When you repeat a line, gesture, or image, you return to it in its original shape. If it gains importance the second or third time around, the action has shifted around it, but the image remains intact. The key line in *Good Will Hunting* remains the same even though the character who speaks it changes. The students in the *Blair Witch Project* return to the same clearing in the woods several times before their demise. Because the location never changes, the characters and the audience both begin to feel that they must be lost, and panic sets in. By the third time, the clearing takes on a menacing quality.

In contrast, you can *reincorporate* a plant in many ways. One of the first scenes in *American Beauty* takes place around a dinner table. This dinner ritual is the plant. The conversation is clipped, tense, and restrained. When the characters return to the dinner table several days later, the scene explodes with accusations and rebuttals. The characters' lives have fallen apart, and so has their false custom. Alan Ball, the screenwriter, continually returns to clichéd family rituals, but he alters them slightly each time to suggest that the changes that have gone on outside the house.

Here's a quick way to define the difference between the two devices:

- ✔ **In repetition:** The plant remains the same, but the action alters around it.
- ✔ **In reincorporation:** The plant changes shape to suggest changes that have occurred in the action.

Plants establish a pattern; the payoff represents the satisfying end to that pattern. Returning to an unaltered image or event several times (repetition), lets the audience view it again, hopefully in a different way. The audience discovers new information as the film progresses, so the image acquires new meaning the second time around. Returning to a slightly altered image or event (reincorporation) helps the audience understand changes in the story as a whole. The image becomes a way to gauge the action. Whether you return to an event or image several times or only once, the process of revisiting grants audiences a way to assess the action and generally results in a feeling of completion. You'll want to track the plants through your second act to determine which ones you use to enhance your story, and which ones you ultimately employ to conclude it.

Continuing Success: Tracking Three Successful Movie Middles

In Chapter 6, I detail five very different but equally compelling movie openings. Because the second act is the longest portion of any script (therefore making my discussion much longer), I decided to cut the number of films from five to three. So here, I break *Jaws, The Untouchables,* and *American Beauty* into their ensuing actions, obstacles, key exposition, and status fluctuations. If you haven't seen any of these films, you may want to rent them before reading the next section, or the outlines may ruin a future surprise. (If you want to know what happens in the other two films from Chapter 6, you'll just have to rent them and find out.)

Jaws

Key actions: The second act of this script takes place in two major parts that are separated by location. The first portion takes place in town; the second takes place on the water. Here are the key actions in chronological order.

TRY IT

A recipe for plot: Take one routine, add an obstacle, and stir

It sometimes helps to consider your plot as a series of patterns or routines. Your job as a writer is then to break that routine with an obstacle of some sort and, thereby, establish a new one.

In this project, you start with a generic pattern or activity and break it with an internal or an external obstacle. After you've done that, see if you can guess what the new routine might be. And if you're very brave, break that new routine with an obstacle and continue the plot.

For example: A woman composes a letter. An external obstacle may be as simple as the pen running out of ink or as dramatic as her mother entering and ripping the letter out of her hands. Her new routine may then be rummaging

around for a writing utensil or chasing her mother around the room, snatching at the letter in her hands. If I break the routine with an internal conflict, say her fear of writing the wrong thing, her new routine may include throwing draft after draft of the letter across the room.

Here are some generic routines to get you started:

- Walking a dog

- Catching a train

- Packing for a trip

- Speaking in front of a crowd

- Climbing a mountain

The mayor decides to keep the beaches open, claiming that the initial death was due to a boating accident. The shark kills a young boy, and his mother offers a $3,000 reward for its capture. A shark hunter named Captain Quint says that he'll kill the creature for $10,000. The marine biologist, Matt Hooper, arrives and discovers the false boating accident report. A tiger shark is captured, prompting the Mayor to announce the threat is gone. The mother finds out that Police Chief Brody knew about the shark and failed to alert anyone. She publicly blames him for the death of her son. Brody and Hooper discover that the tiger shark isn't the killer, but the mayor refuses to listen. Another man is killed the next day in the same area where both Brody's son and the mayor's children are swimming. The mayor signs an agreement to let Brody and Hooper hire Quint to kill the shark. The trio sail out to kill the shark, and it puts up a formidable fight — sinking the boat, separating Hooper from Brody, and eating Quint in the process. When the second act ends, Brody must face the shark alone.

Obstacles: The town and the shark are the two primary antagonists and external obstacles. They present the first obstacle by refusing to close the beaches to the tourists. This conflict becomes more prominent when the tiger shark is caught and everyone assumes that the waters are safe. Brody overcomes this obstacle when the shark threatens the mayor's own children, and he signs an order to destroy it. The battle with the shark is further complicated by the shark's size, strength, and (believe it or not) intelligence, a rickety boat, and an alcoholic, slightly crazy captain. The largest internal obstacle is Brody's fear of water and boats. He overcomes this terror to finish the job.

Exposition: The audience needs to know that it's the Fourth of July weekend, that Brody is afraid of water, that Hooper has never tracked a great white shark before (especially one of this magnitude), and that Quint saw his entire crew get eaten by sharks after a submarine attack in the war. The first pieces of information are conveyed visually and through scattered lines of dialogue. The rest is revealed over the ship's table, moments before the final struggle with the shark.

Status: Status first alters in the political battle between the town and Brody. Brody ultimately triumphs. The battle among the three men is both social and intellectual. Quint owns the ship and has practical knowledge of sharks, Hooper has the scientific data and is equally stubborn. Brody allows them higher status until called upon to fight at the end. Their relationship with the shark is obviously a physical fight to the death — when the second act ends, no one knows which side will triumph.

The Untouchables

Key actions: The second act of this script can also be divided into two parts: one that takes place prior to the selection of Ness's crew and one that takes place after the crew is assembled.

Ness raids a factory that's supposedly smuggling liquor for Capone, based on a tip he receives. The tip is a false one, and he's publicly humiliated. He meets Officer Malone (Sean Connery) in passing and asks him to join the Treasury team. Malone at first declines, but he then changes his mind. They select the second team member, George Stone (Andy Garcia), and with the unwitting help of the Treasury's accountant, successfully raid a secret liquor ware-house. Capone brutally murders the man responsible for the mistake. His crony offers Ness a bribe, which Ness refuses. They threaten Ness's family, who are quickly moved to a safe location. The gang successfully stops an arms shipment and retrieves Capone's financial ledger in the process. Capone begins trial for income-tax evasion. Capone has the accountant killed, at which point Ness almost ends the fight in despair. Malone is also murdered, but he manages to relay information on how to nab Capone's bookkeeper before he dies. At the end of the second act, it remains uncertain whether Ness and Stone will be able to do so without the help of their friends.

Obstacles: The antagonist is obviously Al Capone and his mafia crew. However, Ness also fights corruption within the Treasury itself, the police department, and, eventually, in court. Internal conflicts include Malone's initial fear of death, Ness's devotion to his family, and his concern for their safety.

Exposition: The audience needs to know that Ness begins the journey on his first day on the job, his police experience is limited, his ethics are strong and sound, he desperately loves his wife and child, and his wife is pregnant. The audience discovers all this information in the first ten minutes. Later, it becomes important to know that Malone is a religious man, Stone is a stellar marksman, and Capone will kill his own people if necessary. All these details arrive when you need them — not a moment sooner.

Status: The film works very much like a tennis match. First, Capone wins; then Ness, then Capone, then Ness. They're evenly matched, and although the audience roots for Ness and loathes Capone, the victor remains uncertain.

American Beauty

Key actions: The second act exists in three parts. During the first part, Lester despises his life. In the second part, his life begins to change, and in the third part, he begins to enjoy it again. His wife Carolyn and daughter Jane go through similar changes at exactly the same moments.

Lester is told that he may lose his job unless he writes a report convincing them that he's a valuable employee. Carolyn fails miserably at selling a house. Jane meets the new boy across the street, Ricky Fitts. He silently films her. The audience meets his family — his silent, withdrawn mother and his father, a homophobic, retired military colonel. Lester meets Jane's seductive friend Angela. He becomes infatuated with her. He embarrasses his wife at a social function, leaving her to flirt with a rival real estate tycoon. Lester smokes pot with Ricky. He begins to work out and buy marijuana from Ricky on a regular basis. The family takes the first major turn. Lester blackmails his company into a great severance package and takes a job at a fast-food restaurant. Carolyn begins an affair with the tycoon. Jane begins seeing Ricky. Colonel Fitts suspects him of having sexual relations with Lester. Carolyn buys a gun and takes up shooting lessons. Lester reminds the audience that he'll be dead soon. Their lives take the second major turn. Lester discovers his wife's affair. Jane ends her friendship with Angela. Colonel Fitts kicks Ricky out of the house. Ricky and Jane decide to run away together. Angela decides to sleep with Lester.

Obstacles: Internal obstacles abound in this film, too many, in fact, to list. Suffice it to say that most of the characters are their own antagonists; much of the action involves altering their mind-sets and, thereby, changing the course of their lives. Other obstacles include Colonel Fitts, Lester's boss, and Carolyn's career, but these external obstacles take a back seat to the internal conflicts.

Exposition: Lester provides most of the necessary exposition through his narration. He tells us what his life is like, he tells us what his flaws are, and he tells us what he'd like to change. Colonel Fitts's own comments suggest the homophobia, Ricky tells Jane that he's recently returned from a mental institution, and everything else is revealed visually in scenes or through narration.

Status: All sorts of power changes hands in this film. Sexual tension erupts between Jane and Ricky, Lester and Angela, and Carolyn and the tycoon. Lester defeats his boss; he and Carolyn square off time and again; Angela loses social control over Jane but gains sexual power over Lester; Ricky and his father pit intellect against brute strength. The score is always in flux.

If you rent these films, I encourage you to break them into the individual story components of status, obstacle, actions, and exposition. The pieces will undoubtedly overlap; obstacles cause actions, status shifts result in more obstacles, and so on. Yet by focusing your attention on one task at a time, you soon garner a familiarity with plot structure as a whole. Hopefully, it'll make the constructing of your second act less daunting.

Chapter 8

Plot Part III: Endings

• •

• •

How do you know when your story's finished? It's finished when the characters triumph over adversity, the villain disappears, the conflicts are efficiently resolved, and everyone goes home smiling, of course. You don't believe me? What if I said that your story's finished when the characters, who have undergone so much turmoil that they can hardly stand, finally give up the effort entirely and let the world collapse around them? You still seem skeptical. Well, good for you because, for a strong script, neither of those endings fits the bill.

Regarding your story's conclusion, I have both good news and bad news. The good news is that if all your second-act pieces are in place — if you've crafted dynamic actions, intimidating obstacles, and formidable foes — your ending should write itself. The bad news is that at the end of a first draft, your second-act pieces are rarely in place.

A convincing conclusion is one in which the conflicts that you've inflated in Act Two find resolution, the characters achieve their goals or stop vying for them, and the new world you've created makes some kind of sense — however unorthodox that sense may be. Your ending relies entirely on every moment that precedes it. If the second act offers no solution, your only resort is a forced wave of the magic wand (so to speak) to sum things up, which will leave your audience dissatisfied and confused. This chapter offers suggestions on ways to recheck both your opening and second act to steer them toward the appropriate finale and on how you may craft that finale when you get there. (If you need more info on crafting your opening and second act, see Chapters 6 and 7.)

How Do You Know When You're Done?

The end of your second act is a very precarious place to be. Your protagonist is either embroiled in chaos and ready to abandon hope, or she's just beginning to acknowledge a bright and promising future. The antagonist is closing in, ready to fight to the death if need be, and time is running out. The only question left to answer is, "Will your protagonist be successful?" In other words, will she solve the problem and achieve her goal? After you answer that question and envision a tentative ending for your piece, proceed to the following questions. They may help clarify whether you've discovered the fitting conclusion and how you may approach getting there.

- Has your story been written before? If so, how does it differ from predecessors with a similar concept?

- Do you understand your characters more thoroughly now than when you began?

- Are your "rules" still intact? (See Chapter 6 where I discuss "rules.)

- What have you discovered about your story so far?

- Have your story's central themes or questions changed? If so, what are they now?

- Does each portion of your story address those themes or questions in some way?

- Has your story reached the point you anticipated reaching? If not, are you content with where it is?

- Have your characters changed? Has their world altered? How?

- What has been gained and/or lost for the characters, the environment, and the audience?

The first six questions address elements of your opening and second act, which you may need to adjust in retrospect. If you've discovered a movie that shares too much in common with your own, you'll want to enhance the portions of your script that make it unique. You should know more about your characters now than when you started. If you don't, your action is probably fueled by events rather than people. Go back and see what you can discover in hindsight. The "rules" of your film refer to its consistency. In other words, are you writing the same film now that you were at the beginning? If not — if characters have disappeared, the genre has changed, or the ultimate goal shifted — you'll want to do a continuity check to see where the plot became muddled. The same note applies to your story's central themes and questions. You may find that the themes you arrive at are more compelling than those that began the journey. If that's the case, rewrite your beginning to match your end.

The final three questions on the list speak to the all-important aspects of any film — the elements of discovery and change. Unless your characters have learned something about themselves or the world in which they exist, and unless both venues have changed accordingly, you won't know how to end your story. The film's final moments rely on an acquired knowledge on the part of your characters and, hopefully, in the audience as well.

Tracking the change: What's different now?

A strong story chronicles the most important or compelling moments in a character's life. And the most compelling moments involve the most difficult and, therefore, enlightening transitions. Consider the revealing portions of your own life — moments when you discovered something horrific or awe-inspiring about yourself or your environment. I'd venture to guess that they included or were followed by personal growth and maturity. Your characters will experience the same phenomenon as the script progresses, and what they learn will affect where you lead them, a journey known as the film's *dramatic arc*.

A *dramatic arc* refers to the trajectory of a character, a community, or an environment from one state of being to another. The transition can be monitored through changes in behavior, in points of view, or in moral codes that, in turn, alter the story's action.

Tracking character arcs

Before you begin crafting a conclusion, look back at what you've done so far with an eye toward character change. Hopefully, your characters will alter dramatically. You're tormenting them for a reason, and that reason's not so that they can remain passive or content, right? It's your job to challenge and, if necessary, harass your characters into a new way of life. They'll become the sum of all the experiences you toss at them, so keep track of those experiences and, more importantly, of their effects. In doing so, you'll quickly discover the following:

- Whether the stages of transformation are clear and consistent
- Whether your audience has been privy to the transformation
- Whether you've omitted key moments
- Who your character may ultimately turn out to be

If your character exits one scene as a millionaire and appears two scenes later begging for change on a street corner somewhere, your audience won't trust the transformation. Why should they? *You* might know exactly how he got from one state of being to the next, but don't forget to let your audience in on the actions that brought him there. The most dramatic scenes in this scenario connect the character from wealthy Point A to impoverished Point B. If you show me his gambling habit, the demise of his business, and a hefty divorce settlement that favors his two ex-wives, I'll not only understand his monetary transition, I may even expect it.

The above scenario is an example of an external change, which is generally less difficult to dramatize. Other external changes may affect the following aspects of your character:

- ✔ Appearance
- ✔ Mode of expression
- ✔ Profession and/or financial status
- ✔ Circle of family and/or friends
- ✔ Habits, hobbies, and personal tendencies

Many external changes don't necessitate lengthy dialogue — if they require conversation at all. If your main character begins his journey hobnobbing with the elite and ends warming his hands over a back-alley fire pit with pickpockets, I'll visually note the change in his social circle. In *The Talented Mr. Ripley,* Matt Damon transforms from a middle-class nobody to a mirror image of his upper-class idol with virtually no speaking at all.

External changes generally mark key stages in the main story's dramatic arc. Lester Burnham of *American Beauty* begins working out just as his life begins to improve in all capacities. In *My Fair Lady,* the scene in which Eliza Doolittle speaks with distinction marks the first moment in her transformation from street urchin to a lady. However, shifts in the character's physical person or circumstances may also be the result of some internal transformation. Internal transformations include shifts in the character's:

- ✔ Psychological health
- ✔ Confidence
- ✔ Anxiety
- ✔ Sexuality
- ✔ Opinions or beliefs
- ✔ Passions or dreams
- ✔ Awareness of others
- ✔ Compassion or lack thereof
- ✔ Religion or faith

External changes are simple to dramatize; internal shifts require more thought. Unless you visually re-create the mind or spirit of the character, much as the writers do in ***Being John Malkovich,*** it will be the character's altered behavior that clues me in to the transformation. Brody begins his journey in ***Jaws*** as a man desperately afraid of the water, yet by the end, he's battling the shark alone on the ocean, clutching a piece of driftwood for support. Spielberg illustrates the change in his phobia by scenes in which Brody moves closer and closer to the water. He then makes it a matter of life and death that Brody charter a boat.

You'll also want to track the internal and external shifts for the other characters — antagonist and subplot personnel alike. Though many villains shift from bad to worse, even the slightest transition affects their actions. Capone may remain a monster to the end, but by the film's conclusion, he becomes a desperate monster, and he's learned an important lesson — that he's not untouchable.

After you know what alterations your characters have undergone prior to your resolution, you should be able to determine what the last step in that transformation may be and whether it will aid or prevent the character from achieving her goal. The scenes in which the characters experience that moment become your *climax,* which leads to the *resolution.*

The *climax* represents the most intense and, generally, the largest scene of the film in which the protagonist makes one last attempt at achieving his or her goal. The climax is the culmination of any struggles or transformations the character has experienced prior to it; it marks the story's final battlefield.

The *resolution* occurs immediately after the climax and comprises the film's last scene. This is the time characters and audiences alike absorb the impact of the final battle. It marks the character's first walk as a changed person in the new world of your script.

Altering the world of your script

Characters are so closely linked to their environments that it's often difficult to distinguish changes in one realm from changes in the other. The world of your script will shift as the characters change; in fact, the world may directly reflect their changes, both internal and external. You want to track these transformations through the opening and second act as well in order to better predict where you'll ultimately end up. Here are two important questions to consider while constructing your final landscape:

- ✔ What sort of world have I crafted?
- ✔ Why have I led my audience to that world?

The first question speaks to your script's general climate. By climate, I mean both the actual landscapes and the social, political, and economic conditions, all of which may alter with the action. The climate may change in any of the following ways:

- ✔ Physically
- ✔ Politically
- ✔ Socially
- ✔ Spiritual
- ✔ Ethically
- ✔ Sexually

A change in climate makes something possible that wasn't possible before, or it removes a possibility entirely. In **Lord of the Rings,** a beautiful and serene setting becomes dark and ominous. The landscape shifts and it becomes more difficult for good to prevail. In **The Green Mile,** the spiritual climate shifts. People who once did not believe in the supernatural find themselves witness to it. As a result, they view a convicted murderer with very different eyes. To further understand what I mean by climate, you may want to complete this phrase:

> "My story ends in a world where _____ is no longer possible/acceptable and where _____ can now occur."

You should be able to complete at least one part of that statement at the end of your script. At the end of **The Untouchables,** Chicago is a city where extortion is no longer acceptable and where justice can now occur. At the end of **A Beautiful Mind,** psychological stability is no longer possible, but an honest way of life can now occur. Bear in mind that a shift in one of these realms doesn't necessarily mean that the climate will change within the boundaries of your story. You may only be concerned with leading up to the shift itself; the repercussions may belong in a different script. However, a shift in one of the realms always suggests the possibility of a change in climate. You may explore that change onscreen, or let your audience imagine it long after the credits roll.

The second question speaks to your responsibility as a writer. You're not going on this journey alone; you have an audience behind you. That audience expects to gain or feel something along the way — preferably something grander than disgust or low-brow humor. It wants to watch people do things that ordinary people can't or don't do; it expects to leave the film changed in some way. You're giving the audience a gift of some kind — the gift of laughter, of knowledge, and even of extreme pain if enlightenment is the result. Spielberg's **Schindler's List** is an example of a world full of bigotry, destruction, and death. Yet at the film's conclusion, relatives of the deceased leave stones on the graves, honoring the victims together. The audience may leave feeling mortified and/or ashamed, but it will also remember the victims.

The world you craft need not be neat, predictable, or safe. As a member of the audience, I don't live in a world where all three of those conditions exist, and I might not believe it if I saw it. Your characters need not end up happy or more ethically sound; that phenomenon also rarely occurs in everyday life. However, in order to fully satisfy your audience, the ultimate world of your script should do a few things clearly:

- ✔ It should evolve out of the previous action.

- ✔ It should represent the changes that your main characters have undergone along the way.

- ✔ It should allow or prevent your characters from achieving their goals and/or solving their problems.

- ✔ It should offer hope in some direction.

The last item on that list also speaks to responsibility. Hopefully, your story represents a change for the better or offers that distinct possibility. Yes, your main character may die, but can that death lead to some ultimate good? Lester Burnham's death in **American Beauty** leaves the other characters (and possibly audiences) questioning bitterness in themselves and the life they take for granted. Rhett Butler leaves Scarlett O'Hara in **Gone with the Wind.** The end of that movie is tragic and frightening, but until that point Scarlett took full advantage of her marriage with no clear understanding of who Rhett really was. She treats her marriage much in the way that she moves through life — with little respect for anyone but herself. And as she very much symbolizes the view of the plantation-owning South, there is hope at the end of the film that she may finally recognize this fact about herself and that the Southern tyranny may come to an end. The audience doesn't know if this is the case, but the possibility exists.

Crafting your story's conclusion

An *epiphany* is a sudden intuitive realization, an unexpected comprehension of reality. The key words in that definition are "unexpected" and "realization." In grand cases, epiphanies are accompanied by a sharp intake of breath and a quickening of the heart and mind as they struggle to absorb a new way of understanding something about the world. In more subtle terms, an epiphany feels like a great "Aha!" and a mild relief at the solution to a mystery. Get to know this word epiphany. Sit with it a while and include it in your story. It's the heart of a strong conclusion.

You can conclude your film in numerous ways, yet the classiest endings seem to exist in two parts: the climax and the resolution. In a sense, the rising action runs you up the hill where you fight the final battle (known as the *climax*), and at the end, you roll down the other side of that hill into the resolution. By the end of the second act, you should know roughly what that resolution will be. Even if you're a writer who loathes outlines, you know what your characters want, and you know where they're going. Start painting a picture that tells your audience what *you* already know.

Climax — the final frontier

The climax marks the first and most important part of your story's conclusion. If you've done your job, audiences have some idea of what's coming next, and they're ready for it. Your action up to that point creates expectations that your climax will fulfill. But no pressure, right? With so much riding on this scene, it really helps to take it step by step.

A strong climax will do the following:

- ✔ **Be the grandest scene in your script in weight, scope, and action.** All scenes lead to this one, so don't disappoint your audience by skimming through the climax. Consider your genre. If your film is a romantic comedy, the romance blossoms or almost ends here. If your film is an action/adventure, the greatest, most exciting battle occurs here. If your film is a tragedy, the climax marks the time of greatest loss. Remember that time is running out; the actions that your characters once shied away from must happen now if they're to happen at all. If you make bold decisions anywhere, let it be here.

- ✔ **Toss your protagonist into a moment of choice.** Your characters have undergone changes for a reason. They've acquired skill and knowledge for a reason. They've done so because that expertise will be necessary in the climax. Place your characters in a moment of uncertainty when they must choose which way to act, and let them use their newfound knowledge to decide what to do. If things simply happen to your main character, or around her, the audience will leave dissatisfied, uncertain whether she's truly strong enough to solve the problem or is simply lucky.

- ✔ **Begin at the moment that the protagonist experiences the greatest despair or the first indications of hope.** The choice you make here often determines whether you end triumphantly or with tragic repercussions. A character that starts the climax in anguish has nowhere to go but up. Something will happen in the next moment to convince that character to turn things around, and he'll face the enemy refreshed or, at the very least, determined. On the flip side, a character that's full of great hope at the onset of the climax has the most to lose. The character will either experience that loss in the final scenes or experience it and then make a miraculous recovery at the end.

- ✔ **End when the protagonist resolves his or her problems.** Resolving the problem doesn't necessarily mean achieving the goal. However, if your character doesn't achieve his goal, his failure to do so should somehow solve the problem. Scarlett O'Hara doesn't find romantic fulfillment, but her inability to do so ends her false marriage and puts a dent in her way of life. Luke Skywalker doesn't decisively defeat Darth Vader until the third portion of the *Star Wars Trilogy,* but he nevertheless solves the ultimate problems in the first two films.

Your character is waging a dual war in the climax:

- ✔ **A war with the external antagonist/villain.** Keep track of your villain or your chosen antagonist. That villain has learned alongside the hero, and that villain has acquired a support group alongside the hero. That villain is ready to win, as is the hero. They should be evenly matched.

- ✔ **A war with himself.** Something internal has been holding your character away from complete success. He needs to overcome that something here or use it to his distinct advantage.

Ask yourself what event would force these people together, where would they choose to wage a last war, and who is the strongest of the pair. That scene is your climax.

Your audience should leave your film satisfied. Notice that I don't say thrilled or grief-stricken, but *satisfied.* In Chapter 7, I speak about *reincorporation,* the art of weaving key bits of thematic information continuously through your story. Those bits culminate here. The climax marks the final reincorporation of images, ideas, skills, and traumas. Luke Skywalker loses his aunt and uncle, who act as his parents at the beginning of the *Star Wars Trilogy;* he finds his real father in the trilogy's final climax. George Lucas reincorporates the idea of parenting and guidance one last time, and somehow, the story feels complete. *American Beauty* begins with the caution speech that the main character may die. The speech returns with greater meaning at the end after everyone's world has been drastically altered. Your climax releases the tension that you've constructed between characters, and it completes some pattern, be it behavioral or thematic. The ending of that cycle is very satisfying.

Resolution — the final lap

Your film's resolution is the audience's final grace note, the time to linger with the characters just long enough to feel what's shifted in the world. Here are some final questions that may help you clarify that scene when you get there:

- ✔ **Where is your villain?** What kind of justice reigns in your finale? A truly formidable villain leaves a mark even after death, be it a physical scar on the hero's cheek or his wiser, more wary sensibility.

- ✔ **What has your protagonist lost and gained?** This loss or gain may be as specific as a love interest and as profound as stability, but something is missing from this world, and something exists now that was not there when you began. What is it?

✔ **Was it worth the trip?** Ask this question for the characters and for the audience. What can a human being gain from watching the action? The answer may be "an evening of laughter" or "an acute look at racism." If the audience has gained something or even left with an element of hope, you've done all right.

✔ **What story might begin the way yours now ends?** The ending of every script could mark the beginning of a new one. You're moving your characters from stability into chaos and back to a new (not necessarily secure) stability. One person's finale might be another's opening night.

Your resolution will be short. After all, you solved the problem in the climax. You may just have a few loose ends to tie up. After the explosive and revealing scene between Matt Damon and Robin Williams in *Good Will Hunting*, Damon must still quit his job, pack his belongings, and leave a final note for Williams. The audience needs to see his friends drive up to the house and discover him not there because it completes a pattern established earlier. But these scenes happen quickly. The pervading tension has already been released, and the epiphany has been reached — give us a calm scene or two and let the closing credits roll.

Danger Will Robinson: Threats to an Otherwise Healthy Plot

Much of a first draft is written in a feverish pitch and at a feverish pace. If you let your script sit around for too long in between writing marathons, anxiety will creep up on you along with every other thing you have to do before finishing the script. So, often, the best thing to do is to write the whole thing quickly while caught in the story's grip and wait until you've completed a draft to hunt for those elements trying to sabotage it from within. However, you now have a complete draft. You have a beginning, a middle, and — lo and behold — an ending. Now, you can begin to search for those things that make your plot go clunk in the night instead of zing.

Would that really happen? The probable versus the possible

When you write a script, you make a silent pact with an eventual audience; they're going to trust you, and you're going to preserve that trust. Audiences want you to succeed at your craft. They've paid ten dollars to be here (not to mention ten dollars on popcorn); they want your story to astound them, move them, affect them in some positive way. In other words, they're on your side. That is, they're on your side until the first line of dialogue doesn't ring true, until the first scene with a forced conclusion, until that long-lost character emerges to sum everything up, or until that senior citizen with the broken ankle manages to sprint up six flights of steps at record speed just in time to force his way into the deadbolted room and defeat the sumo wrestler. Do you see where I'm headed? *Plausibility* and lack thereof will be the first thing to make or break your film.

Aristotle said that drama lies in that which is probable, rarely in that which is possible. Plausibility refers to holes in your story's logic, and the more probable your actions are, the fewer holes you'll have. You should ask yourself the same two questions that audiences will ask as they watch:

- ✔ Could this really happen?
- ✔ Could it really happen this way?

Audiences may not think to ask these questions until something in your script suggests that they should. They may pass over the first awkward moment because they've spent money here, and they want to enjoy themselves. The next few moments will set them on edge; they may begin looking for flaws, and by the fourth or fifth error, they'll pick your script apart on the drive home. What sort of moments might grab their attention? All sorts, actually.

A story becomes improbable when

- ✔ **It has glaring historical or factual errors.** Audiences shouldn't consider movies, historical or otherwise, to be entirely factual. They're built on drama, and drama takes liberties. However, if your script takes place in the seventeenth century and a car drives by in the distance, I would have a hard time buying the setting, if not the action itself.

- ✔ **The film's genre shifts or is in question.** The best films combine comedy with drama, romance with adventure, and so on. Yet at its core, a film lives in one area. If it doesn't, if it jumps evenly between two or more categories, it may feel like two films are vying for space, neither of which has time to be complete.

- ✔ **Crucial information comes too easily.** I go to movies to see people struggle, to battle each other for control of something that they want. Your heroes are only strong because an audience witnesses their struggle. Nothing in life is easy. If your hero's life is simple and easy, not only will I refuse to believe it, I may resent it a little as well.

- ✔ **A character's actions contradict each other.** This item refers to consistency, and consistency refers to the ultimate goal. If your character always moves toward one goal, her actions remain consistent in their purpose. If her goal shifts, or if she behaves erratically for seemingly no reason, I'll leave the theater frustrated and bewildered.

- ✔ **A character disappears with hasty explanation or no explanation at all.** This phenomenon occurs either because, in crafting the protagonist, you've forgotten a smaller character or because you found that you had one too many people to track and didn't know how to write one out.

- ✔ **A character bursts onto the action with little or no setup.** This phenomenon occurs either because you knew this person was coming but failed to allow for it in your opening or because you need to solve a problem in the script and are hoping that a new character will do it for you.

- ✔ **Problems are solved without combat of any kind.** Characters are only interesting when they're making choices, gaining knowledge necessary to make choices, or acting on choices that they've already made. They should make events happen, not let events happen to them.

Your opening may solve some of your plausibility difficulties. Those first 15 to 30 pages establish what can and can't happen in the script. If you want me to believe in a car that travels through time, introduce me to its inventor right away *(Back to the Future)*. If you want me to be believe that an island of dinosaurs exists in 2000 *(Jurassic Park)*, take me to that island as soon as possible and prove it to me. If you intend to introduce a character much later, create a world in which people pop in and out — in other words, where I'm used to surprised visits. You might also mention the character in earlier dialogue, so that the name precedes its owner.

There is a distinct difference between *suspension of disbelief* and improbability.

Suspension of disbelief refers to an audience's willingness to believe fantastical or extraordinary situations out of a desire to enjoy the story.

Audiences suspend their disbelief because they're enthralled by the plot, and they want to believe that it could happen. An improbable script presents something as fact that cannot be, but it does little to convince the audience of its worth. It often happens with the best intentions. Writers are on a tight deadline, desperate for a next payment, or they're furious with one stubborn portion of the script and ready to be done with it. In any case, they reach a point where a solution won't present itself, and they quickly formulate some device to solve it for them. In Greek drama, it appears as a *deus ex machina*. A god descends from the heavens to settle old scores and sum information up. In current times, it appears as that lucky tip that happened to solve the case, the one door that happened to be unlocked, or those keys that happened to be left in a getaway car. These solutions are too easy; I feel the writer stepping in. When the writer's hand in the work becomes apparent, the audience's belief in the action diminishes.

How do you avoid implausible action? You may try one or several of the following:

- ✔ **Research, research, research.** The more familiar you are with the world, the less likely that historical or continuity mistakes will occur. You should know more about your story than the audience does. Prove it to them, so they can trust the story and relax.

- ✔ **Allow a character to express the audience's disbelief.** *Back to the Future* and *Jurassic Park* work, in part, because one of the characters is a skeptic. The character takes on the role of the audience in questioning the action. As he or she becomes convinced that the notion is possible, so, too, does the audience.

- ✔ **Prepare the audience for improbabilities in advance.** Those script rules are all important. Look toward possible improbabilities and prepare an audience for them in advance. *Star Wars* tells the audience right away that this is a galaxy long ago and far away. Audiences are immediately prepared for a sci-fi adventure where impossible things are now possible.

- ✔ **Make characters work for information.** Any piece of data that arrives quickly and easily is suspect. Life doesn't work that way. You may write an element of luck into your script, but too much luck is unacceptable.

- ✔ **Let characters solve problems themselves, using skills or knowledge that the audience has witnessed them acquiring.** The audience wants to get to know your protagonists, to learn from them, and to be changed by them. It can't do so if the protagonists don't act for themselves or make choices and follow them through.

Implausibility maligns your audience's trust and, therefore, makes the audience wary of you as a writer and of filmmaking in general. You want your audiences to continue expecting good films, not to be surprised when they finally see one. Eventually, it's your name on the work, and audiences will see the film as an extension of you. Take care with what you present.

Scenes where nothing happens: Two final threats to watch for

Two final threats occur when a writer overwhelms a reader with unrelated action or unimportant dialogue. I call the first threat *cascading* and the second threat *banter.* Ever been to a movie with scene after scene of exciting action or cutting repartee that has little aim or direction? Many things can happen in a scene without anything really *happening.* How? Look at this scene breakdown:

A man robs a bank.

Police follow him to the harbor.

A boat chase ensues.

He is picked up by a helicopter.

He flies to an airstrip, but detectives are waiting.

He charters a jet.

A plane chase ensues.

Aside from the obvious improbability, what's really happening here? A lot of movement, some exciting special effects no doubt, and an element of danger — but beyond that? Not much. When one action follows another with no sense of purpose, you're creating a paper chain, not compelling drama. This is cascading. You cascade a script when you forget to reincorporate knowledge or experience from one action into situations that follow it.

Suppose that a boy goes flying with his father in the opening shots; the audience can see that he idolizes his dad. In a following scene, he plays airplane with his younger brother, explaining how to fly just as he heard his dad explain it to him. So if, at the end of the film, a group of men chase him into the shed where they keep the plane — how do you think he'll escape? Well, if he skateboards out, I'll probably leave the theater. Here, each action builds into the next, and, at some point, previously acquired knowledge is reused. I could've said that the boy flies with his father, he plays airplanes with his brother, the family's attacked, he escapes to the woods, he's chased through town, and so on. But that would be a cascade. The action never lands; it just keeps on coming.

Cascading affects your scene-to-scene structure. Banter works in much the same way, but it affects your dialogue. Remember, I go to the theater to watch characters change and affect each other. I go, in part, to keep score. Consider the following dialogue between two co-workers:

"Hey Jackie, how's your work going?"

"Fine, Grace. And yours?"

"Fine. Great shindig last night."

"It was, wasn't it? How much do you think it cost?"

"I don't know, but it wasn't cheap."

"Was Harry there?"

"I think I saw him. I loved his speech the other day, didn't you?"

And so on. Who's winning in that scene, do you think? It's hard to tell. Any tension on the rise? Doubtful. The problem with the conversation, as it pertains to drama, is that nothing's changing. Neither woman gains or loses status, nor does the conversation seem to be code for another topic. Banter occurs when characters get stuck talking about another event, or when no one is altered by the exchange. If Jackie had just been fired and Grace was purposely hurting her feelings, social tension would exist. I'll watch the scene. If both women are having an affair with Michael, sexual tension will result. I'll watch the scene. As long as someone in the scene is being affected, if that person leaves the scene different (however slightly) than when she went in, you've done your job.

Ultimate Success: Tracking Three Movies through Their Triumphant Conclusions

In this section, I tell you how three films end, and moreover, I break down those endings. I just thought I'd warn you in case you don't already know how these movies end and would rather see or read the endings for yourself first. (Aren't I considerate?)

The three films I skim through here tackle different subjects, different environments, and build completely different people. Yet they share a tight, efficient structure. Every ten minutes, a routine is broken, and an action occurs. The characters gain skills that they use later to further the plot. Every main character, villains included, is given a resolution, if not a joyous one. If you begin analyzing all the films you watch in this manner, you may be amazed at what you discover.

Jaws

Rising Action: The final battle in this film must take place between Brody and the shark. Brody is the one with the fear of water, Brody was responsible for funding the expedition, and Brody is the one propelling the town to take these actions. So the rising action consists of getting him alone. Hooper descends into the water in his observation cage, armed with sedatives meant to end the creature when it approaches. This plan, of course, fails. The cage is destroyed, and Hooper barely escapes to hide behind a reef. Next up — Captain Quint. After destroying the radio in a fit of passion and destroying the boat in foolish pursuit of the shark, Quint takes one last stab at it with his gun and three barrels. He fails, and the shark eats him. Brody is left alone on a sinking ship, facing a very angry shark.

Climax: The shark has a tank of compressed oxygen caught in its mouth. It repeatedly batters the ship until it sinks entirely. Brody faces the beast with a shotgun. The shark turns around and begins swimming toward him. Brody shoots once. Nothing. He shoots again. Still nothing. He continues to shoot, as the shark head right for him. Suddenly, a shot gets in, and the shark explodes.

Resolution: Hooper emerges from beneath the water. He greets an exhausted Brody. They fashion a makeshift raft from the leftover ship and swim back to shore.

The Untouchables

Rising Action: The climax of the film occurs between Ness and Capone, but the action leading to it would suggest that Ness might not have gotten that far. It begins as Ness decides to give up the fight. The accountant is dead, his family's in hiding, his wife has just had a child, and he's exhausted. But Capone won't let him rest. Malone is brutally murdered. He dies in Ness's arms, but he's able to alert him about a train carrying Capone's bookkeeper in the seconds before. Now resolute to avenge his dear friend's death, Ness heads for the train station.

Climax: This film's climatic scene is one of the most tense and well-choreographed scenes in film history. Ness and Stone wait at the train station. At first, no one shows up. A woman begins dragging her baby carriage up the steep stone steps. Worried for her safety, Ness runs down to help her, just as Capone's men show up en masse. As he reaches the top step, the bookkeeper shows up, and the men begin to leave. A shot is fired by one of Capone's gang. The baby carriage tips. As it clatters down the steps in slow motion, Ness and his sharpshooter comrade Stone proceed to kill all Capone's men but one, who uses the bookkeeper as a shield. In the final tense moment, Stone shoots Capone's man in the head, narrowly missing the bookkeeper.

Resolution: Though the climax is over, a few things still need to be solved before the film can end. First, Ness discovers Malone's murderer sitting in the courtroom. After a quick chase scene over the rooftops of Chicago, Ness pushes him off the high-rise onto a car below. Next, he discovers that Capone has bribed both the jury and the judge. He scares the judge into switching juries mid-trial. Capone is furious. Clearly, he'll be sent away. Ness is finally able to approach him in complete victory.

American Beauty

Rising Action: This film spends much of its time helping Lester Burnham take control of his life. When he finally does so, the climax and resolution occur very quickly. The rising action bounces between family members, so every character experiences a climax of some sort. Carolyn's affair comes to an end, her work is in shambles, and she's desperate for some sort of real connection. She purchases a gun. Ricky's father accuses him of seeing Lester, and he kicks him out of the house. Ricky and Jane decide to run away together. Colonel Fitts approaches Lester in the garage and kisses him. Lester tells him that he must have the wrong idea, and Fitts stumbles back home in the rain. Angela and Jane fight; Ricky accuses Angela of being the shallow person that she pretends to be. Angela, vulnerable and upset, decides to sleep with Lester. They try, but she admits that it's her first time, and Lester is unable to follow through with the encounter.

Climax: The final battle also takes place on many fronts. Angela washes her face in the bathroom, Jane and Ricky lie together upstairs, and Carolyn approaches the house with the gun in hand. Lester sits at the kitchen table. Suddenly, a gun goes off, and blood sprays on the white walls. Lester is dead.

Resolution: The final moments of the film are a sweep of sorts. The audience sees Ricky staring at Lester's vacant eyes. Angela turns to listen from upstairs, Carolyn clutches Lester's clothes in the closet, and Colonel Fitts rushes into his house covered in blood. The narration returns, asking us to cherish every moment of our mundane little lives. It is, at once, a tragic and a hopeful finale.

Chapter 9

Character Building

*I*f plot is a story's skeleton, characters are its heart. Astounding events rarely transpire organically — they occur because people make choices. Those choices require action or have consequences that result in action. Your audiences may be enthralled or shocked by a series of high-adventure situations, but they rarely invest in those situations alone. Audiences invest in people — people getting by, people braving the elements, people beating the odds. Without vibrant and compelling characters, your story takes place, but to what end? The events may elicit raised eyebrows, some laughter, perhaps a gasp or two, but so what? Give me someone to care about, and I'll take your film home with me. I may even talk about it the next day.

Creating a character requires the artistry of a painter and the inquisitive nature of an ace reporter. You must illustrate the person physically, crafting a form one brush stroke at a time; and you must interrogate that person, crafting a history one question at a time. Your goal? Create someone true. Whether you portray your character realistically remains to be seen, but I want to believe that he or she can exist. True characters have questions, so will yours. True characters have strengths and weaknesses, so will yours. True characters have distinct ways of moving through the world, so will yours. This chapter provides tips on crafting such characters, physically and emotionally, while offering advice on how to allow your characters to propel the story as a whole.

Portrait of a Person: Constructing a Physical World

Character building has two primary approaches: from the outside in and from the inside out. No one method is correct, and, occasionally, a decision in one approach leads to a discovery in the other. For example, the decision to give your protagonist a limp may spark an important memory that you illustrate later on. The scar on Harry Potter's forehead is the result of childhood trauma. This memory propels the entire series of books and the resulting film. In this way, a physical characteristic can allude to the emotional backstory. I detail backstory in Chapter 5, but I use it here to mean any action that took place prior to your story's beginning. The character-building approach you take depends on what kind of a writer you are and what part of the character suggests itself first. However, because film is a visual medium, audiences will base their first impressions on what they see physically. So I'm going to begin with the visible components — those that are more apparent and accessible — and dive inward from there. Those visible components are

- The character's physical being
- The character's physical environment

Your character's physical being

You know the phrase "Never judge a book by its cover"? That sentiment is both true and false as it pertains to character development. Audiences WILL judge characters by their appearance, and you want them to do so because it gives you a set of expectations to match or contradict. Think about it: A young woman stands on a busy sidewalk at night. She wears tight, revealing clothing, gaudy jewelry, and an excessive amount of makeup. She waves to several cars as they pass by, leaning into a few when they stop to talk. The immediate assumption is that she's either a woman of the night or an undercover cop. If you fulfill these expectations — if it turns out that this young lady is on assignment by the FBI or if she goes home with one of the drivers — audiences will appreciate your continuity, secure that their expectations were correct. If, however, she enters the next scene wearing a business suit and tries a winning case before a jury, audiences will watch to see how these images can both be part of the same person. Either way, you win. Audiences like surprises as much as they enjoy continuity. The movie **Superman** is based on this premise. As Clark Kent, the protagonist is a mundane, bumbling young man. As Superman, he's the extreme opposite. The juxtaposition of the two types makes him dynamic. So although you know and may later prove that appearances can be deceiving, you want audiences to go ahead and judge your characters by their covers. Physical appearance is the first piece of the character puzzle.

Ideally, you make every decision for a reason — from your character's name to the time-worn secret he harbors. In real life, people miss persona details because they don't generally spend enough time with one person to notice everything. In films, an audience follows a character closely for at least two hours. You have to convey years of information in those two hours. Therefore, every choice has the potential to speak volumes. Choose wisely.

The following sections present a few physical attributes to consider.

Your character's name

What's in a name? Possibly everything. A well-chosen name has the capacity to impart or suggest pivotal character information quickly, often prior to the main action in a film. Perhaps the character's title matches his or her personality exactly. James Bond is a slick name, easy to repeat with a monetary connotation; James Bond is a slick man, spoken of often with an eye toward personal gain. Scarlett O'Hara is a volatile, melodramatic Southern belle whose name suggests those qualities. In other words, you may want to choose names based on the images they elicit. If you want to establish someone with a romantic flair quickly, Jane Smith is the wrong choice, but something like Francesca Romani may just fit the bill.

One of the most difficult and important things to do in film is to make internal qualities apparent. Some writers choose names that suggest emotional or psychological characteristics for this reason. These names often have a storybook or mythical air about them. George Lucas utilizes them throughout *Star Wars:* Luke Skywalker's destiny is apparent in his title, and Hans Solo's name encapsulates his aloof and distrusting personality.

Names can suggest cultural or ethnic backgrounds just as Tevya does in *Fiddler on the Roof,* or Vito Corleone does in the *Godfather* series. If your story is historically based, be aware that the names may already carry certain associations. The name Al Capone is linked both to extreme wealth and extreme corruption. Amelia Earhardt's name conjures up adventure, daring, and mystery. Names of any kind, but especially those rooted in history, often attach images to your story before it's told. Your job is to use those images to your advantage or oppose them with images of your own.

In determining your character's name, consider three things:

- ✔ **Length:** The longer the name, the more eccentric, important, or complex the character seems. Shorter names tend to imply grounded, simple, or direct personalities.

- ✔ **Sound:** The sounds of the names you choose may suggest images or simply elicit an emotional response. Isabella Rossellini sounds elegant and a touch exotic. PeeWee Herman sounds immature and cartoonlike.

- ✔ **Meaning:** If you want to suggest a theme or an internal trait with a name, numerous books detail both the history and the definition of personal titles. Baby books often categorize them into names based on cars, countries, animals, colors, gemstones, and so on.

Feeling overwhelmed? Here are some specific questions to help narrow the name search down:

- ✔ What's the story behind your character's name?

- ✔ Is your character named after a friend or relative of hers?

- ✔ If so, did that person have a legacy?

- ✔ How does your character feel about his or her name?

- ✔ How does he or she try to live up to or shrug off the name?

Take some time and care with your decision. When a child comes into the world, a name is chosen based on personality, on relations, and on your personal feelings or aspirations for the child. A character name is no different. Give it some thought.

Your character's appearance

A character's appearance is made up of a variety of factors. Some of those factors are

- ✔ **His physique:** What does he look like physically? Is he short or tall, fat or thin? What color hair, skin, and eyes does he have? Is he physically fit? A character's physique may suggest anything from his worldview to his confidence or insecurities. The difference in size and weight is what initially makes Danny Devito and Arnold Schwartzenegger such an intriguing pair in the movie *Twins.*

- ✔ **Visible scars or physical disabilities:** Scars of any sort suggest history and maturity, and they certainly affect how that character moves through the world. The bearer has been through some trauma or struggle and has survived, albeit slightly scathed. Scars may also represent an internal turmoil that has yet to be worked through. In *Pay It Forward,* Kevin Spacey plays a teacher who was badly burned as a child. His fight to mask the scars on his torso mimics his fight to remain emotionally removed from other people. Frankie's scar in *Frankie and Johnny* is so well hidden that it remains unnoticed until the film's conclusion. However, it remains an integral component of her emotional and physical interactions.

- ✔ **The wardrobe:** Does your character dress to impress, either himself or others? Would I know what he does by what he wears? Is his sense of style or fashion slightly left of center, or do his clothes suggest a type? Molly Ringwald's character in *Pretty in Pink* is what she wears, so is her quirky friend Ducky. Films like *Pretty Woman* and *My Fair Lady* thrive on the makeover of one character's sense of fashion and style. The general message here is what you wear affects how you're perceived and, therefore, who you are.

TRY IT

From a list to a life: Building a generic physical world

Characters are the most personal part of your story. You will undoubtedly put most of your effort as a writer into constructing their form and creating a world for them to walk through. When the process becomes overwhelming — and believe me, it will — it helps to step away from your story and into another one, for however short a stint.

The following project combines several details chosen arbitrarily into a unique physical world. It's fun, it's fast, and best of all — it's just a project. So the pressure's off.

Chose answers for the following categories:

- Two colors
- Two numbers from 4–10
- A number between 80 and 400
- A song
- A country
- A weather condition

- A type of dwelling (house, barn, igloo, or whatever)
- Pick one body part — the head, the torso, the limbs, or the face

Jotted something down? Here's how they fit together. The first four items pertain to your character's physique — the colors match the hair and eyes, the first set of numbers is the height, the second set is the weight, the song is both the character's physical rhythm and somehow pertains to his name. The country is where your story takes place, the weather condition depicts the climate, the type of dwelling might be home or work, and the body part refers to a physical disability. The exact nature of that disability is up to you; it affects whichever body part you selected.

After you've pieced this new and often crazy character together, take a second and imagine him in action. How does he interact with others, whom does he live with, and what does he do all day? You'll be surprised at the scenarios that occur to you when you concentrate on one small portion of an imaginary script.

Appearance is perhaps most striking when it conveys the inner life of your character and the changes therein. Lester Burnham's initial appearance in *American Beauty* suggests a man who's average in all ways. He wears the same type of suit and tie every day, his body lacks the muscle tone of someone physically active, and he's neither short nor tall. When he begins to turn his life around, his appearance changes. He alters his wardrobe, he begins to work out, and his posture improves; the physical alterations suggest the emotional shift.

When you consider your character's appearance, start by answering the following questions:

✔ How much time does your character take getting ready every day?

✔ What does your character do to get ready?

✔ What parts of his or her physique would your character hide and/or flaunt?

✔ What are your character's favorite colors, textures, or looks?

✔ Your character would be most comfortable wearing what?

✔ Your character is most often caught wearing what?

✔ What physical attribute does your character most admire and condemn in other people?

✔ What sort of an impression would your character like to give?

✔ How does your character feel about being noticed?

I spend a great deal of time envisioning my characters physically. First impressions are commonly based on appearance alone. The impressions of audiences are no different. I want their impressions to match my intentions.

Your character's physical environment

Characters spend time in certain places for three primary reasons:

✔ By choice

✔ Out of habit

✔ Out of necessity

Each reason suggests something different about your characters. If they choose to be there, that speaks to who they are and what they want. If they're used to being there, that speaks to their sense of security and routine. If they're forced to be there, that speaks to their level of endurance or to the lengths they'll go to in achieving success. When you peruse the following three environments, ask yourself not only where your character is but also how she feels about being there.

Your character at work

Most simply put, what does your character do for a living? This may be a step toward her career or something she does to put food on the table. She may be a novice or an expert in her field. If it's something she's good at or has done for a number of years, it will affect how she looks at the world and the way she speaks. It should also result in certain talents or access to information that will eventually come in handy. A seasoned waitress will be adept at handling unruly customers; photographers look at the world with selective eyes; a medical student may be too busy to assess the outside world at all.

The movie *The Doctor* is a film about a man so overwhelmed with his career that he loses sight of his patients. *Erin Brockovich* is, in part, about one woman's growing ability to collect information. In building a work environment, keep track of skills the job requires and the benefits it provides. You'll use both later on.

Try to envision the grand scope of each setting and then narrow your focus to specific details. You may imagine rows and rows of gray office cubicles with people in suits talking frantically over the phone, separated from their neighbors by plastic partitions. This is how Lester Burnham's office appears in *American Beauty.* A closer look may reveal photographs on the desk, a favorite poster hung haphazardly on the wall, particular books on the shelves, and so on. Lester's cubicle reveals a distinct lack of anything personal. Every detail offers another clue to the disposition behind it.

Pay particular attention to the relationships your character fosters at work. Who does she work for, who does that person work for, and how long has she known her coworkers? Does your character work amongst friends or rivals? Is she able to trust anyone in her workplace? These relationships may aid or thwart your character in her quest for success, so pinpoint what they are and how they work.

Do I have some starter questions for this section? Of course I do. Try these, and then craft some of your own.

- Does your character work in an office or at home?
- How many jobs does your character have?
- What is the chain of command at work?
- Your character's duties include?
- What are your character's immediate and ultimate professional goals?
- What are the rewards for a job well done and the consequences of failure?

Your character at rest

Your character's home may be a most revealing location. By home, I'm referring to that place your character returns to at the end of the day. This place may or may not be an apartment or house. It may be her place of work, someone else's house, a shelter, a box, or a hole in the ground. What matters is that it's uniquely hers, and it houses what belongings she has.

First, decide how secure the environment is. Is it a refuge or a war zone, some place to escape to or to avoid? If it's safe and familiar, what about it specifically offers comfort? Envision everything from the photos on the walls to the number of windows and the kind of light they allow. This is an ample opportunity to show the literature, art, and music that she surrounds herself with as well. In *About a Boy,* the main character's flat is full of technological gadgets and little else. You get virtually no sense of the man himself or anyone else in his life from the space. Perhaps this is because he has little sense of anyone other than himself at the story's beginning. If your character's home life is taxing or traumatic, it may explain behaviors in other areas of her life. It may determine what she dreams of pursuing. Illustrate which portions of her home are tumultuous and what, if anything, provides solace.

Next, decide whether she lives alone or with someone else. If she lives alone, was everything in her home chosen and designed by her? If so, this is one of the fastest ways for an audience to assess a character. In **_Kissing Jessica Stein,_** Jessica lives in a well-lit loft, surrounded by books, her easel, and paints. She works as a reporter, but her apartment offers a first glimpse of her other love — art. In this setting, anything chosen by the character becomes a reflection of the character in some way. If someone else has chosen and designed the home for her, I'll want to know which portions and why. If she lives with someone else, is it a lover, a roommate, or children? This decision affects her varying responsibilities and ability to maintain and juggle personal connections. Also, it provides an opportunity to illustrate a different side of your character — the mother or girlfriend side perhaps.

Finally, what kind of feeling does the place arouse? Is it an uncomfortable space, original, traditional, eerie, or threatening? How should the audience feel when entering it? After you answer this question, determine what details in the setting suggest that atmosphere.

Here are a few questions that may clarify your character's home environment:

- ✔ Does your character live in a suburb or in a city?
- ✔ Does your character live in a house, an apartment, a shelter, or something else?
- ✔ Is your character's home a stable or unstable place to be?
- ✔ How much pride does your character take in his or her home?
- ✔ How much personal effort has gone into the maintenance of the home?
- ✔ Does your character live alone? With a lover? With a roommate or children?
- ✔ Why does your character live where he or she lives?

Your character in play

Play environments refer not only to those locations your character goes to in her free time but also to any location other than home and work where she spends a reasonable amount of time. I say "in play" because these environments are generally ones in which important action takes place. It need not be a safe environment, and your character need not go there by choice. But she should return to it more than once, and something should change as a result. Play environments include the various bars in *Star Wars,* the woods in *Stand By Me,* and the art museum in *The Thomas Crown Affair.* If your character goes to a library once, you needn't spend much time detailing that library in your mind. If your character spends many scenes in that library, as Morgan Freeman's character does in *Seven,* you may want to explore it with a bit more depth.

As "in play" environments vary drastically from film to film, I include four basic questions to help get you started. Add to the list as more occur to you. These questions will come in handy with each new script you write.

- ✔ Does your character have a circle of friends or one close friend?
- ✔ How does your character know his friends, and how did they meet?
- ✔ Where does your character go to relax?
- ✔ Given your plot, where might the character need to return to for information or aid?

With all these physical attributes and environments, remember that you're offering the audience pieces of a puzzle. Your character is that puzzle. Your physical world may simply set the scene, or it may suggest emotional status or thematic structure. An audience will automatically assume that you've carefully selected each detail for a reason, and they'll continually guess at what that reason may be. Don't disappoint them.

The Good, the Bad, and the Ugly: Constructing an Internal World

Audiences base their first impressions of a character on the physical world that you construct; the internal world provides a steadily unfolding mystery that eventually proves those impressions true or false. Consider the metaphor of a fancy car. The body of the vehicle, its physique, may suggest high-class elegance and durability. If the car handles well and lasts 25 years, your impressions of it were correct. The car is exactly what it advertises to be. If, however, you lift the hood to discover a leaky engine and missing parts, your assumptions were incorrect. The car is a dud in disguise. With characters, you may just as easily discover that the beat-up old Pinto has the engine of a new Corvette and the stamina of a stallion. It all depends on how you envision the internal working with the external. In creating a vibrant internal life for your characters, you're "lifting their hoods" in a sense, revealing what lies beneath.

If you've done your job composing a *backstory* (see Chapter 5), you already know the following things about your character:

> ✔ Her educational background, if any
>
> ✔ Her family background, if any
>
> ✔ Some key memories, including past successes and failures
>
> ✔ Her childhood dreams and aspirations
>
> ✔ The key events that led her to the threshold of your story

Now, you can construct the sum of these parts. Simply put: Who is the person those details have become? Your character's inner world is complex and ever shifting. Portions of it should change dramatically over the course of the film. For now, concentrate on one element at a time, painting each with bold strokes. The stronger your choices today, the stronger and more intriguing your character's choices will be tomorrow.

TRY IT

More questions to get you started

By the time you're finished constructing your character, you may feel that you've put him or her through the Spanish Inquisition. That's all right. In this case, your character will be stronger for it. Here are a few starter questions concerning the inner life of your character. Again, keep a running list of other questions that you come up with as you write.

Dreams, wants, and passions:

✔ What does your character want to achieve financially, ethically, and spiritually?

✔ Would your character pursue these goals on her own, or would it take some effort to convince or force her to do so?

✔ Is your character pursuing these goals for herself, for her friends or family, or for a cause?

Talents and expertise

✔ What skills has your character acquired at work?

✔ What skills has your character acquired in the past?

✔ What talents was your character born with?

✔ What skills will your character need to attain in order to survive your plot?

✔ Who, if anyone, can provide training or expertise for your character?

Internal obstacles

✔ Does your character drink, smoke, or use narcotics? Why?

✔ Who/what does your character adore and why?

✔ Who/what does your character loathe and why?

✔ What is the most trivial thing that your character is afraid of?

✔ What is the most significant thing that your character is afraid of?

✔ How would you describe your character's self-esteem?

✔ What specifically brings your character great joy or great sorrow?

I discuss the primary elements of your character's inner world in the next three sections.

Dreams, wants, and passions

In order to generate a dynamic script, you must know three things:

- What your character wants
- How badly your character wants it
- What your character's prepared to do to get it

Compelling characters establish themselves early in the film with a dream or a desire, and that longing fuels the ensuing action — all of it. The dream may have originated in the past. Perhaps the character's harbored it for years, and your story is his or her opportunity to pursue it. Perhaps the character's forgotten all about it, and you're about to jog his or her memory. The desire may begin as a subtle tug at the character's heart and grow in urgency as the story progresses, or it may be palpable from the start and become more desperate with every new scene. In *Rear Window,* Jimmy Stewart's curiosity over events he witnesses in a neighbor's apartment steadily becomes an obsession and, finally, a frantic need to stop what he thinks has transpired. By contrast, Elliot Ness begins his journey in *The Untouchables* with a passion to rid Chicago of corruption; that passion immediately underscores all his dialogue and action. The goal becomes a matter of life and death later when his family is threatened and his friends are killed. How you manipulate the need is up to you — but your character must have one. Without that overriding passion, your character is like a car without any gas for the trip.

Talents and expertise

Your characters are good at something, and if they're not, they will be by the end of your film. Remember, audiences go to the movies to see people with extraordinary skills braving extraordinary circumstances OR to see people utilizing average skills to survive extraordinary circumstances. Did you catch the comparison? Both scenarios require skills of some kind.

A character's skills may be any of the following or a combination of several:

- Artistic
- Athletic
- Technological

- ✔ Scientific
- ✔ Academic
- ✔ Mechanical
- ✔ Interpersonal
- ✔ Parental
- ✔ Financial
- ✔ Economic
- ✔ Strategic
- ✔ Political
- ✔ Magical

Your character may be good at many things. Novelists fill pages with descriptions of the characters' numerous talents. In a film, though, time is money. Choose pertinent skills — skills that will advance your story's action. The young girl in *Jurassic Park* may be good at checkers for all I know, but checkers won't save her and the others from the raptor. On the other hand, her computer skills will. So, that's the skill highlighted in the film.

Your character's talent may be his personality. Main characters need not be likable. Likeable characters are often dull. They may be power-hungry brokers, unscrupulous lawyers, or deadbeat dads — if they're in some way compelling, I'll watch them. Your character may be incredibly intelligent, witty, powerful, or seductive. None of these qualities suggest that he's a fun-loving or kind person, but they have the capacity to pull me in. They're qualities that I'd like to acquire, so I'll watch someone who wields them.

If your character doesn't excel in any one area, audiences love to see that character learn. The training sequences in *Karate Kid, Star Wars, Chariots of Fire,* and *Rocky* are a few examples of films capitalizing on this technique. These films allow the audience to train beside the character, to assess first-hand any changes that he may undergo in the process. The *Harry Potter* series is charming, in part, because the characters are studying the art of magic. The audience observes them using a wand and a broomstick and practicing spells for the first time, and, in so doing, the audience learns along with them.

Internal obstacles

No true character is perfect. Characters who are talented, intelligent, funny, good-looking, and well-off without personal flaws to balance them out aren't only impossible to believe — they're also maddening. Every person in your play, no matter how surreal or magical your landscape, has some internal demon to wrestle with before the story is over. This demon comes in many forms. It may be

- **A mental or emotional illness:** Does your character suffer from depression, a learning disability, insomnia, amnesia, or some similar problem? These illnesses have the capacity to serve as metaphors for other problems in your character's life. They also clearly set restrictions on that character's behavior and outlook on life.

- **A past trauma:** Perhaps something from your character's backstory still haunts him or her. This may be a memory or trait they've always struggled to overcome, or something revived by events in the current plotline.

- **An addiction or obsession:** Any urge your character can't control has the power to be destructive. Addictions and obsessions can determine what and whom your character notices, and they can manipulate everything that the character says and does.

- **An overriding passion:** Like the previous item, passions here refer to emotions so strong that they control your character's ability to think and act rationally. These passions can include anger, fear, lust, vengeance, greed, indolence, ignorance, and envy, among others. Anger and fear are the two most common overriding passions in films today.

Often, these obstacles provide your character with his or her main objective. Coupled with external conflicts that the antagonists provide, these inner flaws create the tension that holds your action together. Main characters generally face up to and/or conquer the primary obstacles in the film's climax.

From the Inside Out: Making the Inner World Visible

As I said earlier, one of the screenwriter's greatest challenges lies in finding ways to suggest a character's inner world visually. In plays, characters reveal their fears, feelings, and regrets through dialogue. Novelists fill endless pages with descriptions of their characters' emotional states. Screenplays, however, unfold pictorially, and a person's inner world is often physically imperceptible. Your character may expend remarkable amounts of energy maintaining a serene front when, in fact, he's dying inside. He may manage anger by donning a stoic facade or use humor to ward off fear. These tendencies are particularly problematic because a character's inner life changes as the action affects it. You need to find a way to establish where your character begins internally and illustrate any shifts along the way. So how does a writer visually reveal what lies beneath the physique? The following techniques may help answer that question.

Balancing character dialogue with character action

Sometimes, characters reveal themselves, and sometimes, they're revealed by others. Generally, audiences grow to understand them in three primary ways:

- Through what they say about themselves
- Through what other people say about them
- Through what they do

The first two options rely on dialogue, so bear in mind that characters need a motivation to speak. In screen life, as in real life, people rarely offer information, especially personal information, without some incentive. They're cajoled, threatened, or seduced into doing so. They gain something by revealing themselves. In *Jaws,* Captain Quint seems like a drunken and slightly mad fisherman with a penchant for catching sharks. For much of the film, he seems to hunt the beast solely for money, yet his growing obsession begins to suggest otherwise. Finally, Quinn relays the story of the crew of his ship that was consumed by sharks before his eyes. This crucial piece of information concretely explains his erratic behavior throughout. Yet the writers wait until moments before the climax to reveal it. Why? It's stronger storytelling. Quinn doesn't trust easily; he wouldn't logically have revealed that information earlier. The other characters must joke him into confession. He tells the story almost without meaning to. The result is a powerful, realistic scene. So before your characters talk about themselves or about others, ask yourself this question: What's in it for them?

Also, bear in mind that audiences like to earn the story as well. Easy information is unrealistic and generally disappointing. Never provide a piece of the puzzle until you're sure that someone's after it. The information is worth more if a character and, therefore, the audience have to work to acquire it. The discovery is only as grand as the search itself.

Of the three methods, the third is the strongest. The phrase "actions speak louder than words" is a screenwriting mantra. A character's actions are always based on some inner need. Therefore, they offer the most honest glimpse of his personality. Here's an example: You meet a young man. He looks kindhearted. He speaks at great length about the good deeds he's done. His friends and neighbors swear that he's a man of his word. Yet an hour later, he kills two elderly women and steals their money. What have you discovered? He's a ruthless killer and a liar. Other characters may not know that, but you do. You've seen him in action.

After you determine what character detail you want to divulge, consider who might reveal it and how an audience will know that it's true. When in doubt, rely on action and save your breath.

Crafting concrete character goals

If your characters seek happiness, revenge, true love, justice, power, or retribution, they're in the market for an *abstract goal.* Abstract goals are theoretical or ethical in nature and lack a specific form. Is there something wrong with that? Yes and no. When a character is after something that's solely abstract, tracking his or her success rate can be difficult. He wants to be happy; that's fine, but how will I know when he gets there? Happy means many things to many people. So, for that matter, do power, love, and revenge. They're grand, undefined desires.

For this reason, I encourage you to make your goals concrete. By *concrete,* I mean give them a form, define specifically what "happy" looks like in your film. In *Braveheart,* Mel Gibson's character seeks retribution for the treatment of his people and the murder of his wife. Retribution is his abstract goal. He'll achieve it when the law grants his people the right to manage their own land and when the villain is dead. Those goals are his concrete goals, his definition of retribution. Concrete goals allow audiences to track how close or far away the hero is from success. I can watch Mel Gibson chase the villain, and I can know that he's won when he's the last man standing at the end of the film.

Concrete goals suggest their abstract counterparts. Elliot Ness wants to rid Chicago of corruption; he wants justice. In putting Al Capone and his henchmen behind bars, he achieves the concrete and, therefore, the abstract goal of justice. Think of one as the physical form of the other. Without a concrete goal, your character may win or lose without your audience even knowing.

Providing character opportunities

You've already determined your characters' talents. Now, craft opportunities in which they can utilize them. In *Gone with the Wind,* Scarlett O'Hara is an accomplished flirt. She demonstrates her prowess when she surrounds herself with men at a gala, making them all compete to see who can fetch her dessert. Ferris Bueller, from the film *Ferris Bueller's Day Off,* is an expert liar. He feigns a temperature; he impersonates his girlfriend's father; he lies to friends, family, and authority figures alike in order to avoid going to school. If your character begins the journey with skills or expertise, find a way to demonstrate their ability early on.

If your character acquires skills or talents during the story, craft scenes in which he learns the skills and then provide an opportunity for him to use those new skills later — preferably while fighting the antagonist. These scenes become checkpoints for the audience as they track how your characters are changing. Be aware that a growing talent also suggests a growth in maturity and spirit. Luke Skywalker becomes a Jedi knight over time — every other scene tests his skills — and as his expertise grows, so does his confidence and determination. So equip your characters with some original talent, prepare them to acquire more, and then decide what opportunities might reveal and eventually test those skills.

Establishing routines that change

In *About a Boy,* Hugh Grant plays a character who spends his afternoons watching television alone in his flat. One day, a young boy blackmails his way into that routine until, eventually, Grant can't spend the afternoon without him. This simple routine and the shift therein both suggest his emotional journey from a man more comfortable alone to a man who relies on others.

Habits and routines provide instant access to a character's true nature. People engage in them because they always have, and because doing so is comforting. These routines, therefore, are glimpses into a character's past or current emotional state. As your characters change, their habits change; they may eventually abandon those habits altogether. After you know your character fairly well, crafting routines is a simple and satisfying way to make the inner world visible.

Forcing your characters to choose

Characters aren't just what they do; they're what they choose to do. In other words, don't let life happen to your characters; let your characters happen to life. A character's inner strengths and weaknesses are instantly apparent when he or she is confronted with a difficult choice. Audiences assess characters by the choices they make. Here's a look at how the process works:

- ✔ **The film:** *The Untouchables*
- ✔ **The character:** Elliot Ness, Chicago Treasury officer.
- ✔ **The choices:** To accept a bribe from Al Capone and back off the case OR to refuse the bribe, thereby incurring Capone's wrath but maintaining moral dignity.
- ✔ **The decision:** Ness refuses the bribe in front of witnesses.
- ✔ **The audience's verdict:** Ness is a man of honor and his word. He's committed to putting Capone away and brave enough to start the fight.

Your goal with this technique is twofold. First, make the choice a difficult one. If Ness takes the bribe, Capone leaves him alone and his family lives comfortably for a very long time. With a wife he loves and a new child on the way, it's a tough decision. Second, put something personal at risk. If Ness takes the bribe, he loses his dignity and self-respect; if he doesn't, he may lose his life. Tough decisions beg the question, "What would you do?" and involve an audience in rooting for an outcome. One choice has the power to clearly define a character. Craft options that test the character's strength, ethics, and spirit throughout your script.

Using a mentor

A mentor or trusted confidante provides interesting avenues into the main character. A mentor has an inherently higher status; he or she knows something that the character wants or needs to know — the mentor's wiser. This places the hero in a state of vulnerability and weakness, in which all sorts of inner conflicts might arise. In *Good Will Hunting,* Matt Damon plays a young genius, Will, a man consumed by quiet anger rooted in his childhood. With everyone else he is aloof, funny, or noncommittal. He's only vulnerable with his psychiatrist, played by Robin Williams, and only then after many angry sessions. Through Williams, audiences glimpse a younger, more hopeful side of Will that they may otherwise not have seen.

A mentor is in a position to teach the hero a new ability or way of life. The audience, therefore, learns along with the hero, becoming an active part of the adventure. Through Mr. Miyagi in *The Karate Kid,* you learn control; through Gandalf in *Lord of the Rings,* you learn the bravery of a selfless act; through Obi One Kenobi in *Star Wars,* you learn to fight for the good. In tutoring the hero, mentors educate the audience as well.

Finally, a mentor forces the hero to answer for himself and to make difficult choices. A strong mentor expects the protagonist's weaknesses to become strengths. In training the protagonist, those weaknesses emerge. A mentor removes facades that a protagonist might don in other settings and forces him to rethink past behaviors and habits. The resulting interrogation may tax the hero beyond endurance, but it's a dynamic way for the audience to get to know your character at his core.

Using a narrator

Narration is challenging to maneuver gracefully, and, unfortunately, it's a device that's often abused. Narrators are commonly the protagonists, though on occasion someone else chimes in. For example, the narrator in *I Remember Mama* is the main character's daughter, now grown up.

If you can relay the story any other way, avoid narration. The strongest narrators, Lester Burnham in *American Beauty,* for example, have a desperate need to speak directly to the audience. They're delivering a message. Lester tells the story immediately after his death, as if on his way out of consciousness. His message is both a warning and a hopeful prayer, and it certainly warrants a direct voice. He's an exception.

Many writers utilize narrators because they don't know how to convey plot information. Narrators become an easy way to introduce characters, to relay backstory, to explain events. In most instances, this information would be better off in action. Film is, after all, a visual medium. Why *tell* me something when you can *show* me something equally compelling? For example, **Radio Flyer** begins and ends with narration, but the meat of the film stands without it. It seems a weaker choice in this film because you so readily forget the narrator's presence. If you're interested in a clear example of how a film changes as a result of narration, compare the original **Blade Runner,** which uses narration, with the director's cut where it's been removed.

If you're thinking about using a narrator, give her a reason to speak, a unique voice, and a vibrant perspective. If these details don't readily present themselves, consider a different technique.

Chapter 10

Say What? Constructing Dynamic Dialogue

Dialogue: What is it? It's words, it's sounds, it's rhythm — simply put, it's music. Perhaps this is why great dialogue, like great music, soars off the page, and why awkward dialogue clunks about or flat-lines halfway through a scene. Your script is your symphony. When a symphonic composer wants a section of the music to swell, he calls upon the strings. Should he require a wail, a squeak, or a piercing melodic line, the reeds are close at hand. And if the piece demands a backbeat or punctuation, he need look no further than the percussionist.

Much of a writer's orchestra is made up of characters. Their words, silences, the pace and quality with which they speak — these are their instruments. A skilled screenwriter, like a composer, knows which voices together or in succession produce the most compelling moments. He knows which words escalate a conflict and which diffuse it. He knows that words spoken by one character may cause friction, but spoken by another, they offer solace. All in all, he knows who to point the baton at to create the desired effect.

How does he know all this? Film language is a craft. The required musical ear emerges after years of writing, and even then, it may elude you at times. Professional writers often find character voices difficult to define until part way through a draft. The road to an effective exchange is paved with patience, research, and hours spent talking to yourself in private (and sometimes in public). In other words, it takes practice. However, powerful dialogue springs from character. If you're comfortable with your musicians and what skills they possess, you'll eventually conduct them with clarity, depth, and precision.

But before your characters can perform, they need practice, and before you can conduct them, you need practice, too. This chapter provides that opportunity for practice by breaking dialogue into two components — diction and music — and then suggesting effective ways to pull them together in conversation.

Diction: What's in a Word?

If scores consisted of similar instruments playing similar notes, the resulting music would be rather dull. Rather dull? It would be downright monotonous. The same principle holds true for films. The quality of your dialogue depends on a combination of unique voices singing different tunes. The key word here is *unique,* and a unique voice begins with a unique vocabulary. If you can envision your character in detail, if you've jotted down her background, her work life, and her inner qualities, the time's come to let her speak. What she finally says is known as diction.

In the music world, diction refers to the enunciation and pronunciation of words, or the singer's lyrical clarity. In the writing world, diction has a different meaning. *Diction,* as it pertains to films, refers to a character's distinct choice and use of words. Factors determining this vocabulary include the character's education, profession, geographic location, and overriding emotional state.

Find a comfortable seat in any public place and eavesdrop for a while. You'll notice the same conversations being held in a variety of ways. Consider this selection that's loosely based on a woman speaking to her young child in a fast-food restaurant:

> "Quit it, Sammy. I said put that thing down. I ain't sayin' it again, you heard me the last four times, I know you did. Now, I can take it, or I can break it — what's it gonna be?"

It may not be verbal fireworks, but it's a distinct voice fueled by a clear frustration. Now, I'll rewrite the clip in an alternate diction. See if you can pinpoint the distinction.

> "Now Samuel, stop that. I would appreciate it if you would put that thing away. I've asked you nicely several times, and I'm certain you've heard each request. Now, you have a choice. You can either give me the toy, or I can toss it in the garbage."

Hear the difference? Can you verbalize the exact nature of the change? The first woman says exactly what she feels without ornamentation. Her words are short and clipped. As a result, her anger comes across loud and clear.

The second woman speaks with larger words and more complete sentences that seem to contain her irritation. Her speech is more orderly and precise, as if chosen in advanced or pulled from a book on parent-child confrontation. Yet the two women are saying essentially the same thing. Understanding diction is like discovering a new language. Listening for and locating the variations in that language is the first stage. The second stage involves understanding what those variations convey to a listener. In other words, what does a character's diction suggest about him as a person?

Isn't versus ain't: Diction's determining factors

How do you craft a character's diction? If you've spent a length of time researching her background and illustrating her present circumstances, you have all the information that you need. Diction is primarily determined by four factors that you've already explored while developing your character. These four factors are

- Education
- Profession
- Geographic location (past and present)
- Overriding emotion

Every character discovery you've made thus far can be suggested with a variety of words and phrases. The remaining process involves selecting which exact words from that list communicate those discoveries to an audience. As I detail each factor individually, revisit your research and listen. Character voices either behave as shy, unwilling children or eager participants, ready to show off. In any case, consider yourself a reporter searching for the perfect quote. Have a pencil handy.

Your character's education

Intelligence exists in many forms. The character Mark Van Doren in **Quiz Show** is a college professor from a world-renowned literary family. Reporter Dick Goodwin, in that same film, may not hail from an Ivy League school, but he uncovers a historical scandal most newspapers overlooked. The characters in **The Sting** successfully con a league of con artists. One of the young men in **Hoop Dreams** survives the inner city to become a successful ball player. Are these men equally intelligent? Yes, in different ways. In establishing your character's education, contemplate which of the following forms of intelligence matches his own.

✔ **Academic:** How much schooling does your character have? Someone with a grade-school education may speak differently from someone with a doctoral degree. What subjects in particular catch his fancy? The literature buff, the math whiz, and the aeronautical engineer — these people express themselves in diverse ways. Degrees of academic intelligence are often delineated by verbal complexity or lack thereof. The English professor in *Wit* often sounds as if she's spouting a textbook. Her students and, therefore, the audience may require a translator to process what she says. If a character speaks primarily with one or two syllable words, limited vocabulary, and incorrect grammar, such as Billy Bob Thornton's character in *Sling Blade,* an audience generally assumes that his schooling has been minimal.

✔ **Intuitive:** Some characters possess an instinctual intelligence, a sort of sixth sense that they're born with or gain through traumatic experience. From Sherlock Holmes to Yoda, these characters act on spontaneous impulse, rarely on lessons learned in school. Reporters, detectives, and responsible parents often demonstrate this strength; characters in horror films, tragically, do not. For this reason, reporters and detectives in other film genres generally uncover the crime, while characters in horror films become the victims of one.

✔ **Acquired:** This type of intelligence is also called "survival sense." Characters who possess it choose their words carefully, certain that what they say could result in trouble or heartache. Any child who survives the inner city of a John Singleton or a Spike Lee film does so because he's learned how to. He has acquired street smarts. Francis Capra's character in *A Bronx Tale* and Frankie in *Frankie and Johnny* dodge the Mafia and a life of physical abuse, respectively. Those experiences mold their vocabulary.

Obviously, these types of intelligences may overlap. A duality of language makes characters mysterious and compelling. Matt Damon's character in *Good Will Hunting* has a blue-collar, poverty-stricken background, a grade-school education, and the intelligence of a Rhodes scholar. He can maintain a conversation with his working-class Boston friends and college physicists alike. The switch from one diction to another keeps the audience and other characters on their toes.

Your character's profession

Your character's choice of work often defines how she views the world and, therefore, what she has to say. A writer, for instance, may speak in metaphors or have an unusually developed vocabulary. Politicians speak in vague, noncommittal phrases to avoid offending voters. A rhyme that I've adopted over the years goes, "If a job affects your point of view, it probably affects your diction, too." In other words, let what your characters do for a living color how they express views, opinions, and beliefs. This is often true in real life, and so could be true on the screen.

Specific professions also require specialized or technical language, known as jargon. If I can determine your character's profession by her vocabulary, you've probably correctly identified that jargon. These Jargon Alerts throughout the book, for instance, define screenwriting terminology; a character's jargon reveals her line of work.

Every occupation comes with a list of terms and phrases learned on the job or required to do the job. Here are a few examples of phrases commonly heard in certain work professions:

- **Wait staff:** "The usual," "He's a regular," "cup of joe," "table four," "order up," "stiffed the tip," "over-easy or sunny side up," "soup du jour," "straight-up or on the rocks"

- **Actor:** "upstaged," "on cue," "heads up," "black-list," "hit your mark," "from the top," "ingénue," "blocking," to "go up" on your lines, "curtain," "flies," "wing space," "apron," "understudy," "dark night," "talent on the set," "slate"

- **Lawyer:** "verdict," "approach the bench," "plea bargain," "manslaughter," "assault and battery," "hung jury," "beat the rap," "the jury will disregard," "stricken from the record," "take the stand," "pro bono"

Do you know what these terms mean? If you're writing about waitresses, actors, or lawyers you should. The lists for these professions are endless, so imagine the lists that follow others. What would the television show *E.R.* be without medical lingo, or *Hoosiers* be without basketball terminology? Original jargon abounds in films like *Star Wars* and *Star Trek.* These sci-fi adventures are believable, in part, because of that jargon and the serious way in which it's delivered. Audiences buy it because the writers took it seriously.

Some writers believe that jargon suggests a stereotype rather than a three-dimensional person. They contend that lawyers, doctors, teachers, and so on speak in unique ways that generally have nothing to do with their jobs. This argument is valid, and over-reliance on jargon can rob characters of their distinct voices. However, writers choose professions for their characters because they help define their behavior and personality. If you're not familiar with the necessary terms, if you don't employ them when required, audiences may dismiss your characters as phony or incomplete.

Your character's geographic location

Where your character grew up and where he's from now may affect the way he speaks. As a general rule, I don't advise spelling out a dialect — you're liable to wind up with dialogue like:

> "I'ma goin' ta hafta take that there knife away from ya'll, do ya hear? Ifn ya don't put it away right quick."

I'm exaggerating a bit, but I have encountered phrases that I'm sure the writer understood, but which resemble hieroglyphics to anyone else. Sounding out dialects and transcribing them to the page slows readers down and irritates actors. However, certain regions abound in colorful phrases, phrases like "not the brightest porch light on the block" and "dumber than a box of rocks" and (my personal favorite) "a shuffle short of a winning card," for instance. These colloquialisms are known as slang, and to miss them is to miss a verbal gold mine.

Slang refers to nontraditional language that's specific to a certain culture and/or geographical region. It consists of words and phrases peculiar to that group of people.

The only way to really absorb the language of a group of people is to immerse yourself in it for a concentrated length of time. If it's impossible to visit the region, track down interviews or recordings made by people from the area. Read literature from the region or make a phone call and talk to a local. If you're creating slang for a fictional group, listen to conversations in your own neighborhood and record any slang you hear. Those recordings should give your fictitious expressions a hint of authenticity, though the phrases themselves are unique.

Certain regions or peer groups add, abbreviate, or drop words from sentences entirely. Canadians, for example, tend to end sentences with "eh?" Pittsburgh natives say "don and arond" instead of "down and around" and "yins" instead of "you guys." In some places your characters may say "goin'" instead of "going" or replace "fabulous" with "fab" or "fabola." The word "like" or "all" may replace the verb "to say," and "totally" may become an adverb for all seasons, as in the sentence:

> She was like "you should totally do this," and I was all "you totally know I just can't."

Again, I'm exaggerating for effect here, but sentences like this one abound amid the younger generation. Movies like *Heathers* and *Clueless* capitalized on expressions like these and were unexpected hits. They took an unusual vocabulary and stretched it to ridiculous proportions. Knowing and utilizing slang when necessary lends credibility to both your characters and their environments.

Your character's overriding emotion

Characters exhibit a wide range of emotions over the course of a film. However, most human beings have one emotional state that they return to in between dramatic events. I call this their overriding emotion, their default state of mind, and it certainly affects how they communicate.

Consider whether your character adopts any of the following dominant emotional states:

- ✔ Anger
- ✔ Fear
- ✔ Hope
- ✔ Wonder
- ✔ Joy
- ✔ Greed

Cautious personalities generally say little, and when they do speak, they use carefully chosen neutral words. Many angry people curse their way through life. David Mamet's characters capitalize on this colorful, albeit potentially offensive, language time and again. Artistic or particularly vibrant personalities may speak in sweeping generalizations or use words that call up images of grandeur. Norma Desmond of **Sunset Boulevard** fame was one such character; Orson Welles himself was another. Revolutionaries or group leaders share this tendency, which is why many speeches include some image-based metaphor like "a bridge to the future," "soar like the eagle," or "smoke the enemy out of his hole." Audiences can see these phrases, which makes them particularly effective, especially in film.

In many situations, your characters will assume a vocabulary that they don't usually employ. Perhaps, as Carolyn does in **American Beauty,** they desperately want to impress someone whom they admire. Maybe they do so out of a desire to fit in, as Shannon Dougherty does in **Heathers.** Matt Damon's role in **The Talented Mr. Ripley** goes to great lengths to assume someone else's identity, voice and all. Whatever your character's reasons for altering his vocabulary, knowing what base diction he'll return to when the façade deteriorates is helpful to you as writer. This is his true diction, and it eventually reveals the factors used to construct it.

The highs and the lows of language

Human beings can be classified by a variety of conditions — by finances, social status, political power, physical appearance, and so on. Each one of these classifications exists on a scale. Those people with the "most" and "least" of that condition make up the respective ends of the scale, and most everyone else falls somewhere in the middle. Language is no exception to this rule. Words, like people, can be classified into groups: High diction and low diction mark the ends of the scale with middle-grade words in between. These groups are based on education, profession, and upbringing.

Putting words in your character's mouth

Here's a fun and simple way to generate the beginning of a clear diction. Take a look at this list of a few neutral phrases. (By neutral, I mean that they don't suggest any type or level of diction.) Now, give yourself two or three minutes on each one, jotting down as many different ways to express the thought as you can think of in the allotted time. Feel free to make expressions up if they occur to you.

✔ Hello

✔ Goodbye

✔ I love you

✔ I hate you

✔ Get lost

✔ That's great

✔ Have a nice day

After you complete the lists, think about your character. Circle any of the phrases that you came up with that your character might use. If you can't find one that fits, think of one now. Try this project with other neutral phrases. Eventually, your character's voice should emerge.

High diction: The prince

In politics or economics, the level of status is determined by the degree of power or the amount of money that a person controls. With appearance, the person deemed most attractive holds court, and on down the line. With language, the classification of "high" vocabulary doesn't necessarily determine a character's power or prestige. It can, however, suggest a certain degree of education, professional training, a historical setting, and, perhaps, a privileged lifestyle.

Consider the following example. In speaking to a friend, I might say:

> "You know, I just finished a book that you have to read. It was great."

This is not an example of particularly high diction; it's rather neutral or middle range in fact. It might be hard to distinguish my education, profession, or socio-economic standing from that sentence. Now I'll rewrite it, using high diction:

> "I have just completed the most tremendous novella. You simply must peruse it when you have a moment to spare; it is undeniably compelling and persuasive."

Although I may not imagine this person in detail, the words "novella," "peruse," and "persuasive" suggest character possibilities. Most people don't speak this way today, so if your story takes place now, this character will most definitely stand out. And what if you're writing a period piece? Might a Victorian lady use these words? Perhaps your character spent her childhood obsessed with language; perhaps she enjoys showing off her verbal prowess or likes to hear herself speak. There are innumerable reasons for choosing high diction, and it's worth picking up a dictionary just to have these words at your disposal.

A quick way to differentiate between high and low diction is to note the word's structural degree of complexity. High-diction words are generally multi-syllabic, technically verbose, or ornate in style. They generally comprise the well-spoken phrases of the elite, the academic flourishes of a professor, and the technical jargon of a lawyer or renowned physicist. They fuel the literary Van Dorens of *Quiz Show* and every character in an Oscar Wilde piece. They are uncommon and often grandiose. They may also come from an unlikely source. In *Good Will Hunting,* Matt Damon spends much of the film speaking in middle-grade, everyday diction. However, in a classroom setting, he uses high diction, surprising university professors, award-winning theorists, and possibly the audience. Allowing characters to speak against expectation is a quick way to grab an audience's attention.

Low diction: The pauper

Low diction, by contrast, is strictly functional; it gets the job done with little or no flourish. Characters who speak with low diction may have little schooling, or may not care to draw attention to what schooling they've had. They often hold down unpretentious, blue-collar jobs. They speak with direct, monosyllabic words and without artifice. Low diction is rarely concerned with grammatical precision and tends to rely heavily on slang. Low diction is often associated with street language for this reason. It's not a language picked up in school; it's picked up by necessity and experience. It may be passed down by friends and family. Low diction is the language of the main characters in *Sling Blade,* of Jackie Gleason in *The Honeymooners,* and of Sylvester Stallone in *Rocky.* An example of low diction might be:

> "Hey. Cut that out. You gonna talk to me 'cause I ain't got all day. You either say what you have to say now, or I'm gone. I've got other things I could be doin', you know?"

Notice that I'm spelling certain words to read the way I hear them? That's another way to distinguish between high and low diction. High diction is concerned with precision of speech; low diction is not. Don't worry if it's not clear right now. The distinction between high and low diction often comes after a great deal of comparison. Here are a few examples of words from both categories to get you started.

Low Diction	High Diction
Nice	Astounding, divine, splendid
Hate	Loathe, detest, despise
Glad	Delighted, elated, jubilant
Bad	Unfavorable, detrimental, atrocious
Mean	Nasty, spiteful, vicious

Bear in mind that a character's level of diction isn't always an indication of true intelligence, prestige, or profession. The wisest person in the room may be the working-class servant, as is the case in **Gosford Park.** Someone with the diction of a scholar may, in fact, work as a janitor, as Will does in **Good Will Hunting.** Your character may choose a lower diction than he or she is capable of to blend in, to nab information, to avoid pretension. Yet at some point, his or her true verbal palette will emerge. That palette may be a mixture of the two dictions.

Most people speak with a combination of dictions, and this is called *middle diction.* Middle diction is a more common, more neutral way of speaking, and perhaps this is the type of character that you want to suggest. However, middle diction doesn't jump off the page or the screen as readily as high and low diction because audiences are used to it. If you want an immediately distinct character voice, a character I can identify with my eyes closed, you may want to look at other options. You're a writer, and words are your tools. If you have a clear understanding of the weight and scope of each word, you'll continually craft unique voices.

Name That Tune: Crafting Your Character's Music

A well-crafted verbal exchange is like a catchy song. Diction provides the lyrics; music provides the tune. Dialogue relies on the sounds of words as well as their definitions, on the rhythm of a conversation as well as its meaning. If you block the literal significance of a discussion and isolate the sounds that it's made up of, you discover a rhythm holding the entire exchange together. Shakespeare wrote in the unstressed-stressed pattern of iambic pentameter. Why? Because it mimics the cadence of natural speech. It's lilting. The dialogue of David Mamet and Oliver Stone explodes off the page. Why? They use explosive words in an explosive way. The result is verbal fireworks.

Compare these two examples. The first is from *Under Milkwood,* a radio play by Dylan Thomas. The second is from Sam Shepard's *Cowboy Mouth.*

> "It is Spring, moonless night in the small town, starless and bible-black, the cobblestreets silent and the hunched courters-and-rabbits wood limping invisible down to the sloeblack, slow, black, crowblack, fishing-boat bobbing sea."

> "I don't need no black baby lamb with a bell in its tail and I ain't gettin' no cradle for no dead crow. I have a baby! My own baby! With its own cradle! You've stolen me away from my baby's cradle!"

Out of context, these passages may make no sense, yet each one has a distinct sound and rhythm. The first one is not unlike a lullaby, lilting and slow. The second passage uses hard consonants and repetition to drive its meaning home. Both selections are held together not by the choice of words alone, but by the sound of each word in conjunction with the others, by the felt melody those sounds create together. They're held together, in part, by music.

The music component of dialogue is responsible for any mounting tension or emotional undercurrent in a scene. After you know what types of phrases your character utters, rework them with an ear toward melody and percussion. Which voices enhance each other? Which are combative? What is the character's state of mind at the time he speaks? How can you convey that state of mind through sound alone? Joy, fear, anger, grief, awe — these emotions have unmistakable rhythms; listen for them around you, examine their form, and then try to recreate them on the page. Like a catchy song, eventually, they'll stick with you.

Sound 101: Using poetry as a guide

The terms *alliteration* and *assonance* are often used in poetry, where an ill-chosen sound can make or break the piece. Alliteration refers to the repetition of consonants and the effect of that repetition on the listener's ear. Imagine a tiny percussionist sitting inside each word, matching an instrument to each consonant and sounding them in succession. Perhaps he pounds the hard "d's" out on a kettledrum and taps the "t's" out on a snare. Maybe he selects wood blocks to create the "ch" sounds and shakes a rain stick for an "sh." In any case, he repeats the sounds of each word in such a way that they produce an audible rhythm. That rhythm is alliteration.

Consider these examples:

> "Hollywood is jam-packed with professional people pounding on doors." The repeated "p" here creates the sound of those people in action.

"The wind whistles through the willow tree." The "wh" sound here becomes the wind.

"Terrific, I say. Terrific. It's utterly and totally terrific." This sentence is explosive in part because of the resounding "t's."

Alliteration is helpful when you want to punch a line or emphasize it for your audience. It also tends to speed a line up. Alliteration can produce the biting anger of Don Corleone or Michael Palin's stutter in *A Fish Called Wanda.*

If it's punctuation or percussion that you're after, alliteration's your approach. If you're trying to produce a specific tone, it's assonance you're after.

Assonance is the repetition of a vowel sound within a phrase. Assonance creates the pitch or timbre of a conversation.

When repeated in direct succession, vowels can mimic the human voice. A sentence full of vowels may produce a subtle moan, wail, squeal, or cry. In this way, assonance helps to create an emotional soundscape for a phrase, a speech, and possibly an entire conversation.

Consider these examples:

"Don't go. I won't know what to do with myself all alone." The long "o's" in this sentence underscore its mournful request. They help the request linger long enough for the other character, and, therefore, an audience, to hear it.

"It rained on my birthday. A cold rain that refused to abate until the guests had gone away." The long "a" sounds here emphasize the sadness of the speaker.

"I will fly higher than ever before. I will fly until your eyes cannot detect me and I become the sky itself." The repeated long "i's" here accentuate the speaker's determination. The phrase has the sound of a victory cry.

If alliteration speeds a sentence up, assonance slows it down. If alliteration provides a backbeat for the conversation, assonance heightens the mood. Together, they help a writer generate a distinct palette and rhythm for a character's voice.

Fascinating rhythm: Crafting your script's pulse

Clichés abound depicting the body's physical response to a grand emotion. When struck by love, hearts beat wildly against the chest, and knees grow weak. When scared, a person's pulse begins to race, and her mouth goes dry. Angry people stomp and growl and spit, or they stare coldly ahead with little or no expression. All these responses are easy to see, but what if you close your eyes? Would you hear them as well? Chances are that you would because every emotion has an accompanying verbal pulse — a rhythm that gives it away.

Of course, every sentiment sounds slightly different in different mouths, but something about the way a character speaks should eventually suggest the way that he really feels. As you eavesdrop on conversations around you, listen for a few key rhythmic elements:

- ✔ Punctuation
- ✔ Repetition
- ✔ The use of silence

Punctuation

Punctuation, or lack thereof, is often considered the key to realistic-sounding dialogue. First consider interruption, which appears in your script as a dash. People often interrupt themselves mid-sentence. Why? Perhaps they're excited over something and get ahead of themselves as they speak.

> "I can't begin to tell you how wonderful it all was — did I mention the food, oh the food was just — and the wine? Out of this world — and the service?"

You get the picture. The speaker can't relay the information as fast as her brain recalls it. Another form of interruption occurs when people think ideas through as they talk:

> "It's best if the reception starts at noon, yes noon — or maybe one. That might be better. And the cake should be chocolate — oh, but Sal can't eat chocolate, better make it vanilla. I called the musicians — wait, did I call the musicians?"

The more thoughts that occur to them, the more interruptions occur. Speakers also commonly interrupt or overlap each other, especially when in the throes of some grand passion. One person's thought is triggered by a word or phrase directly before it. The tendency is to speak immediately upon hearing that trigger word, regardless of whether you interrupt someone to do so. In this following dialogue example, see if you can identify which words trigger the next line.

> "So, I had lunch with Daphne the other day, and —"
>
> "Daphne. I haven't seen her in, well I can't think of the last time we —"

"She mentioned you hadn't called. I told her you were busy and —"

"Of course she did. She always was one to keep track of those sorts of —"

"Now, now. There's no need to start in on —"

"Really though. What right has she to talk about our friendship with —"

"The same right as you, I suppose."

Each line has a trigger word. Can you sense them? The urge to speak generally occurs well before the current speaker is finished talking. Following that urge usually results in an interruption.

A trail off, represented in a script by an ellipses (. . .) also punctuates everyday conversation. The trail off is generally used when a person forgets what she's trying to say, is searching for just the right phrase, or is trying to buy herself some time. If your character frequently trails off mid-thought, she may also be a dreamer.

The punctuation and grammar of your dialogue need not be technically correct. Phrases that look like questions may end forcefully with an exclamation point or a period. Nouns may replace verbs in sentence structure and vice versa. People speak in fragments; so will your characters. So don't dot all your i's or cross all your t's. Unless your character's an English buff, a refined aristocrat, or a robot, doing so will sound unnatural. Again, I emphasize that this rule holds true for dialogue. You'll probably want other portions of your screenplay — your scene descriptions, for example — to remain grammatically correct (see Chapter 4 for info on punctuating your script).

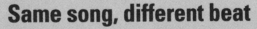

Same song, different beat

Here's part of a generic speech:

"When I came home and you weren't here, I knew. I thought, if his shoes are here, he's coming back. If his shoes are gone, then so is he. Gone for good. Then I searched everywhere. No shoes."

Now, here's a rewrite that I've done with the rhythm of joy behind it:

"When I came home and you weren't here well I just knew. I just knew it and I thought,

if his shoes are here, I thought, then he's coming back BUT if his shoes are gone? If his shoes are gone? Then so is he. Gone, gone, gone for good. And guess what? No shoes!"

Try reworking this speech again with the music of love and fear in mind. Feel free to repeat words, add connecting words, or omit some entirely. You're changing the rhythm but leaving the sentiment intact.

Repetition: You can say that again

Repetition is a valuable and multifaceted tool. It may be used to emphasize a point:

> "We get the job done, do you hear me? We get. The job. Done."

Or it may be used to create the stutter of confusion, love, or fear:

> "What I meant was, what I meant to say just then, was to ask, that is I would like to ask, to know, I would like very much to know if you might consider, just consider mind you, going out sometime."

It may be also be used to portray eagerness or demand:

> "Did you get it? Well? Did you? Did you get the job?"

As a writer, you must find a way to create heightened and carefully selected dialogue under the guise of naturalistic conversation. Punctuation and repetition make that task considerably easier.

The sound of silence

Dialogue isn't made up of words alone. Silences are as important and, sometimes, more important for conveying intent on-screen. If words are implied, a silence may take the place of an entire conversation.

I should make the distinction between a natural pause in conversation and the beats or silences that you'll use sparingly throughout your script in place of words. If I wrote in every natural pause, I'd add at least ten unnecessary pages to my screenplay. Leave natural pauses to the actors. If your scenario is strong enough and your character voices clear, a good actor will know how to say the line.

Beats are faster than silences. Both tools let a writer do one of two things:

- ✔ Emphasize the last line spoken
- ✔ Suggest to readers and audience alike that some nonverbal exchange is taking place.

If your last line is a humdinger, if you want your audience to remember it, take a beat after it. This beat allows the line to linger briefly before the next action directs attention elsewhere. If two characters are engaged in some nonverbal exchange, use a silence. This type of pause is your way of saying, "There's a scene going on; you just can't hear it." Composers use grace notes throughout a score to let the music breathe. Writers use silence.

Practice rewriting generic or otherwise neutral dialogue with these three musical elements, or layer them into a scene from your script. You should be able to say essentially the same thing with different emotions in mind and, therefore, with varying rhythms.

Putting It Together: Letting Your Characters Speak

Okay, you've chosen a vocabulary, a sound, and a rhythm for your characters. You're ready to write an entire scene. Where do you begin? You might simply start writing and see where the discourse takes you. However, if you're pressed for time or want to approach the task in a more organized fashion, you may find it helpful to outline a few things about the scene in advance.

Setting the scene

Here are a few elements to consider immediately before you write any scene, but especially one with dialogue.

- ✔ **Which roles are your characters playing now?** Each character plays a variety of different roles throughout her day. Each role speaks with a different voice. Your protagonist might be a mother, a friend, a sister, and a boss. As the mother, she might be nurturing and kind; as a boss, demanding and curt. Before crafting your scene, determine what relationship the characters have and how that relationship affects their dialogue.

- ✔ **What is the status or perceived status between the characters?** When a veteran employee addresses the new hire, he may instantly assume higher status. After all, he knows the company fairly well, so he has knowledge to impart. His dialogue may, therefore, be pompous, authoritative, or stern. If he later discovers that the new hire will soon be his boss, that diction may change. Determine the perceived level of status between the characters in advance.

- ✔ **What does each character want?** What your characters say in a scene is determined by what they hope to gain from each other. Your characters may flat out demand what they want, or the dialogue may code for what's really being discussed. Before you start writing, try to determine what each character wants and who, if anyone, will get it.

- ✔ **What will change during, or as a result of, the exchange?** Every strong scene relies on tension, on risk, or on mystery. Scenes in which friends discuss the weather are dull because nothing is taking place; no one is being changed by the experience. If they're talking about the weather to avoid talking about an impending medical operation, the scene becomes more interesting. Ask yourself what will be gained or lost in each exchange for the characters and for the audience.

After you've outlined these four things, you're ready to write. By this time, the characters should have plenty to say. After all, they've waited all this time to say it. However, if you get stuck, you can always return to one component of their voices — the diction, the music, or the rhythm — and see what's lacking. You also have an outline of the scene's action and objective to keep you afloat.

Dialogue do's and don'ts

The challenge of great dialogue is that it has to accomplish specific tasks while drawing little attention to itself. Remember that you're creating the illusion of average conversation, but there's really nothing average about it. Characters perform extraordinary actions, and they're also able to articulate thoughts and emotions that many people never express.

Developing good dialogue

Strong dialogue does the following:

- Combines distinct voices
- Reveals character and character relationships
- Propels the action forward
- Conveys pertinent information or exposition
- Prepares an audience for events to come
- Grows out of events in the past

If your dialogue seems flat or uninteresting, check to see if it's accomplishing at least two of these goals. If it's not, revise it with another one in mind. If it is accomplishing two things on this list but it still feels flat, look at the character relationships more closely. Most dialogue feels flat because, in a sense, it's not moving forward. In other words, the lines don't know what they want to accomplish, so they're not accomplishing anything. In the most interesting dialogue, characters want something from each other, and they switch tactics according to how close or far they are from obtaining it. Can your characters more actively try to acquire, convince, elicit, or demand some response from the others? If you know what your language is doing in each scene, it won't remain flat for long.

Going into a scene with these dialogue goals in mind is helpful. However, you can enhance one or two facets of the exchange after you've written it. Here are a few ways to rework it:

- **Speak it out loud**. If you stumble over the words, an actor will, too. If it sounds strange in your mouth, you've probably done a nice job of creating a unique voice.

- **Let other people read it out loud.** Sometimes, you can't tell what's wrong with an exchange until you've heard it. The dialogue may sound great in your head and lousy out loud. See what an objective reader has to say.

- **Build your scene toward some point**. Every line, every speech, and every scene culminates in some resounding moment. Know what shift your scene is building toward and eliminate any detail that distracts an audience from it. If the man gets the girl at the end of the scene, make it difficult for him to do so, but not impossible.

- **When in doubt, cut it out.** Too many images, too many silences, too many words clutter up the action. You have minutes of screen time for every scene; sometimes, seconds. One image can speak volumes; one well-phrased line may resonate for pages. The more images or catchy lines that you have in one scene, the weaker they all become. Let them stand alone.

Avoiding bad dialogue

If you know what kind of dialogue to avoid in advance, you may be better equipped to write a convincing scene. Take a look at these top six dialogue offenders, so that you can avoid these pitfalls:

1) Too "on the money"

This type of dialogue tells rather than suggests. In these scenes, characters divulge information with seemingly no reason to do so. As a result, the dialogue sounds manufactured instead of organic.

> "Dad, I can't tell you how glad I am that you called. I've been waiting all these years for some sign that you missed me."

> "Of course I missed you, honey. I've been so miserable here alone. Just hearing your voice makes me want to cry."

The conversation would sound more natural with silences, hesitancy to speak, or awkward stops and starts. They're speaking for the first time after an extended absence — how comfortable can they be? Here's how I might rework it:

"Dad, I can't tell you I don't know how to, I just I'm just really glad you called."

"Well. I missed you. I missed your voice."

Note that what's left unsaid is often inherent in what's said. The daughter doesn't need to tell her dad that she's waited all these years for a sign from him, because it's inherent in how difficult it is for her to speak with him.

2) Too repetitious

Repetition is a great tool for crafting rhythms. However, like any technique, it can become overbearing. Repetition of first names, phrases, or ideas has a tendency to slip into first-draft dialogue uninvited and overlooked.

"Larry, can you hand me that wrench?"

"This wrench? Sure thing, Phil, I'd be happy to."

"Thanks, Lar, this wrench works on everything."

"No problem, Phil. I've got a wrench like that at home."

For some reason, first names are often emphasized in first drafts, though we rarely use them more than once or twice in everyday conversations. They slow down your line, so strike them whenever you can. The dialogue sounds better if you keep the first line and a few words more, and then cut the rest. For example:

"Hey, Larry. Can you hand me that wrench?"

"Sure thing."

"Thanks. It's amazing, this wrench. Works on everything."

"Yeah, I've got one at home."

It's still not an inherently dramatic moment, but at least the speech patterns resemble those of a real conversation.

3) Too similar

When characters begin to sound alike, scenes become about information and not about people. If I can close my eyes and identify a speaker by the sound of her voice, you've done a good job crafting the dialogue. If I can exchange names in a scene without it mattering, you've got work to do.

"Did you go to the party last night?"

"Yeah. Were you there?"

"Yeah. It was great, huh?"

"Pretty great."

First of all, nothing's happening in the scene. No one's being affected; they're stuck in the realm of banter. Also, the characters have the same voice. Here's a tip: If you glance at your page and notice that every character has roughly the same number of lines in each section, your characters probably need some work. Here's a potential rewrite:

"Did you go to the party last night?"

"Hell yes. Never miss a party, man. Never, never, never miss a party. Were you there?

"Yeah. It was great, huh?"

"Great is not the word. It was stellar, man; that party was stellar."

Again, the dramatic potential is iffy, but at least there are two distinct voices in this conversation.

4) Too long or wordy

Lengthy dialogue often suggests a novice writer. You don't need very many words in film because pictures do most of the work. Opinionated discourse and philosophical discussions have no place in drama unless the fate of the world rests on the outcome of that debate. Characters raving about a cause or standing on a soapbox should be sent home.

"The campus didn't act on this one because the administration doesn't care. Most large organizations are so adept at sending a messenger to do their work for them, or putting someone on hold while they grab lunch, or nodding and looking the other way that they've forgotten how to answer an honest question. It would be too easy. Nothing happens anymore without red tape. If a question doesn't come with red tape, they'll put some on it, wind it up, and hire someone to take it off. This wasn't always the case, but it is now. Good luck trying to get the campus to act; I'll be surprised if you even get a foot in the door."

The speech exists entirely of words and opinions. Nothing new is said after the second line; ideas are merely reiterated. If you cut it by a third and give the person a clear reason for ranting, the speech may get interesting. Here's a potential reworking:

"The campus didn't act, because the administration doesn't care. I repeat, it doesn't care. You think they'll listen to you now? No way. They'll get some secretary to intercept you, they'll put you on hold, they'll nod and then look the other way. By the time they're done with you, you'll be nothing but a mound of red tape with no idea of why you went to them in the first place. No, it's a lost cause tryin' to get this administration to act. Won't even get your foot in the door."

5) Too contradictory

When a character says one thing about himself and behaves in a way that contradicts the claim, that character becomes interesting. When a character is scared to death of the dark but overcomes this fear in the next moment, the two pieces of information contradict each other in a confusing, inconsistent manner.

"Don't go down there; it's dark."

"I'm not afraid of the dark."

"You're deathly afraid of the dark."

"You're right, let's go back."

"No, I think we should go down there."

Both these characters contradict each other. The scene goes nowhere, and I'm no closer to understanding the characters than I was when the dialogue began. I'd rather see both characters stick to their views for a while and let them change attitudes over the course of an entire script. For instance:

"Don't go down there, it's dark."

"I'm not afraid of the dark."

"And I hear something. Come on, come back up."

"No way. I'm no sissy. You cower up here if you want, but I want to know what it is. Once and for all."

The points of view are clear here. One character can certainly become braver as the story goes on, but it's unrealistic for it to occur mid-dialogue."

6) Too reflective

Shakespeare's characters speak their real thoughts in asides to the audience. Realistic drama rarely utilizes this option, so seeing someone try the equivalent is always odd. People don't usually talk to themselves, nor do they utter speeches under their breath.

"Hal,"

(under his breath)

"I wish I understood it. All this anger between them, all the bitterness. But I don't. I don't understand it, and I wish I'd never come."

It's not realistic; it's entirely too long; it tells, but it doesn't show. This sentiment could easily be communicated through a quick look and a pause.

I include these dialogue faux pas as examples of what to avoid. In reality, you'll find them slipping into your work time and again. That's routine. Strike them out and write something in their place. Dialogue is difficult. You're creating the illusion of spontaneity and reality — yet in actuality, you're carefully constructing each moment. The fastest way to become more adept at crafting conversation is to try, fail, and try again. Listening, reading, and constant practice translating what you hear and read onto the page — these are your tickets to strong dialogue.

Chapter 11

Maintaining an Audience's Trust: A Screenwriter's Responsibility

Cinema is fast becoming a medium in which any visual effect is both technologically and financially possible. Its audience also extends beyond that of other mediums, reaching millions of people every year. These elements in combination make film an incredibly exciting art form but a potentially dangerous one as well. Why dangerous? Perhaps you've heard the saying "With power comes responsibility" or a variation of it. Nowhere is that sentiment more applicable than in film, and the responsibility falls to the screenwriter first. Every time you begin a project, the resulting work may affect children, adolescents, and adults from differing cultures and educational backgrounds. What you write may be seen, heard, and, quite possibly, believed by those viewers. And your name's on the material.

So before you toss a script out there, take another look through it. Have you written a responsible script? If you're not sure, read on. This chapter explores what a writer's duties may or may not be and how to shape a work so that it remains true to the subject and to its audience.

Screenwriting and Ethics

Because film is so accessible, so much like a window to the world, it's easy to assume that screenwriters should strive above all to create the illusion of reality. In other words, the more real the action appears, the more successful the script seems to be. Yet in truth, the screenwriter's objective isn't always simply to mirror reality, nor should it be. The screenwriter's job isn't to re-create life but to design it. The difference between these tasks is subtle but vast.

If I record the conversations around me and transcribe them onto the page, I'm re-creating life. The result may sound convincing, but it begs the question: So what? I'm not *writing* the discourse; I'm simply writing it down — a big difference. But if I spend time replaying the conversations, weighing one section against another, selecting between them and then reconnecting those portions, I'm designing life. I have a grand scheme in mind. Writers create a text in this way. Even when they're adapting from a source or pulling from historical events, they're selecting which pieces to include and how to present them with a grand scheme in mind.

Responsible writers ask two central questions at some point in their process:

- ✔ What kind of world do I want to design?
- ✔ Why design that world in place of others?

Implicit in these questions is the idea of choice. Between you and every creative decision lie at least three options. Will your character survive, perish, or simply leave the story? Should you kill a character on-screen or off-screen or begin the action and then cut to another moment? Do you set the scene in Paris, Prague, or Rome? Sometimes, you make a choice based on logic — he's Italian, so the memory scenes take place in Florence. Sometimes, you make a choice based on style — that dark alleyway fits the *film noir* genre better than a crowded street because film noir is a style that relies heavily on shadow and mystique. These decisions often take care of themselves; they just make sense. The more difficult choices — how do you kill a character on-screen, how explicit is your language, is a scene funny or offensive — are based on ethics.

Artists sometimes bristle at the word *ethics*. And yet, every script exists in an ethical realm. The study of ethics is the study of human motivation. You're presenting work to an audience, and that audience will weigh the choices that you've made therein. They'll search for motivations for each character action, and they'll judge those characters accordingly. Are the characters honorable or despicable, do they elicit praise or disdain, are they trustworthy or two-faced, why do they behave the way that they do? These questions are ethical questions, and because it's your job to guide an audience through your piece, they merit your attention.

Unfortunately, "ethical" has come to mean "family oriented" or "innocuous." Under this definition, films with violence, cursing, and sexual content become unethical, forcing artists to censor themselves in undesirable ways. I'm not using the term in this way. Many of the most troublesome and thought-provoking films are written for ethical purposes. Charlie Chaplin's **The Great Dictator** and Steven Spielberg's **Schindler's List** tackle the Holocaust in ethical ways. They're not meant to be comfortable or easy to watch; they're meant to invite debate. **Guess Who's Coming to Dinner** takes on interracial relationships. I doubt that this film made everyone in the first audiences comfortable, but it was written for ethical reasons. Because film is a social medium designed to elicit audience response, screenwriting is an inherently ethical craft. Screenwriters, then, are automatically moralists as well as storytellers.

Screenwriting and Responsibility

So what do ethics have to do with responsibility? Well, in a sense, you're responsible for considering what ethics you present. Why? Someone's going to watch them; you're not on this journey alone. In other words, be aware of what you suggest. Know why you're writing the script. Screenwriters have a threefold responsibility. They have to consider themselves, the material, and the audience

If you write an irresponsible script, all three of these entities suffer, but consider this: The medium itself also suffers. Audiences enter a theater wanting to enjoy themselves and wanting to discover something along the way. They enter with expectations. If you fulfill those expectations, even in a small way, they're more likely to trust that the next film will, too. If I see three action films in a row that offer special effects and little else, I'm likely to assume that the whole genre's lost its touch.

What are you willing to put your name on?

Right now, the script is yours and within your control. It may not be yours in the near future; it may be *optioned* (purchased for consideration) or purchased to produce outright, and what it becomes after that sale is out of your hands. But right now, it's your story. How do you want to tell it? What do you want it to say? Because you're putting your name on this script, you need to be responsible to yourself in this way first.

Writers approach material for any number of reasons, and they usually hope to interest an audience in the same things. What affects you in the material may similarly affect an audience. Moreover, you can enhance those qualities in your script so that they have the desired effect.

Being responsible to yourself also means remembering why you're writing the story and maintaining the integrity of its ideal. What's sacred in your script? The depth of character? The thoughts and opinions expressed? The way that certain events transpire? List those details now and make sure that you accomplish them. Just as actors sign contracts stipulating what they will and will not do on-screen, writers make an agreement with themselves. That agreement may include the following statements:

✔ I will write stories that I believe in.

✔ I will entertain several options before I choose one.

✔ I will keep my audience in mind.

✔ I will remember what drew me to the story in the first place.

✔ I will do the best that I can.

Your intentions may shift along the way. Let them. This story is your opportunity to explore a new world, to ask difficult questions, to inspire yourself and others. This vision may change radically in the hands of business executives, but a responsibly written script is more likely to become a responsible film.

Approaching difficult subject matter

So you're writing a film about warring gangs in the inner city. Right away, the subject matter evokes images of guns, blood, drugs, murder, and danger on multiple levels. You may feel the need to include these details for the sake of accuracy, but before you craft scenes full of graphic violence, ask yourself, "How is the story best served?" To tell a story clearly, you have to consider both the material and the audience. On-screen violence may seem realistic, but if audiences spend two hours with their eyes closed, they'll miss your story. The question, "How do I approach that material responsibly?" really asks, "How do I do justice to the story?"

Violence, abrasive language, and sexual content offer distinct challenges. If you err on the side of caution, you risk credibility. If you opt for completely realistic, you risk distancing your audience from the narrative. I usually ask writers to consider three truths before choosing an approach:

✔ **Images linger.** I've said it before, and I'll say it again: Film is a visual medium. Your audiences are more likely to leave the theater with a series of images in their minds than they are to leave considering a grand message. Which images do you want them to retain? Is your film really about a naked actress, or is it about two people falling in love? Do you want them to remember a gunshot to the head, or two children huddled together listening to that gunshot? Is it important to watch a man strike a woman, or to see her walking through public places wearing sunglasses and covering her mouth with one hand? The images that linger come to represent the story itself. How is your story best served?

✔ **Words have weight.** The film *RKO 281* contains a line that suggests that great speeches change the world. And they do. Why are presidential speeches so important? Why choose the wording on advertisements with so much care? Words are a writer's tools. They're the vehicle between your mind and someone else's. They're active and can, therefore, inspire action.

As cinema is a public forum, the language that your characters use also enters a collective vocabulary. Those words not only remain with audiences, they also become more common as they're used more frequently. So consider your language carefully. Again, you're not re-creating life, you're designing it. This task isn't an easy one, especially where language is concerned. If you're simply pounding out words without consideration, you're writing carelessly. Many screenwriters seem to have forgotten this fact.

↙ **What attracts also distracts.** Many films these days openly advertise graphic violence and sexual content. Why? Because sex and violence sell tickets. Advertising agencies know it; so do film executives. Although using these elements may make sense for financiers, it's a dangerous practice for screenwriters, whose first priority is to a story, not a violent moment or a sexual scene. Consider the problem of nudity. Audiences may flock to a film to see Mel Gibson's backside. But the moment that the scene occurs, those people are thinking, "That's Mel Gibson's backside." They're not involved in the story.

Screenwriters must walk a fine line between what draws an audience in and out of a narrative. Assess current films and discover where that line lies. That knowledge will come in handy when it's time to craft an intimate scene of your own.

The Immunity Factor

When you first see a film, everything's new. You watch in a state of naïveté, during which many things may surprise, shock, or intrigue you. In other words, you're actively involved. After a while, you become more sophisticated about its design, and you develop certain expectations. If those expectations aren't circumvented, the film eventually becomes old hat, and you begin to imagine events before they actually transpire. You may cease to think about the movie; you may even begin planning the rest of your day. You've become immune to any potential impact that the film may otherwise have had.

It's an aging process of sorts and can be detrimental to any artist who doesn't foresee it and plan accordingly. This immunity can happen to entire genres just as it happens during the course of a single film. The phrase "If you've seen one action film, you've seen them all" speaks to the dilemma, and it becomes dangerous where difficult subject matter is concerned. You probably don't want audiences saying, "If you've seen one drive-by shooting, you've seen them all," and yet films with excessive violence inoculate audiences to its effects in just this way. After several scenes where cursing prevails, I cease to hear the words. In movies with high sexual content, intimacy may lose meaning altogether.

So how do you protect your work against this process? Begin by asking yourself these questions:

- ✔ What do you want an audience to simply accept?
- ✔ What do you want an audience to hear and/or remember?
- ✔ What surprises do you have in store?
- ✔ What might be more powerful *suggested* rather than presented outright?

Part of your responsibility, to both the story and to audiences, is to wake them up. With a nudge in the right direction, people's imaginations will concoct scenes more gruesome, delightful, terrifying, or inspiring than you may be capable of writing. Never underestimate the power of suggested violence or sexual contact, and whatever you do, don't let audiences become immune to the very thing that you need to convey. Write a film that challenges their expectations or demands that they create new ones.

Finally, before you send a script anywhere, imagine different kinds of audience members for it. Imagine a child in the theater, a young woman, an elderly man. Imagine a victim of violence or sexual abuse. Imagine someone who's fought a war or lived through the events that you're dramatizing. Will they be adversely affected by what they see? This procedure doesn't mean that you'll change the script to fit their needs; you may not. You may feel strongly that it's important in your piece to dramatize war in a graphic, realistic way. *Saving Private Ryan* and *Platoon* are examples of such films. However, if you've thought about the audience that this subject matter may disturb, you can craft a marketing strategy that warns the audience in advance. You might put it on your list of priorities when speaking to executives about the film. After a script hits production, the advertising campaign may be out of your hands. But it's your script first, so the responsibility for your audience begins with you.

A strong script is probably written for several kinds of audiences. But if you know who it's *not* intended for in advance, you'll be better able to market the script responsibly later on.

Part III
Turning Your Story into a Script

The 5th Wave   By Rich Tennant

©RICHTENNANT

"The margins on your screenplay are soooo even, Ms. Holly, and the type so black and crisp. I'm sure whatever the story's about is also good, but with centered headlines and flush left columns like this, we'd be fools not to make your movie!"

In this part . . .

Here's where the process gets technical. You've developed an idea into a story. You know what's going to happen, who it's happening to and how it's going to end. Great. So what make that story a screenplay instead of some other sort of text? Its organization, artistically and technically, that's what. This part is about mapping the story out and piecing it together on the page. From setting your margins and pounding out a draft, to revising it until you're satisfied. This is where the story becomes a film.

Chapter 12

Mapping Out Your Screenplay

• •

In This Chapter

▶ Telling your story in a nutshell

▶ Treating your story to a treatment

▶ Choosing the outline that's right for you

▶ A project to get you started

• •

*W*riters spend months constructing characters, choosing locations, researching events, and conceptualizing the "look" or the "angle" that their stories will take. Yet, despite this preparation, few screenwriters jump immediately into composing a first draft. Why? They don't know where to start. Or they know where to start, but they don't know what comes directly after or what the first scenes are moving toward. More often, they've envisioned the beginning, the middle, and the end of the story, but they have only a vague idea of how to get from point to point.

A full-length screenplay is a vast project, around 100 pages long, hinged together by countless visual moments. Ideally, no script detail is wasted; each component drives the story toward some culminating event. In other words, the writer reveals every piece of information for a specific reason. Can you visualize all those pieces yet? If the answer is no, don't worry. Most seasoned writers can't, either. It's a lot to consider all at once. So when you complete the initial research, you have two choices: start writing immediately and risk staring at a computer screen for hours, wondering what comes next, or plot the story out in advance.

This chapter is all about the second choice. I show you how to plot out your story, from the initial premise to a working outline. You'll still stare at the screen for hours — even an outline can't cure that — but at least you won't be wondering what comes next.

Conceptualizing Your Concept

If your script makes it to an agent or a producer, here are a few questions that you'll hear quite often:

- ✔ "What's the hook?"
- ✔ "Does it have audience appeal?"
- ✔ "Remind me again — it's like what two films?"
- ✔ "Where's the big event?"
- ✔ "Yeah, but, what's it *about?*"

These questions are really asking the same thing — namely, "What's your film's concept?" The *hook* is a detail from your story that ropes an audience in. The *big event* is usually the first major turning point in the protagonist's journey. In some films, the hook and the big event are the same thing. In *Jaws,* for instance, the shark attack is what hooks an audience into the film and what changes the protagonist's life forever. The film's concept combines these items with the central conflict. In other words, it's your premise. After all your research, you may find it odd to return to the beginning, but before you map out a script, you have to revisit the original idea. Do you have a three- to five-sentence *nutshell synopsis?* (See Chapter 5 if you don't have one and want to know how to create one.) If so, now's the time to turn that synopsis into one of two things: a logline or a question. You may want to take a stab at both.

A *logline* is a one- or two-sentence encapsulation of your story. It highlights character, conflict, and those aspects of your piece that make it unique. It's significantly shorter than a synopsis.

Here are a few examples from established films. I include both a logline and a question for each:

- ✔ *E.T.:* When an alien lands in a young boy's backyard, that boy and his family struggle to send it back home before it's too late.

  or: What happens when an alien lands in a young boy's backyard and finds itself unable to get back home?

- ✔ *The Untouchables:* When Elliot Ness accepts a position in the Treasury Department, he and his band of "Untouchables" wage a full-scale street war against crime boss Al Capone.

  or: Treasury agent Elliot Ness attempts to rid Chicago of Al Capone and his gang. Who will be left standing at the battle's conclusion?

Even epic-length films can be whittled down to size:

 ✔ *Lord of the Rings:* A ring of power surfaces after years in hiding, and many forces seek its dark authority. The fate of Middle Earth depends on the hobbit Frodo, bearer of the ring, and his decision over its demise.

 or: The dark ring of power is entrusted to the hobbit Frodo. Will he find a way to destroy it? Will it be lost along the way? Or will its power turn him toward the evil?

 ✔ *Raiders of the Lost Ark:* Artifacts unearthed in Egypt reveal the whereabouts of the mythic Lost Ark of the Covenant. Only one man stands between Hitler's Nazi regime and the Ark's fabled power — archaeologist and university professor Indiana Jones.

 or: Artifacts unearthed in Egypt reveal the whereabouts of the mythic Lost Ark of the Covenant, an object fabled to possess measureless power. Will Hitler and his Nazi regime find the Ark and harness this power? Or will Indiana Jones beat them to it?

Do you see how these snippets depict the crux of each film? These snippets are film concepts. From a business perspective, more films are bought and sold over concept than on full drafts, outlines, or other literature combined. From an artistic perspective, the concept is your greatest ally when writing the first draft. It keeps you on track when the story eludes you. It also fuels the eventual outline.

So after you condense the story into a few sentences, or a well-phrased question, double-check that the following elements are true:

 ✔ Your concept is clear and easily understood.

 ✔ It suggests the largest conflict in the film.

 ✔ It suggests a cast of characters.

 ✔ It suggests what's unique about the story.

 ✔ It suggests what may be familiar to an audience.

 ✔ It suggests what's easily marketable in the story.

 ✔ It suggests dynamic action.

As a final challenge, layer in character motivation. In other words, your characters want something for a reason. What is that reason? Elliot Ness is ethically opposed to Al Capone. Frodo must destroy the ring or be destroyed himself. Usually, your film provides life-or-death consequences, or the characters perceive them to be life-or-death. Add those consequences to your premise. And take your time. A clear concept provides the foundation for every draft of the script that you write thereafter.

How to Treat Your Treatment

If you had to write reports in school, you're probably familiar with a *treatment*. Most class projects require a cover page that explains what topics the report includes and what it ultimately proves. A treatment is the screenwriting equivalent of that cover page, albeit slightly more entertaining.

To be more specific, a *treatment* is a narrative summation of your story. It's part synopsis and part short story. It runs anywhere from 4 to 20 pages in length, depending on the scope of your film, and it describes each act of your script in chronological order.

In five-page treatments, Page 1 is dedicated to Act I, Pages 2 through 4 illustrate Act II, and Page 5 sums up Act III. A film's second act is generally twice as long as the first or third and, therefore, requires more explanation. Most screenplay treatments run 15 to 20 pages in length. If your film is three hours long, or includes several subplots, it may require a few more pages. Treatments that run longer than 20 pages are generally overwritten and overwhelming to the eye. After all, most first acts are about 30 pages; you may as well start writing the script.

Considerations before you begin

There are two kinds of treatments: the one that you write for studios or agents and the one that you write for you. I talk about marketing treatments in Chapter 18. You're writing this first treatment for you, so concentrate on depicting the following elements clearly:

- ✔ **A brief description of your main characters (villains included):** Character introductions are important. You (and eventually your audience) will judge the character's initial actions on that introduction. The characters will also change as your story unfolds. If they make strong first impressions, you'll be better able to recognize those changes as they occur. So think: What do your characters look like? How do they spend time? What are their individual rhythms, physical and language-based? In other words, what are they like when they first enter the scene in five sentences or less?

- ✔ **An immediate sense of their goals and motivations:** Most stories entail what people want and how they're going to get it. You'll probably want to reveal the first part of that statement, the "what people want" bit, early on. If you establish character goals quickly, you'll have more time to pursue them.

Hopefully, you have some idea of where each scene is going. In other words, you've envisioned the story's conclusion. With that end in mind, you can highlight the moments that take you there within each scene. To rewrite my previous example then, I must decide where that moment may lead. When I imagine the tour guide's raging crush on this boy and determine that this event propels her to ask him out, I can add the scene to my outline. The rewritten version might look like this:

Act I, Scene 6 — Ext. Campus Street — Day

A tour guide wearily corrals the crowd into a designated area.

She recites various facts about the architecture on campus.

Suddenly, she is interrupted by a boy on a bike. He calls out her name and waves.

He passes her, as if in slow motion, revealing in detail his blue eyes and dazzling smile.

She watches him ride off, oblivious to the tour group that she's supposedly in charge of.

She finally looks at them for a second, then takes off after him, calling his name as she runs.

The heading of each scene in an outline corresponds to the slug line that will eventually appear in your script. Slug lines include the basic information needed to set up a shot. I talk about them at greater length in Chapter 15, if you want the whole scoop, but for your purposes here, just remember to include a rough indication of where the scene fits in the chronology of your story, a sense of location, and a sense of time. If the following scene in the tour guide drama takes place in the bookstore where she tracks the boy down, the next portion of the outline should begin:

Act I, Scene 7 — Int. Bookstore — Day

If you want to be even more specific about time here, the next portion may also read:

Act I, Scene 7 — Int. Bookstore — Moments later

Outlines help you organize the action. Planning so much in advance may seem odd at first, but eventually, this blueprint becomes second nature and, in many cases, necessary.

A sentence outline (or beat sheet) does the following:

✔ **The platfor**
event? Wha
job, family,
basically, ar
protagonist.

✔ **The catalyst**
launches the
as simple as
it's a catalys

✔ **Plot Point I:**
does he or sl
when your cl
does so willi

✔ **Plot Point II:**
decides to fac
a moment of
to give up, or
forging ahead

✔ **Climax:** What
ticular attenti
force behave i

✔ **Resolution:** W
the film look li

I discuss these plot
list provides an ove
important events, to
scatter the same inf
tions throughout. Co
do you know your cl
entire script? Where
information, do som
your drama. You may
or constructing a nev
able with the process

Putting it or

Like the concept, you
Artistically, you want
characters. From a bu
ity. So although you ca
ing guidelines usually

✔ Treatr
imme
takes

✔ They'
becor

✔ They'
or ed

✔ They

✔ They
(Dial
whic

✔ They

✔ They

•

c
o
he
j
pa
wa
hi

✔ The
rea

You can
now, con
while, so
as its dra
remain v
together

gu
es
ef
of
le

Exploring

An outli
you're v
list of tl
a treatr
smaller
reveals

✔ Runs in chronological order from Act I through Act III

✔ Is broken into sequences introduced by the act number, the location, and the time of day

✔ Is broken down within each sequence into individual actions. Each action gets one or two sentences of description

✔ Highlights the characters, situation, and, sometimes, the pace of each scene

Think that's the only kind of outline to explore? Think again. The next example fleshes the story out even further.

One step at a time

The sentence outline is like a writer's grocery list. It's typed directly into the computer or written into a notepad. Some writers post it by their desks, some carry it around, and many check off the scenes as they go. One of the strengths of the sentence outline is that it exists in one piece. Eventually, however, you may want greater flexibility with your outline. You may want to switch scenes around or remove some entirely and watch the story change accordingly. When and if this becomes the case for your story, the time's arrived for the step outline.

Step outlines are traditionally written with 3 x 5-inch note cards. The slug line or scene heading goes somewhere at the top, followed by a short description of the action in that moment. For example:

Act I, Scene 8 — Int. School Hallway — Day

Miriam approaches her locker. It appears to have been broken into. The door has a giant dent, and her books and papers are strewn across the floor. Worse, the letter is no longer taped to the inside wall.

What's the difference between this form and the last one? Detail. In the sentence outline, you summarize the action in each scene. In a step-by-step outline, you envision every visual moment that makes up those actions. For instance, consider the moment where the tour guide sees the boy on the bike smile at her. This one sentence may be made up of several fleeting bits: A shot of her turning around to watch him ride by, a shot of his face, a shot of his mouth calling her name, a close shot of his eyes as he winks, and then a shot of him riding down the street. Each one of those flashes might receive an individual note card in the step-by-step outline.

In the example of Miriam at her locker, the card concentrates on the locker from one person's point of view. If someone taps Miriam on the shoulder and she whirls around, the ensuing interaction merits a new card.

Some writers further classify each card in the following ways:

- **Organization by location:** Several moments may take place in one location. If you add that location at the top of each card, you can tell how many shots make up each sequence. The "living room" sequence may be made up of several note cards.

- **A character list:** Try recording the characters in each scene on the card. This log allows you to determine how often a character speaks, when he or she may need to speak, and who he or she interacts with on a regular basis. The list also helps you track each character's journey individually should the need arise.

- **A note on plot:** Is this scene pivotal to the main plot or to a subplot? Indicating that information on each card helps to determine when a subplot scene may be necessary, when the subplot has been overextended, and when two plots intersect.

- **Scene strength:** You may want to delineate the strength of each scene in a word or two on each card. For instance, is the scene primarily fueled by character, dialogue, plot, exposition, or theme?

How much or how little you include on each card is up to you. For some writers, three or four sentences of description is enough; other writers go so far as to color code their cards by act, strong point, or sequence locale. Directors and cinematographers create storyboards for the film. They break the film down into pictures that will become each shot.

This step-by-step outline is your storyboard. Do you need to use 3 x 5-inch cards? Absolutely not. This method allows you to rearrange individual parts, however. The ability to spread the scenes out in front of you and mix and match until you're satisfied with a chronology is invaluable. You may choose to cut and paste on a computer or use a page per action instead, but whatever you do, choose a form that can be easily rearranged.

What to Do When the Outline's Through

If you're satisfied with your story at this point, the next step is to start writing. However, few writers complete an outline satisfied. If you don't have large portions of the script to be reworked, you almost certainly have moments that are out of place or missing entirely. Here are a few questions to ask yourself after you've completed one or both of the previously mentioned outlines:

- Do you have long sequences of dialogue or action? How might you break these sequences up so that they don't become monotonous?

- Are the characters' goals clear? Are they obtained in the end?

- Do your characters acquire new skills or information along the way? In which scenes?

- What relationships exist at the end that did not exist at the beginning? Do you have enough scenes to plausibly support that interaction?

- Is your villain fully represented?

- Are your subplots represented? Do they support the main plot?

- Is each scene motivated by a preceding scene or moment? In other words, does every scene inspire another to occur?

- Does each scene propel a reader to the climax in some way?

- Is enough backstory introduced to successfully frame the action?

- Does the choice of location strengthen the theme or the action?

- Does your script contain surprises? If so, where are they?

Be on the alert for too many scenes in one location, or of one quality in succession. Your script is like a visual symphony, too much of one melodic line quickly becomes repetitive. Break up action-packed scenes with moments of budding character relationships. Break up image with dialogue. Find any way you can to vary the form and content of your story.

Also, beware of action that happens to or around the protagonist. You want the protagonist to happen to the script, not the other way around. Force your character to make choices — the scenes will suddenly become active and dynamic.

When you're finished, spread the cards out in front of you and sit with them for a few hours. Even if you're satisfied with a sequence of events, try rearranging one or two cards. Try envisioning your piece with alternate opening and closing images. Force yourself to remove three moments. Which three will they be? You're creating a visual piece, so being able to see the entire project in front of you is very helpful. Tell the story out loud and see how it sounds, based on your short descriptions of each moment. It may take a week, it may take a month. By the time you're finished pouring through the cards, you'll know the story inside and out — which is convenient because the next step is composing a first draft!

Outlining someone else's story

This project is familiar to many television writers who rely on it to acquire a feel for any new series. It's helpful to feature-film writers as well, especially because outlining someone else's script is easier than outlining your own.

Tape an episode of your favorite TV show or rent your favorite film. You can do this project with a piece of paper or with note cards. If it's a TV show, watch the whole thing once through; if it's a film, choose a portion of it to watch. Take note of the following details:

- Order of locations
- Character introductions
- Major events
- Minor events
- Actions that caused other actions

When you're through, watch the piece again. Keep the pause button handy for this part. See if you can construct a sentence or a step-by-step outline of what you see. Finally, watch the sequence again with outline in hand to see what you missed. By the time you're through with this project, you'll know the story, the genre, and the structure of the piece that you selected. You'll also know how to approach an outline of your own work.

Chapter 13

Surviving Writer's Block

• •

• •

1f you've ever taken up exercise, you know what writer's block feels like. You're running on that treadmill, your pulse rate is high, your breathing is steady, you feel invigorated and alive. "This is easy," you think, and for a while, it is. Then, all of a sudden — bam! Your muscles tense up, your legs give way, you're winded, and you have to stop. The impetus and the desire to run are gone, seemingly forever. The next day, beginning again is infinitely more difficult, if not impossible.

Writers experience this same cycle. One minute, characters speak unbidden, and images fly across the page; the next minute nothing, no pictures, no voices, no sense of what comes next. It's called *writer's block,* the not-so-great equalizer. It strikes without discrimination and without warning. It leaves you uncertain of how to proceed and panicked that you can't proceed at all.

But what is writer's block really? Is it an affliction or a natural part of the creative process? Is it to be feared or embraced? Is there anything you can do to avoid it? And what, oh what, do you do when it finds you? If you've ever experienced writer's block, or if you're curious about how to handle it when you do, read on. This chapter takes on all those questions and more.

From Panic to Peace: Switching Mindsets

In conversation, writer's block sounds like a disease. It certainly has all the symptoms: confusion, lightheadedness, loss of appetite, insomnia, restlessness, headaches, and nausea. I know a writer who hyperventilates at the mere thought of writer's block, and another writer who swears that she can sense its approach by the twitch in her left hand. Every year, a student asks me if I believe that writer's block is contagious. I usually say, "No, I do not," but I know why they're uneasy. Writer's block seems to carry more legends than any other part of the artistic process. Horror stories abound, from novelists unable to complete more than one novel to dramatists with award-winning ideas abandoning projects halfway through the first draft. People hear these stories and develop all sorts of misconceptions. A few years ago, I began compiling a list of these fallacies. The following are among the most common:

- Writer's block means that you're a bad writer.
- Writer's block means that your story isn't worth telling.
- If you enjoy time away from your work, you're not really a writer.
- Some writers don't experience writer's block.
- Writer's block means that you're not psychologically ready to write this story yet.
- After you've written several screenplays, writer's block disappears.
- If you ignore the problem, it will go away.
- If you tell people that you're experiencing a block, they'll think that you're inexperienced or mediocre at your craft.
- If you don't find a way around writer's block, you'll never be able to accept work with a deadline.
- Writer's block is something you have to face alone.

None of these things are true, yet they're only a few of the beliefs circulating among writers. With all this bad press, it's no wonder people fear the ordeal.

Surprisingly, though, writer's block isn't something to fear. In fact, fear is the problem. Look at other professions. Would anyone expect a doctor to offer diagnosis after diagnosis without pausing for thought? I doubt it. Would anyone expect a teacher to understand students at a glance or fault her for puzzling over them until she determines how each one should be taught? I hope not. Yet many writers expect to maintain a breakneck pace and a rigorous schedule without allowing for an occasional question, a pause or — heaven forbid — a moment of indecision. Why? Because they're afraid, and thus, they're artistically exhausted. Fear is the culprit behind virtually all forms of writer's block. If you look closely, you can see it lurking behind each one.

The top ten reasons for writer's block

Writing is a private process, so finding an explanation for every creative obstacle is difficult. However, as most writers experience the same stages of the creative process, they share the problems with each process as well. You can, therefore, trace the most frequent blocks to one of the following causes:

✓ **Something about the story needs to change.** After you've outlined a script, you'll probably write it scene by scene. However, stories change as you write them, and you'll probably deviate from that outline a bit, sometimes a great deal. Unfortunately, tracking larger changes in structure can be difficult when you're entrenched in the details of scene work, and you may finish one scene only to find yourself confused as to how the next should look.

✓ **You've written past your initial design.** Your story develops as you write, so the landscape and the characters in the second portion may not match their original images. Writers often become frustrated by plot and character inconsistencies halfway through a script, fearing that the story has gotten away from them.

✓ **You're under a strict deadline.** Some people work well under pressure; others do not. Although deadlines provide clear artistic goals, they also require a strict schedule and a pace that allows little time to daydream — let alone question a script. The pressure of meeting those demands often makes it impossible to do so.

✓ **Your expectations are unreasonable.** Writers aren't robots, so you shouldn't be expected to churn out the same material in the same way every time you write. Some days, you'll produce a lot of work; other days, you'll produce none. Some days, your writing will be palpable and precise; other days, it will drag across the page begging you to hit the delete key. Impossible expectations put undue pressure on you, as an artist, and they virtually ensure failure of some sort.

✓ **The last thing you wrote was fantastic/wretched.** The last thing you wrote was successful, so this one might be a flop. The last thing you wrote was unique, so this one might be clichéd. The first script was horrific; this one might be worse. If thoughts of what your script "might be" keep you from writing, these thoughts "might be" your block.

✓ **You're unable to admit uncertainty.** Today's society doesn't applaud indecision, and it certainly doesn't reward hesitation. People, therefore, feel a need to provide answers instead of asking questions. Writers are no exception. Without a ready answer, many writers panic and can't write at all.

✓ **You're facing a pivotal script decision.** When facing a pivotal decision, some writers trace each option through the remainder of the story as if it were a game of chess. They're afraid of making the "wrong" choices, so they don't make any. This deliberation often lasts a long time, and as a result, little work gets done.

✓ **You write quickly.** I know what you're thinking: If writing quickly is a problem, send it your way. Writing quickly can be an asset, but it can just as easily be a curse. In your artistic frenzy, you may lose sight of the story as a whole. When you finally do come up for air, you may have to take a while to assess what you've written and what to write next.

✔ **You're constantly interrupted.** Few people can write in the 15 minutes between phone calls and meetings. Your imagination needs time to shift into working mode, to focus on your characters again and determine where you left off. Interruptions make it impossible to switch into working mode and, therefore, to work at all.

✔ **You don't allow time for a personal life.** Although you need uninterrupted time alone with your work, you also need time away from it. Many writers view "free time" as wasted time and fear that they'll lose momentum if they don't spend every minute with the characters. Yet without time off, you may end up with one-dimensional characters and contrived plot points.

Notice a pattern? Unrealistic expectations, excessive pressure to succeed, lack of personal time — these factors underscore the entire list, and they're all fueled by fear. You're afraid to fail, or afraid to succeed, or afraid to succeed and then fail. In any case, fear is what's stopping your pen.

Can you avoid this predicament? No. But you can survive it. The first order of business involves a change in attitude. Despite the symptoms, writer's block is not a disease; it's a natural part of the creative process — maybe even an important part. Nine times out of ten, writer's block means that you're on the verge of some productive change. Your story is about to shift, and you need to stop for a moment in order to discover how. Tedious and irritating as it may be, writer's block may be beneficial. Here are a few things that it may suggest:

✔ **Your abilities as a storyteller are improving.** Writers sharpen their skills as they write. Perhaps you're becoming more adept at the craft, and your imagination needs time to adjust. If you stop and reread your work, you may be able to catch the improvement on the page.

✔ **The characters have something unexpected to say.** When people spend enough time together, they can close their eyes and re-create the sound of the other person's voice. The same process occurs as you get to know your characters. If you spend enough time with them, they'll start speaking to you. You know them better now than when you first began writing, so don't be surprised if they're telling you something new.

✔ **Your reason for writing the story has changed.** Some people have a clear reason for writing from the very beginning. Others do not. Events that you discover as you write quite possibly may change your reason for finishing the project. If you didn't have a reason when you began, you'll probably find one as you go. Use the extra time that writer's block bestows on you to reconsider that position.

✔ **Your subplot is becoming more important.** Subplots have a way of becoming more dynamic as a script develops. As subplots tend to carry the movie's theme, they often threaten to overshadow the main plot. Your creative block may be fueled by that subplot, tugging at your sleeve for attention.

✔ **You forgot a critical piece of information.** If you're entrenched in the work and writing at a fast pace, you can easily lose sight of backstory and exposition. After all, you understand the story; *you* don't need that piece of information. Your audience will need it, though. Double-check that you've included all the information that an audience needs to understand the world of your script.

Creative blocks are like red flags meant to catch your attention. If you ignore them, they just get larger. If you become angry with them, you exhaust yourself beating them down. Instead, consider them a warning and try to discover what they have to say. Maybe — and this is most often the case — you just need to relax. Take a breath. You have nothing to fear; if anything, something exciting is in store for you and your story. You're about to learn something new.

A survival guide

Are you breathing? Good. If you've reached a creative standstill, the best thing to do is direct your attention away from the block and all the horrible things that might happen if you're stuck forever. You're not stuck forever; you're just stuck now, and now is the time to concentrate on other things. Here are a few "other things" that you may want to try when writer's block strikes:

✔ **Do something else.** Sometimes, you just need a break from the computer or from your notepad, even if it's just for a hour. The best ideas always find me in the shower or in the car. So take a drive, go play golf, have lunch with a friend, take a long walk, or indulge in a nap. Trick your mind into thinking that you just don't care about that script. Answers often arrive when you least expect them.

✔ **Switch projects.** John Logan, writer of *Gladiator* and *Any Given Sunday,* likes to juggle several projects at once. Why would anyone do that? First, doing so diverts your mind from the creative impasse and keeps you writing at the same time. Also, what you learn on one project may clarify a problem in another. If you try this strategy, make sure that the projects are at different stages of development. If you're in the first draft of script one, for example, script two should be in development or revisions. Otherwise, you risk ending up with not one, but two cases of writer's block.

✔ **Outline the script.** You probably outlined your script before you began writing, but it never hurts to do it again. Outline what you've already written first, and then move on to what you intend to include later. If your story has changed, the outline will show you how. Tracing the steps leading to the block may lead to the next scene.

✔ **Read, read, read.** Other artists offer techniques, dramatic examples, and inspiration. You needn't limit yourself to screenplays; read literature, poetry, and nonfiction, too. Read newspapers or old letters. Read anything that ropes you into a world other than your own or the one that you're creating.

✔ **Return to research.** In Chapter 4, I detail the creative process. Part of that process involves the *saturation stage,* where a writer seeks creative input of all kinds that may inform her script. Return to that stage now. Visit museums, collect photographs, listen to music, eavesdrop on conversations, and record what you hear. You've written part of the story, so your imagination knows what to look for now. You may discover details that you missed the first time around.

✔ **Try alternate forms of writing.** By "alternate," I mean try writing something other than a screenplay. Write a letter, send an e-mail, start a diary, or give yourself an assignment and write for an hour. Like switching projects, this strategy also redirects your concentration while keeping your imagination alert.

✔ **Sleep on it.** If you've been tackling a block for a while, you're probably tense and exhausted. Go to bed. Your mind still works while your body sleeps. You'll definitely wake up refreshed. You may even wake up with an answer.

You'll discover many more avenues through creative standstills as you go. Do what works for you — just don't give up. The worst thing that you can do is push the script aside completely. You're almost always abandoning something worth keeping, and more writer's block is waiting for you ahead. If you don't overcome it now, how will you survive it the next time?

Reevaluating Your Routine

A solid work regime helps writers coast through creative blocks with their sanity intact. It also cuts the frequency of the encounters in half. If you think that your routine could stand a change, try one or all of the following suggestions:

✔ **Write at the same time every day.** As I say in Chapter 4, the more habitual your writing routine is, the better. If your schedule allows you to write from 9 a.m. to noon every day, your imagination will adjust accordingly. Pretty soon, you'll be in working mode by the time you sit down, and if the muse is looking for you, she'll know where to go and when.

✔ **Set aside preparation time.** Preparation time includes anything and everything you do to prepare yourself to write. I keep a "later" list near me at all times. This list reminds me of the parts of the script that I intend to write later. It includes character details, events, pieces of conversation, or images that occur unexpectedly. This way, I always have something I can work on when the current scene eludes me. Some writers spend an hour each day dreaming up tomorrow's scenes. Doing so leaves them ready for the next day, but more importantly, it leaves them excited to begin again.

✔ **Set clear goals.** Some writers try to finish a certain number of pages each day; some writers set aside a certain amount of time. When three hours are done, so are they. You may find it easier to work through choice moments, completing a scene or a monologue for instance. The specific goal is entirely up to you, but do try to achieve it. You'll always feel better if you end each day with some sort of success.

✔ **Devise an opening ritual.** Sometimes, the imagination takes a while to warm up. Find a way to help it out, and start each day with that procedure. Some people write three to five pages of stream-of-consciousness thought each morning. Writing letters or rereading past work also prepares the imagination to begin. The opening ritual is yet another way to make the writing process habitual.

✔ **Keep a writing journal.** Writing journals are different from diaries. Everything in a diary is personal; it grants writers an outlet for pent-up anger, joy, and pain. Keeping a diary is a form of therapy. Writing journals are reserved for your work. Give yourself an assignment and record it here. Stuck on a scene? Write it out in prose form in your journal. If you're a pen writer (as opposed to a computer writer), maybe your whole first draft belongs here. In this way, you separate unwanted emotion and personal judgment from dramatic writing.

✔ **Stop when you know what comes next.** Here's a piece of advice from Ernest Hemingway. He used to tell young writers to stop writing when they could envision what the next moment in the story would be. That way, they'd always have a place to begin.

These techniques won't stop writer's block entirely, but they'll help to make it less frequent. They represent the personal side of the process, measures that you take on your own. If you plan on writing professionally, you may also want to seek the help of others.

Seeking Outside Help

Writing is often a lonely endeavor. It requires a great deal of time away from family, friends, and the outside world in general, which can be disconcerting for all involved. However, you needn't cut yourself off entirely while completing a script. Writer's block is the perfect opportunity to enlist support. Here are several ways that your colleagues and loved ones can become involved in the process:

✔ **Share your schedule.** Alerting other people of your writing schedule is advantageous in two ways. If people know when you work, they're less likely to interrupt while you're working. Also, if they know your goals in advance, they may be able to help you accomplish them. Not all writers make a living at their craft, and the encouragement of friends and family often takes the place of financial support.

✔ **Write with others.** Do you know any writers? Meet them for a few hours and write together. If you arrange the meeting, you'll most likely show up, which means that work will probably get done. If a script problem arises, there's someone across from you to help. Watch out though — you may have to enforce strict "no gabbing" rules to ensure that work gets done.

✔ **Join a writing group.** Writing groups usually meet once a week or once a month, and they can be a wonderful place to workshop new scripts as well as to make connections. Every writing group is structured differently. Some groups simply present and discuss new work. Other groups include writing projects for participants to try in between sessions. Some are mediated by an instructor and may charge a joining fee; others are more informal. I encourage you to try several before committing to one. Writing groups often post information on how to join at local libraries, universities, and frequently in writing journals or magazines. If you can't find one, you can always start a group yourself.

✔ **Talk it out.** I'm of two minds on this method. I usually suggest waiting to talk about a story until the idea's fleshed out and there's at least one outline in place. In the early stages, you really can't talk about an idea until the desire and the immediate need to write it disappear. Wait until you're developing scenes, and then seek advice. A new ear picks up details that you've long since forgotten, and remember, other people don't know the story yet. Their questions and reactions will quickly reveal any confusing or inconsistent moments. You may also consider this discussion to be your first pitch. How can you sell the story from the start?

✔ **Plan group readings.** Do you know any actors? Do you have any dramatic friends or family members? Invite them to read a few scenes out loud. Assign someone to read the description as well. There's no substitute for hearing your words out loud. If they flop in your living room, they'll likely flop with actors. But if they fly now, they'll likely fly on-screen.

A strong support group may help you end the period of writer's block more quickly. Having the support certainly makes the process bearable at the very least. So the next time you're in a creative rut, don't rant and rave in private. Rant and rave with others.

All in all, the best advice I've ever gotten about writer's block was from an old colleague who said, "Don't let it eat you alive; use it to sharpen your teeth." Writer's block isn't an end; it's a beginning. Use the break to reflect on your story and sharpen your skill. If it's true that human beings grow the most during times of struggle, you'll be infinitely wiser by the time your script is complete.

TRY IT

Knocking your block off

Here's a project that I use on the first day of workshops and anytime thereafter when a student gets stuck. It's a timed writing. In this case, you'll be writing for two minutes, and you'll be using a *tag line,* which is the first phrase you write and the phrase you return to if you can think of nothing else to write.

The rules of the timed writing are simple:

✔ Keep your hand moving on the page. If you can't think of anything to say, continue to write the tag line until something occurs to you.

✔ There are no expected responses. You're recording your thoughts as you think them; go where they take you.

✔ Pay no attention to grammar or spelling. They're entirely unimportant in this exercise.

✔ Don't censor yourself. Go for the jugular, so to speak.

✔ Stop writing when the time is over, even if you're mid-sentence.

So, those are the rules. Here are two tag lines. Write for a minute and a half on each one. The tag lines are:

✔ "Today I am . . ."

✔ "Tomorrow I see . . ."

After you've written your responses, read them out loud. Circle any phrase or image that sparks your fancy. Did you learn anything? You might also try combining the two reactions in some way. After you're done, you can choose tag lines that direct your energy toward a specific script. Here are five such tag lines to get you started:

✔ "I see someone who . . ."

✔ "If you listen closely, you'll hear . . ."

✔ "The room resembles a . . ."

✔ "The music of the moment sounds like . . ."

✔ "Soon I expect that . . ."

Chapter 14

Formatting Your Screenplay

• •

In This Chapter

▶ Setting up your page

▶ Scripting character introductions

▶ Writing compelling description

▶ Understanding the camera

▶ Looking at some helpful beginning examples

• •

Skim a few books on how to land a great job and you'll notice at least one similarity: They all reserve a section, if not a chapter, on first impressions. If you walk into an interview looking like you just rolled out of a bed and proceed to speak in half sentences or grunts while tugging at a hole in your shoe, you're not leaving with the job. If you walk into the interview in a ball gown or a tux, singing your extensive credentials and qualifications, you're not leaving with the job. To land the position, you should look and sound like you mean business. You should be clear, confident, and concise. You have a first impression to make, so make it well.

In screenwriting, your format is your best shot at a good first impression. In a way, it's your first interview. If your format looks professional, the readers will assume that you're a professional. If your format suggests confidence and skill, the readers will be confident in your skill. Unlike plays and novels where the structure is fairly loose, screenplays are written within precise guidelines and restrictions. Your challenge as a screenwriter is to tell a unique story within those guidelines. Even if you're writing for the fun of it and have no intention of sending your script out, a screenplay isn't a screenplay without the format. It's merely a set of ideas with no vehicle.

This chapter guides you through the basic screenplay format to help lift your ideas from the outline stage to the printed page. It also highlights the tools that you need to make a good first impression.

How the Screenplay Looks on the Page

As a screenwriter, your job is to immerse the readers into your story. Those readers may be editors, agents, producers, studio execs, actors or directors — anyone you hope to interest in your piece. You want their eyes moving down one page and onto the next without having to stop or flip back in confusion. For that reason, the screenwriting format is designed to fade into the background. Once mastered, it allows a screenwriter to convey location, character, and action in a quick and efficient manner. It also enables a screenwriter to design the mood, angle, and pace of a scene without drawing attention to the mechanics involved.

Imagine a blank page. In the screenwriting format, six parts are all vying for space on that page. Those parts are

- **The description:** the description of the location, the characters, and any action indicated throughout the scene (The description is sometimes referred to as "the business" of the scene.)

- **The character name:** the person doing the talking

- **The character dialogue:** what that person says

- **Parenthetical directions:** how the person says a line, or what he's doing as he says it

- **Transitional directions:** any camera information or indications of how the scene should be visualized and/or read

- **The page number.**

Each component has its own placement on the page, and a reader should be able to distinguish one component from the other at a glance. Together, these components convey all the necessary information to an audience.

Setting your typeface and your margins

The proper typeface for your script is Courier font or another font with equal proportions. In general, that means that there are approximately ten spaces to every inch of line. Why this rule? This type size insures that, on average, one page of script reads at one minute — a detail very helpful to directors trying to determine the running time of an individual scene or of the script as a whole.

After you set your typeface, program your computer or word processor to remember the following marginal guidelines for each formatting section.

- **Left margin:** 1½ inches
- **Right margin:** 1 inch
- **Top margin:** 1 inch
- **Bottom margin:** 1 inch
- **Description:** runs the length of the page (after you've set your margins)
- **Character name:** 4 inches from the left-hand side of the page (2½ inches from the left margin)
- **Dialogue:** begins 2½ inches from the left-hand side of the page (1 inch from the left margin) and ends at 6½ inches from the left-hand side of the page (5 inches from the left margin).
- **Parentheticals:** 3½ inches from the left-hand side of the page (2 inches from the left margin)
- **Page numbers:** ½ inch from the top of the page, ½ inch from the right-hand side of the page

Transitional directions (which mainly convey camera information) take several forms and, therefore, have several placements on the page. I detail those forms later in the chapter.

The method behind this margin madness is simple: Actors concentrate on dialogue; directors look for the composition and pace of each scene. If your format is correctly aligned, everyone's happy. You've created special compartments for each element. A glance down the left-hand side of the page reveals the primary locations and actions of each scene. A glance down the center provides the character list and accompanying dialogue. This structure lets a reader concentrate on one portion of the scene at a time.

Spacing your script correctly

A screenplay is not a novel. A screenplay is comprised of quick visual clips. Your images should be strong and easily accessible. If you lump three or four images together on the page, they'll be neither. Seeing blocks of text with little or no interruption can be very daunting to a reader. If I get tired just glancing at your script, I'll be unlikely to start reading it and even less likely to finish it. Your format is an invitation to read. Here's how to space your screenplay to highlight each image in a visually inviting way.

Single space:

- All description
- All lines of dialogue

   ✔ All parentheticals

   ✔ All camera directions, sound cues and visual effects

   ✔ Between the character name and the ensuing dialogue

Double space:

   ✔ Between paragraphs of lengthy description

   ✔ Between the end of a dialogue clip and a new speaker's name

   ✔ Between the end of a dialogue clip and a new description

   ✔ Between the *slug line* (see the "Key Formatting Elements" section later in this chapter) and the description

Triple space:

   ✔ Before starting a new scene

Screenwriting software: Let the computer do the formatting

Some writers find the screenwriting format to be overly complex and time consuming. After all, you want to spend your time concentrating on the story, not the look of the page. If the many facets of formatting are frustrating you, it might be time to purchase some screenwriting software. Screenwriting systems abound these days, so peruse your options carefully. The best packages do the following:

  ✔ Format and paginate your script as you write

  ✔ Provide templates for movie scripts, teleplays, and stage plays

  ✔ Offer direct Web links to screenwriting sites

  ✔ Organize your notes for quick reference

  ✔ Help you register your scripts online with the Writer's Guild of America

  ✔ Provide troubleshooting advice from professionals on everything from character development to writer's block

  ✔ Help turn your script into a stage play or novel (should you want to)

I encourage you to investigate your software options online prior to purchasing anything. Some systems focus on story and/or character development; others, on formatting only. Of the systems available, the three most common are

Final Draft: www.finaldraft.com or www.bcsoftware.com; 800-231-4055

Scriptware: www.scriptware.com; 800-799-7090

Movie Magic Screenwriter: www.screenplay.com

All three of these systems are compatible with Macintosh and Microsoft Word, and all three offer a similar array of features. My personal favorite is Movie Magic, as it includes a program with built in 3 x 5 note cards that you can rearrange and print. It also tends to be less expensive at $169. Many systems run between $200 and $300.

After you become familiar with the formatting parameters, you have a choice to make. How do you want to bounce between them? You may set your tabs in advance and tab from one element to the next. (Be aware that this method makes editing fairly cumbersome because any textual alteration disturbs the spacing.) As a second choice, most computers allow you to define new styles (dialogue, name, and parentheticals, for instance) and assign them to a keystroke. One key takes you to the dialogue box, another to the name, and so on. On most computers this feature is found in the toolbar at the top of your page under Format. A quick scroll down the Format list should reveal the Styles component (Formatting and Styles in Microsoft computers). Click on that option and follow the directions from there. Defining your styles makes editing easier as you rework each section individually. Or, as a final option, you may choose a program designed to format the script for you.

Key Formatting Elements

Here's a dilemma: You're an aspiring screenwriter struggling to format your script correctly. You have a lot to say and little time in which to say it. You must speak volumes in three or four sentences that aren't cluttered with adjectives or adverbs. You can't be terse or verbose; you must land somewhere in between. To top these requirements off, you want the script to smack with a unique style and flair. Now, how are you going to do all that?

In a first draft, your primary objective is to get the information onto the page. You can trim, twist, and tweak it into a work of art later, but for now, craft one element at a time with an eye toward story. What's happening, who's it happening to, why is it important, and how efficiently can you let an audience know these things? The format can help direct your information to a location in which it will stand out because every section has a distinct set of tasks.

Character introductions

Always capitalize every letter of a character's name when she first appears. This layout indicates a new figure on the protagonist's or audience's horizon and focuses the attention, however briefly, on a new energy in the script. From that point on, only capitalize every letter of the character's name prior to her dialogue.

When you introduce a character, give a brief but telling description, and then plunge her into the action. For example:

> MOLLY MALONE, a thirtysomething former beauty queen, strides confidently into the room.

I use all capital letters for Molly's full name this first time and then type it normally throughout the ensuing text. If she first arrives as a mere figure or a silhouette, the initial description might read as follows:

> The FIGURE of a woman stands in the doorway. The moon shines from behind, silhouetting her ample form.

This is the first character description. When Molly moves into the scene, the description then reads:

> The figure steps firmly into the room. Enter MOLLY MALONE, a thirty-something former beauty queen with the confidence of a bobcat and the claws to match.

I've capitalized both introductions, first the figure, then Molly Malone, emphasizing the transition from the suggestion of a character to the full character herself.

Here are a few more details to keep in mind when crafting character introductions:

Use full names for the character's initial introduction and one part of the name thereafter

My character's full name is Molly Malone. I let the reader know this as soon as she enters, but thereafter, I refer to her as either "Molly" or "Malone" in both description and in dialogue. If your character's full name is Mr. Nelson, refer to him as "Nelson" for the rest of the text.

Allow incidental characters to remain incidental characters

Your script may call for a waitress, a busboy, a nurse, a ticket agent, a guard, a clerk, and so on. These characters are functional roles and will return in your story sparingly, if at all. Therefore, their introduction need only be minimal. For example:

> The WAITRESS, clearly a veteran server, brings him his coffee and winks in passing.

> Two ARMED GUARDS barrel past, shoving people out of their way as they charge after him.

> The HOTEL CLERK checks the bill and glares at him before disappearing into the back room.

More description than this is unnecessary and distracting. It diverts attention from your main character and the scene's action. Capitalize incidental characters' titles, suggest an age or distinguishing characteristic if necessary, but don't linger on them. They're meant to fulfill a functional role and disappear.

Avoid using names of real actors

You may imagine your main character as an Al Pacino type or a Meryl Streep knockout. You may imagine as much, but don't include those details in your description. Actors reading your script want to imagine themselves (who else?) in the role. They'll be discouraged at best and insulted at worst to see someone else's name on the part.

Avoid detailed description of age or physical characteristics unless pertinent to the story

Consider this character description:

> Sarah Smith, a 29-year-old, 5-foot-10-inch strawberry blonde, strolls into the office.

No specific look says 29 years old, so unless the script centers around her fear of growing older or of an impending birthday, you'd do better to say "late 20s" or "pushing 30" in this description.

You're trying to capture the character's essence. I want a suggestion of age and type, yes, but more importantly, I want a peek at her fundamental nature. If her vital statistics — hair, eyes, height, weight, exact age, and so on — help suggest that nature, include them. It's important, for example, that Erin Brockovich wears tight, revealing clothing. Her physique becomes an asset to her in the quest for information. However, if these details are unimportant to the story, including them simply alienates a plethora of shorter, nonredhead actresses, who may be more talented, from the role. Why alienate talent unnecessarily?

Avoid overly brief and overly long character descriptions

Here are two examples of awkward introductions:

Too brief:

> Leslie Bell, a typist in her midtwenties, jogs through Central Park.

What does a typist look like, exactly? I'm not sure. Does a typist suggest a certain type of person? Not really. This description provides information but fails to suggest a picture of the person in question.

Too long:

> Leslie Bell, a short, skinny powerhouse in her midtwenties, with dimples and a persistent twinkle in her green eyes, sprints through Central Park in her purple Adidas sportswear with a water bottle in one hand and her Sony Walkman in the other. She sports matching cross-trainers, which

seem to be of the expensive variety, but a closer look reveals the soles to be worn thin. She stares ahead, her gaze fixed on some unseen finish line, and her brow is furrowed in determination.

This moment provides more details than a reader can possibly absorb. Character descriptions should be short, no longer than two sentences if possible. Adjectives and adverbs are the enemies of clear writing. When possible, eliminate them. Does the running suit absolutely have to be purple, or does the Walkman need to be a Sony? Probably not. When in doubt, cut it out.

Here's a possible reworked version of the description:

> Leslie Bell, a powerhouse of a woman in her midtwenties, sprints through Central Park, her eyes fixed ahead. A quick glance at her shoes reveals that the soles are worn thin.

This rewrite may even be too long for some tastes. However, I've consolidated it to include the most telling details, those that suggest a person behind the physique.

A capable introduction of a minor character offers the necessary information without detracting attention from more important players in the scene. On the other hand, a compelling main-character introduction shouts, "Here I am! Watch me!" and follows the character into action.

Cinematic description

Screenwriting is a visual art, so visual description makes up at least half of every strong script. Screenplay description includes

- The slug line.
- A description of each location.
- The choreography of characters in a scene.
- Any and all ensuing action

Slug lines

The first line of every scene is called a *slug line*. Slug lines break the script into individual shots, guiding readers through changes in time and locale.

Master slug lines are informative tags that appear at the beginning of every scene. They provide the following information:

✔ Whether a scene takes place inside or outside (INT./EXT.)

✔ The scene's location

✔ Whether it's day or night

Subsidiary slug lines, also known as abbreviated slug lines, indicate that the action has switched to a different area of the same general location. Because time also remains consistent, subsidiary slug lines only include the new location. They may also be used to call attention to one important object in the scene. In this case, the line consists of the object alone.

Slug lines are important and, therefore, always capitalized. They run from the left-hand margin to the right and are generally one line in length. If they run longer, break the line at a logical point and continue writing immediately below the first line without skipping a space.

A typical master slug line looks like this:

    INT. AIRPORT TERMINAL — NIGHT

Notice that I'm not including scene or act numbers here. Scene and act numbers are only used in outlines should the writer wish to organize the scenes prior to writing the draft. Never include them in a working draft, as they distract a reader from your story. The director and cinematographer will number scenes for the shooting script in production.

Slug lines should be as standardized as possible. They're designed to quickly establish the general location and time of each shot. For this reason, *interior* and *exterior* are always abbreviated (INT. and EXT.) You skip a space and provide a more detailed description immediately after the slug line. For example:

    INT. AIRPORT TERMINAL — NIGHT

    The terminal is all but deserted. An elderly MAN and a teenage GIRL slump on chairs at opposite ends of the space. He is asleep. She is not.

If your action then switches to the check-in counter, you might follow this description with a subsidiary slug line.

    THE CHECK-IN COUNTER

    Two AGENTS wearily type information into the computer. One looks up, gives the girl the once-over, then returns to his work.

If he notices that she has a tattoo, an alternate subsidiary slug line may be used.

One looks up and gives the girl the once-over. His eyes linger on her shoulder and

HER TATTOO

of a dragon with a sword in its mouth. Then he returns to his work.

This line suggests that the camera lingers on the image of that dragon. Perhaps it will be important later. Generally, slug lines require no more information than this. The following exceptions to this rule are called *extensions* and should be used sparingly.

- **An establishing shot.** Establishing shots are designed to orient a reader to a new location. If my film begins during a poetry lecture in a high-school classroom and then jumps to the dining room of an obviously wealthy estate, my audience will have no idea where that dining room is in relation to the school. To solve this problem, I add an establishing shot of the outside of the estate and then move to the dining room. In this sort of a slug line, the word ESTABLISHING follows the DAY or NIGHT direction.

     EXT. GEORGIAN MANSION — DAY — ESTABLISHING

- **A stock shot.** Stock shots are images that will be pulled from previously filmed footage. They're clips from other movies, newsreels, documentaries, and so on that are now "in stock" at a film library, waiting to be reused. Skylines and historical landmarks are prime stock material, as are beach, woodland, or generic neighborhood shots. You format stock shots in the following way:

     EXT. THE CHICAGO SKYLINE — DAY (STOCK)

- **An indication of specific time or season.** If your film takes place in 1776, this is an important detail to include in the slug line. If the film bounces between time frames, doing so becomes even more important. If your action spans several seasons, you may add that detail to the line as well.

     EXT. THE CHICAGO SKYLINE — DAY (WINTER)

     EXT. PARIS — DAY (1885)

Remember, a reader will read these distinctions, but a movie audience only knows what it sees. Always follow a slug line with some description of the location that indicates how an audience might know that it's winter or 1885.

Sound and special effects

Detail both sounds and special effects in the general description of a scene and write them, using all capital letters. With sound cues, capitalize the sound of the effect. For instance, the WHISTLE of a train, or the KNOCKING on the door. The capitalization is reserved for those sounds made by outside forces or off-camera. Sounds made by characters in scene are not written using all capital letters.

Special effects are sometimes abbreviated FX or SPFX, but this term is generally reserved for shooting scripts. If you envision special effects in a scene, describe them in such a way that a director can envision them, too. For example:

EXT. PARKING LOT — DAY

Without warning, the station wagon explodes, spewing flames and smoke onto the nearby cars.

Location, choreography, and action

Most cinematic description is composed of single-spaced prose paragraphs that run from the left-hand margin to the right. They're generally no more than three or four sentences in length, if that. Readers like to see as much white space as text, so reserve a separate paragraph for each shot. Double-space between these paragraphs. Doing so divides the action clearly on the page. For instance:

INT. FAMILY ROOM — DAY

Two small GIRLS press their faces to the window and exhale. They pull back and giggle at the prints they've left on the glass. One draws a heart in the print, then slashes at it with her finger.

A WOMAN tiptoes up behind them, ready to pounce. The oldest girl spins around seconds before her hand reaches their shoulders.

When describing location, avoid including too many physical details. Close your eyes and envision the setting, and then describe any essentials that the camera will pick up. If the shot is of two children at their family room drawing table, I might need to see the trail of crayons leading from the door to the table, but I probably don't need to know what color the wallpaper is or how many pictures are hung on the walls.

The other type of description appears in the parenthetical portion of the script. Parentheticals are typed in lowercase letters and are offset by parentheses. They generally depict how a line should be said. For instance:

SANDY
(softly — after a beat)
I don't think that's going to happen.

These descriptions are only necessary if nothing else in the scene suggests how a line should be read. Strong actors often discover the intent naturally.

Parentheticals are also reserved for choreography that occurs while a character is speaking.

A film's *choreography,* also known as the blocking, refers to the actors' physical movement in the scene. For example: Sarah hurries to pick up the phone.

Parenthetical action looks like this:

> SARAH
> (hurrying to answer the telephone)
> I don't think that's going to happen.

If the parenthetical description runs over the allotted space, wrap it around. If it runs longer than two lines, that's a sure sign that the text is too long for a parenthetical. Rewrite the action in a general margin-to-margin description. For example, if Sarah hurries to answer the phone but hesitates with her hand on the receiver, put that line in the general description box. It's too long for a parenthetical.

All description follows the same basic rules as character introduction: Be clear, be compelling, and be concise.

Camera concerns

You're a writer; your job is to tell the story. The director and cinematographer will rewrite that story in a language designed for the camera. Therefore, your concern isn't the camera or its terminology. In fact, technical jargon will distance a reader from the world of your story.

The script that you're crafting is known as a *presentation script,* or the *reader's script,* which is the version designed to seduce a reader into seeing the film. Any technical encumbrances, such as camera angles and scene numbers, are removed to let the story emerge.

The *production script,* or the *shooting script,* is the director and/or cinematographer's script. A much later draft, it includes technical notations, such as camera angles, special effects, and editing requirements.

That said, you may find it helpful to understand the camera and its associated terms so that you can visualize the scene and emphasize the details of your film. You can then write each scene to suggest an angle, without employing the technical term. If you know what a close-up is and you want to use it in a shot, you can rework your description to suggest it.

For instance, if Henry proposes to Sarah in the scene and you want a close-up of the diamond ring, you might write the scene in one of two ways:

Henry pulls a box from his coat pocket. He opens it to reveal a large

DIAMOND RING

He takes Sarah's hand and slips the ring on her finger.

Or:

Henry pulls a box from his coat pocket and opens the lid. Inside the box is a large diamond ring. It sparkles in the light.

He takes Sarah's hand and slips the ring on her finger.

In both cases, the description suggests that a close-up is needed, without jarring the reader with terminology. In order to remain true to this description, a director would have to linger for a second on the diamond ring itself, prior to the shot where Henry slips the ring on her finger. Without the close-up indication, the description would read:

Henry pulls a box from his coat pocket and opens the lid. He removes a ring from the box and slips it on Sarah's finger.

Whenever possible, imply the necessary camera angle. Doing so not only keeps a reader locked into your story but also hones your writing skills.

The following sections cover some basic camera directions, but be warned: I include these camera directions as an overview of what kind of shots are possible within the world of your script. I strongly advise you never to include the technical jargon in the reader's script, however. It distracts a reader's attention away from your story, and universally annoys directors and cinematographers who may envision a shot differently than the writer. So if you're interested in utilizing one or several of these effects, craft description that conveys the effect without calling attention to the camera itself.

Intercut

This direction indicates that two scenes are occurring simultaneously in separate locations. This term appears in all caps as the slug line or in the description. See the following examples:

INTERCUTTING

Sarah shopping in preparation for the date, Henry dressing in front of his mirror.

Or:

SARAH AND HENRY

The scene INTERCUTS between Sarah shopping for the date and Henry dressing in front of his mirror.

The writer then describes individual moments of each scene without using a subsidiary slug line to bounce between then.

Insert

A writer uses this direction when he or she wants to highlight an object in the scene or include a detail that's outside the scene but important to it. To complete an insert, do one of three things: Return to the dialogue, switch locations with a new slug line, or type BACK TO SCENE at the end.

INSERT — PHOTOGRAPH

Small scissors cut around the woman's face, removing her from the image.

BACK TO SCENE

Series of shots

This technique serves as a way to abridge action sequences into a number of short moments involving the main character, usually without dialogue. The format is as follows:

Type SERIES OF SHOTS in place of a slug line, skip a space, and then list a short description of each shot. Skip a space between each description. You may assign a letter to each shot, but many screenwriters opt not to. End the series by typing END SERIES OF SHOTS.

SERIES OF SHOTS

A) Sarah and Henry notice each other across a dance floor.

B) Sarah and Henry dance together at their wedding.

C) Sarah lies in a hospital bed, watching Henry hold their newborn baby.

END SERIES OF SHOTS

A series of shots has a distinct beginning, middle, and end, and is often used to dramatize a passage of time. It's different from (but often confused with) a montage.

Montage

A *montage* is the dissolving of two or more shots into each other to create a desired effect, usually an association of ideas. These shots need not include the main character, and they don't have a beginning, middle, and end. They're formatted in the same way as a series of shots.

MONTAGE

A) Hands shuffle a deck of cards.

B) A screen door SLAMS shut.

C) An unshaven face leers in the darkness.

D) The cards scatter across a table.

END OF MONTAGE

A montage is often used in dream or nightmare sequences. Because of the surreal feeling it evokes, your best bet it to use it sparingly, if at all.

Close-up

A *close-up* is a shot that emphasizes a detail in a scene. It's often abbreviated to CU in shooting scripts, as follows:

CU — IMMENSE DIAMOND RING

Angle on

This shot suggests another view of a previous shot. Here's an example:

ANGLE ON girl staring down from the tree.

POV

Shorthand for *point of view,* this direction implies that the scene is being viewed from another character's perspective. You must identify whose point of view it is and what exactly he sees. If the POV alternates within a scene, employ the term REVERSE POV.

SARAH'S POV — HENRY

He stares at her across the table, then pushes the letter her way.

HENRY

He wants you to have this.

REVERSE POV

Sarah takes the letter and rips it in half.

SARAH

As usual, we want different things.

Split screen

This shot indicates two subjects in different locations on-screen simultaneously. **When Harry Met Sally** uses this shot when the protagonists share a phone conversation from separate bedrooms.

Sally dials Harry's number.

SPLIT SCREEN

Harry and Sally lie in their beds watching the same film on TV.

The split scene shot conveys a distinct film style and is rarely used.

Super

Shorthand for *superimpose,* this term is used if another element is being superimposed over the action of a scene. A super is often used to show dates, locations, or translation texts.

> The yacht barrels toward the shore. The mainland looms ahead.
>
> SUPER — MARSEILLES 1921

Terms that defy categorization

A few formatting details don't fit into a particular category. I tentatively label them "transitional directions." These terms help readers follow your action, and they tell them how to read the script.

Fade in

Every screenplay begins with these words. They suggest the movement from darkness to an image on the screen. They're typed in all caps at the left-hand margin followed by a double space and the first slug line.

> FADE IN:
>
> EXT. COLLEGE LIBRARY — DAY

Fade out

These words end a screenplay. They're typed two spaces below the final line of the script, flush to the right margin. After FADE OUT, writers generally space down six lines and type THE END in the center of the page.

> Henry and Sarah link arms and walk into the sunset.
>
> FADE OUT.
>
> THE END

VO

VO is shorthand for voice-over. This direction is used when the audience hears a character speak who's not in the scene. It's often used to underscore a scene with narration.

> EXT. SUBURBAN HOUSE — DAY

The ranch-style house is in desperate need of attention. Weeds obscure the front path, and the remaining shutters threaten to fall any day now.

HENRY (VO)

I've always thought my neighbor's house would look better as a parking lot or a strip mall.

OS

Shorthand for off-screen, this abbreviation is used when a character speaks outside the camera's view, or when the audience hears a sound but doesn't see where it's coming from.

A door SLAMS OS, then FOOTSTEPS hurry toward him.

Or:

SARAH (OS)

As usual, we want different things.

Cut to

This term was used to cut quickly between scenes, but it's rarely used anymore. It appears at the bottom of a scene, to the right-hand side.

Henry pulls Sarah close, and they begin to waltz.

CUT TO:

Dissolve to

This direction is used in place of the CUT TO when you want to suggest a slow transition from one scene to the next. You may dissolve to suggest the passage of time between one shot and another, or because you want the effect of one image fading into the next.

Continuation

When a scene or a speech is interrupted by a page break, type MORE in parentheses at the end of the last line on the first page, and then type CONT'D after the character's name on the next page.

HENRY

I wish you'd thought of this sooner. It would have

(MORE)

————————page break————————

> HENRY (CONT'D)
>
> Saved us so much time if you had.

When a speaker is interrupted by an action, use a dash to suggest the interruption, type the action, then type "continuing" in a parenthetical after the character's name when he starts speaking again.

> HENRY
>
> I do wish you'd thought of this sooner. It —

Sarah hands him the plane tickets and her purse.

> HENRY
> (continuing)
>
> Would have saved us so much time.

As with all creative elements, formatting takes time. Screenwriting is an art, and as every artist differs, so will every format. The key rule to remember with presentation is this: If it doesn't look right, it's probably not right.

A Sample Scene

The format becomes clear when you see it on the page. I've included a small sample to help clarify both the spacing and several key formatting components. You can also find screenplays online or at your local library or bookstore. The more you read, the more ingrained the format will become.

"A DIME A DOZEN"

FADE IN:

                    EXT. A COUNTRY ROAD - DAY

The road is empty. Fields of corn stretch beyond it for miles and
miles. Nothing but green and gold.

                         ELLEN (VO)
               I used to think there were places that time didn't touch.
               Places too small, or insignificant, or out of the way to
               consider.

An abandoned tractor lies by the side of the road. A scarecrow leans
in one of the fields with a crow perched on his head.

                         ELLEN (VO)
               Where people do as they've always done and the days
               just go on and on and . . . on. Places like my home town.

The sound of a car ENGINE RUMBLING farther off. It grows louder over
the following speech.
                         ELLEN (VO)
               Now though, I wonder. I wonder if time's just waiting.
               Waiting for the moment, that pivotal moment . . . when
               everything falls apart.

A sleek black car barrels down the road spinning dust in its wake.

EXT. A ROAD-SIDE FRUIT STAND - DAY

DARRYL HOPKINS, the 75 year old owner of the stand helps RUTH MADSON,
60, load bags onto her bicycle.

The black car streaks past them. Pebbles fly up around its tires.
A few of them slam into the base of Ruth's bike

Darryl spins around fast enough to catch the

LICENSE PLATE

which reads PUMA 300.

                         DARRYL
               Puma.

```
                            RUTH
                        (whistling)
                    You know what that means.


                            DARRYL
                    Trouble


                            RUTH
                    Trouble with six cylinders.


                            DARRYL
                    Car like that? Going that fast? More like eight.


                            RUTH
                    Trouble with a toothpick.

They exchange a glance, then look back at the road. The car has
disappeared.
EXT SIDE OF THE ROAD - MOMENTS LATER

Two children, wide-eyed ABBEY REYNOLDS, 8, and her friend ELLEN
KURTZ, 13, walk home from school. Abbey carries a multi-colored
pinwheel.

                            ABBEY
                        (chanting to herself)
                    Two, four, six, eight, who do we appreciate? Abbey,
                    Abbey, gooooo Abbey.


                            ELLEN
                    Hurry up, Abbey, we're going to belate. Not that it
                    matters.


                            ABBEY
                    If it doesn't matter, why're we hurrying?


                            ELLEN
                    Because I'm not getting in trouble for something that
                    doesn't even matter, understand?


                            ABBEY
                    Who did she say was coming?


                            ELLEN
                    Someone she knew in school. Someone she wants us to
                    meet.
```

                              ABBEY
                    Is he nice?

                              ELLEN
                    How do I know if he's nice?

                              ABBEY
                    Is he funny?

                              ELLEN
                    Cut it out.

An ENGINE ROARS behind them. They stop walking and turn towards
the sound.

The black car streaks past them. Abbey's pinwheel twirls furiously
in her hand.

                              ABBEY
                    Whoa, did you see that?

                              ELLEN
                    I saw it.

                              ABBEY
                    Was that him?

                              ELLEN
                    Maybe. But I sort of hope not.

The two girls look at each other, then start running down the road.
The top of Abbey's pinwheel twirls off its handle as she runs and
falls to the ground.

Chapter 15

Putting It Together: Structuring Your First Draft

*E*very writer reaches a point where the cup of possibilities runneth over. The head spins with evocative environments, fleeting conversations, feats of strength and daring, impossible odds, side-splitting witticisms, moments of grief and agony, and, above all, hope. You can't possibly absorb any more. And what do you have to show for it? An outline, a treatment, maybe a pile of notes.

At this stage of the writing process, you're like a field guide. You have a destination in mind and a troupe of individuals (otherwise known as your audience) behind you, ready to follow your every move. You have a sense of what you'll encounter along the way, and you know why it's important that you try to make it out with everyone intact. You're looking for the roadmap. In screenwriting terms, you're looking for the *structure*. This chapter illustrates one structure in particular, the three-act structure, designed to help you and your travel-mates reach your ultimate destinations.

Navigating the Three-Act Structure

Every great story is composed of three principal segments: a beginning, middle, and ending. In screenwriting, those segments are known as Act I, Act II, and Act III. Without a strong opening, no one wants to watch your film.

Without a strong middle, the audience will lose interest partway through. Without a strong ending, well, that's like the radio cutting out on the last line of your favorite song. The audience leaves unresolved — confused at best, angry at worst — and wondering what it just saw.

The lengths of each act may differ film to film. As movies are getting longer, so are their acts. But traditionally, feature films run from 90 to 120 pages in length, which is roughly two hours of screen time. Each act is then tentatively broken down into the following number of pages:

- ✔ Act I: pages 1–30
- ✔ Act II: pages 31–90
- ✔ Act III: pages 91–120

How important are these divisions? There are variations to be sure, but if you're a new writer, you should try to stick to industry standards the first few times you craft a script. Why? The most important reason is perhaps only obvious after you complete a first draft. The three-act structure is a strong organization of text. Stories seem to fall into it naturally, and they were falling into it well before Aristotle publicly analyzed the structure's worth in 320 B.C. (more on Aristotle's *Poetics* in Chapter 5). Like any craft, if you understand the basic rules, you'll be better equipped to alter them, when necessary, later on.

Also, many agencies and film companies give new scripts what's known as the *five-and-dime treatment*. They read the first five pages of your script and the last ten and determine its worth from there. If you've followed the three-act structure, which calls for a bang-up opening and a swift conclusion, you may just make the cut. If a producer notices that your script is less than 90 pages long, he may assume that your story doesn't have enough punch to make a feature film. If he notices that it's more than 120 pages, he may doubt your ability to streamline action. Your best bet is to fall somewhere in between until he knows and trusts your work.

The three-act structure isn't a formula; it's a guide. It won't write your film for you or hinder your creativity, but it does provide a solid foundation on which to build. Each act traditionally contains several landmark moments. By "landmark," I mean scenes that help structure the action or pivotal moments in your story. Again, these landmarks are simply suggestions for how to structure your piece. They're not meant to provide a formula.

Act 1: Introductions

Every act in the three-act structure has a set of tasks to accomplish. The first act serves as your audience's introduction to the entire world of the script — people, places, time frame, and all. Remember that your audience members begin in a neutral darkness. In their advance toward some new awareness, they're not unlike visitors in a foreign country. You need to orient them fairly quickly to the story that's about to unfold. So, the first act is all about setup.

Your opening moments

If I could offer you only one piece of advice concerning your first act, it would be this: Begin with an image. Stories that begin with anything else, voices in darkness or immediate dialogue, for instance, are often difficult to absorb. A strong opening image can convey backdrop, character, and pervading mood in seconds. That image might also convey a theme for your piece. *The Untouchables* opens with the planting of a bomb in a local establishment and its inevitable explosion. An innocent girl dies in that explosion, which quickly suggests the depth of corruption responsible for such an action. It visually pits good against evil from the start.

The eye picks up details much more quickly than the ear, and nothing's more disconcerting than staring at talking heads. In a way, you haven't earned the right to open verbally. As someone in the audience, I don't yet know the people speaking; I haven't decided whether they're interesting enough to pursue. Let me watch them for a bit, assess their actions, and make some initial assumptions. Doing so keeps me actively involved in guessing what your story will be.

Also, everything that happens in the first moments of a film is important. If you provide vital information verbally, I'm likely to miss it in my quest to appraise the environment visually. People come to the movies to see pictures in motion. Why begin with anything else?

The first ten pages

If your opening image grabs my attention, you have roughly ten pages after that opening to convince me that your film is worth watching. Don't believe me? The next time you go to a movie, ask yourself how you feel about it after the first ten minutes. If you're bored or confused, you'll likely deem it a failure. If you're riveted, odds are that you'll consider it a success.

The first ten pages provide an initial criterion on which to judge the ensuing story. They should provide just enough information to establish a clear world without giving too much of the eventual plot away, and they should create enough mystery to keep me wondering what's in store. Your first ten pages should accomplish the following tasks:

- Introduce the main characters
- Establish the primary environments

✔ Convey a distinct mood or atmosphere

✔ Establish the time period

✔ Illustrate a routine or way of life

✔ Provide any relevant *backstory* (events that transpired before the story began)

✔ Introduce the antagonist

If you haven't already settled on an ending to your script, now is the time to do it. If you don't know where the script is going, how will you determine which pieces of information to highlight at the beginning?

Everything that happens now is a setup for what comes next. So you have to know what comes next.

Some films reveal the antagonist as the villain right away. The opening text of *The Untouchables* delineates Al Capone as the film's key scoundrel. The shark in *Jaws* consumes its first victim in the first five minutes. By contrast, the true murderer in *Ghost* seems to be a nice guy until well after the protagonist is killed. When you reveal the villain is up to you; you certainly don't have to do so in the first ten pages. However, make the conflict clear shortly thereafter. If you wait much longer, you risk having a restless audience that's impatient for the action to begin.

The inciting incident

The *inciting incident,* also known as the *catalyst,* marks the film's first turning point. It tilts the story from order to chaos, from complacency to combat. It's the point of no return. In this moment, you answer two questions:

✔ What do your characters want?

✔ What might prevent them from getting it?

Together, these queries make up the film's *premise,* or what it's ultimately about. In *Lord of the Rings,* one hobbit wants to rid Middle Earth of an evil force. The Dark Lord and human greed stand in his way. In both *Ordinary People* and *Good Will Hunting,* young men struggle to forgive and forget their tortuous past. Personal demons and unsympathetic adults stand in their way. A strong premise clearly defines a need and an impediment. As soon as an audience senses these details, you can pose the central question:

Will your protagonist(s) succeed?

If the answer is yes, you may have a happy ending; if it's no, a tragedy is in the works. Your inciting incident isn't complete until you pose this question.

Until then, audiences wait. They wait for action; they wait for intent; they wait to be told what they're waiting for.

An inciting incident generally occurs in one of the following ways:

- ✔ An action plunges the characters into conflict.

- ✔ A piece of critical information arrives.

- ✔ A sequence of small events prepares an audience for the story.

In *Jaws,* a shark attacks a young woman, an action that begins the hunt. In *American Beauty,* Lester Burnham receives word that his job is in jeopardy, a piece of information that sends him over the edge. In the final method, the inciting incident takes the form of several events and is, therefore, the most subtle of the three. The film *Zorro* is a clear example of this technique. Two brothers witness Zorro attempting to thwart an execution. They save his life in the process, and he rewards them with a silver medallion. Government troops then invade his house, kill his wife, abduct his child, and throw him in jail. Years pass before he escapes. Meanwhile, the brothers, now grown up, also flee government soldiers. When one of them is killed, the other falls into a great depression and would risk his life avenging the death, if he wasn't first intercepted by (who else?) Zorro. All these events prepare an audience for the real story, which involves the training of a new masked hero. This preparation obviously takes longer than ten pages, but the result is the same.

Plot point one

Plot point one is the first big turning point in your script. It occurs at the end of the first act, approximately 30 pages into the action, and propels an audience into Act II. It must do the following things:

- ✔ Push the action in a new direction

- ✔ Force the protagonist to make a choice and take a risk

- ✔ Raise the central question for the first or second time

- ✔ Raise the stakes

Pivotal events, like plot point one, are usually surprises. Audiences know that something grand will happen eventually. They might even know what the result of that event will be. But don't allow them to guess the details of the event itself or you'll spoil the surprise. *Star Wars* audiences know that Luke Skywalker will eventually be called away from the safety of his family and into training. They may also guess that, as a result, he will have to fight Darth Vader, but they don't know exactly how these proceedings will transpire. Stories that hint too thoroughly at upcoming events become overly predictable and less exciting to watch.

In *Zorro,* the young brother meets his future mentor. He must choose to fight the villain now or follow this instructor and heed his advice to wait. His decision tilts the plot toward the true story — the training of a legend. In *The Untouchables,* Malone joins Ness's force, and together, they enlist a team of crusaders. From that point on, it's them against Capone's small army. The first plot point may be as shocking as the death of a loved one or as gentle as the touch of a hand. Both actions have the power to launch a great story.

Act II: Salting the Wound

If Act I ends by asking, "What does your protagonist want?" Act II continually begs the question, "What will she do to get it?" In many cases, Act II tests not only what your character will do, but also what your character will *endure* to get it. Act II isn't unlike a video game with life or death odds. Each level pits the protagonist against stronger resistance, be it outside forces or internal demons. The protagonist must defeat them all in order to succeed. Traditionally, these conflicts arrive more quickly and more frequently as the story progresses, with the most difficult antagonist lying in wait until the end.

Don't put the toughest obstacle first, or you'll have nowhere to go but down. The audience might as well go home.

Your job in Act II is to create a snowball effect with your action. One moment adds to the next and the next until the action barrels toward some culminating event. Harnessing the momentum so that you can steer it without slowing it down is a constant challenge. Because Act II is twice as long as the first and final acts, writers commonly bemoan "second-act problems" as the task of keeping track of the various characters, their conflicts, and their goals becomes unwieldy. Here are a few checkpoints to help you manage the second-act madness:

- Make the conflict personal.
- Let the protagonist fail at least once.
- Allow the antagonist to succeed, perhaps several times.
- Teach the protagonist a new skill.
- Test the protagonist's current abilities and/or expertise.
- Further explore the subplot.

Think about how each of those points affects the action. First, your protagonist needs a personal stake in the conflict, or she might jump ship halfway through. Zorro and his apprentice, for example, desire revenge for the murder of their loved ones. Theirs is a highly personal fight.

Next, the occasional failures of your protagonist create extraordinary odds, especially if the antagonist thrives during this time. Audiences can't be sure that the protagonist will prevail; they can only hope she will. Both Zorro and his apprentice fail to protect their loved ones. They err in other ways throughout the film, but these initial failures prove them capable of personal defeat.

Finally, human beings are not perfect; neither is your protagonist. A protagonist who learns from her mistakes and who acquires new skills to help her succeed is that much more human. If she triumphs despite startling odds, using abilities both new and acquired, you've crafted an inspiring tale that audiences can relate to. Zorro's apprentice doesn't become the masked avenger until he's undergone rigorous training. He has natural talents that help guide him, but he must also acquire new skills before he can succeed.

The second act is often dedicated to raising the stakes in one or all of these ways. These points strengthen your script's conflict and make the protagonist's success that much more important.

Know where the action is

Even if your second act boasts all the items in the preceding bulleted list, its structure still may elude you. Here's where the formula for action comes in handy: Actions cause other actions to occur. Try structuring your plot with the following techniques in mind.

Create scenes that result in other scenes

When you're overwhelmed with the multiple plotlines of Act II, it may help to follow the rules of action strictly. That means structuring each action so that it causes not only a future scene but the next future scene. Here's a sequence from the second act of *The Untouchables*.

1. Ness successfully raids Capone's illegal liquor warehouse.

2. Capone sends him a bribe to stop the raids.

3. Ness publicly refuses the bribe.

4. Capone's thugs threaten Ness's family.

5. Ness moves his family to a safe location and retaliates with another successful raid.

6. In this raid, he confiscates Capone's financial records.

7. His accountant pursues Capone for income-tax evasion.

8. Capone has the accountant killed.

The action in this second act is tight; every scene sparks the next. The cause and effect relationship holds the act together, refusing to let it stray into banter or unimportant events. You can do this as well. The trick is to create action that's so poignant, so shocking, so revealing that it demands a quick response.

Create strong impediments

An *impediment* is an unforeseeable detail or event that forces the protagonist to switch tactics or formulate another plan. Suppose that your main character spends his entire journey searching for one corner of a treasure map. If he finds the person with the map but that person doesn't speak English, that's an impediment. If that person swallows the map in the protagonist's struggle to obtain it, that's another impediment. In the first example, the hero needs a new tactic. In the second, he needs a new plan.

Tactics refer to the specific methods that a character employs to reach a desired end. Seduction, bribery, bartering, guilt, pleas, tricks, and threats are among the most common.

Impediments force the character to make a different choice and act upon it, often immediately. By seeing what choice the character makes, the audience gets an opportunity to glimpse his true nature. What lengths will he go to, how quickly does he think, what skills can he muster to proceed? Here's a tip: Be sure to let him find the answer and choose the new route himself. Don't contrive an easy answer for him. If your character's running from an army of opponents, let him hunt, dig, or swing himself out of harm's way. You may simply toss him a hiding place, but where's the fun in that?

Plant future conflicts

Plants are conflicts that you foreshadow in an early scene and bring to fruition later. The audience anticipates that they'll be a problem eventually and watches for the moment to arrive. Your job is to provide that later moment. If your character boasts of skills that he doesn't have, he should be called to use those nonexistent skills. If your character hates spiders as Jeff Daniels does in *Arachnophobia,* he'll have to battle one eventually. In *Jaws,* the police chief professes a fear of the water hours before he must tackle a creature of the sea. If you plant the potential for these scenes in the first act, let them payoff in the second. Or, plant them early in Act II, and let them pay off at the end. If your audience watches for them, you've created dramatic tension. If it forgets about them, they're in for a satisfactory reminder.

The "about-face"

Much like the military command, an "about-face" is an abrupt and complete turnaround in the action. The turnaround may be physical or emotional in nature. If your characters hate each other, as they do initially in *When Harry Met Sally,* they'll love each other by the end. If your character struggles to maintain a solid job, as Lester Burnham does in *American Beauty,* he'll switch to an opposing career or abandon it completely. The "about-face" is as exciting as a breakthrough. Both moments force the characters into a new understanding and an opposite path. Use this technique sparingly, so that it doesn't loose its punch, but when the opportunity to use the about-face arises, take it. Audiences love the surprise.

The midpoint: A halfway house

One more thing may help structure the action of Act II — the creation of a *midpoint.* Can you guess where this turning point lands? If you said halfway through the script (around pages 60–65), you guessed correctly. More importantly, this event divides the second act in half, providing much-needed structure in a portion of your story that's so immense.

In *When Harry Met Sally,* the protagonists sleep together. They don't mean to; it just happens, and the action reverses from there. In *The Untouchables,* the accountant is murdered, making the battle between Ness and Capone personal and deadly. Not every script has a midpoint; some stories don't require one. How do you know if yours does? If you're looking for a landmark to steer the first 30 pages of your second act toward the last 30 pages, a strong midpoint is it. Otherwise, build your action consistently toward the next major plot point at the end of Act II.

Plot point two

Plot point two occurs at the end of the second act, roughly around pages 80–85. It mimics the tasks of the first plot point: It broaches the central question again, propels the action in a new direction, raises the stakes, and forces a risk and a choice. However, at its conclusion, you will do two things:

> Remind the audience of a ticking time clock

And either

> Lift the protagonist's spirits

Or

> Crush the protagonist's will

In *The Untouchables,* Malone is brutally murdered, and Ness's wife faces raising their newborn child under the constant surveillance of strangers.

Personal guilt and exhaustion force Ness to consider calling it quits. By contrast, Lester Burnham decides to sleep with his daughter's best friend at the end of Act II. His eventual refusal to go through with the act brings him closer to his estranged wife and daughter. He ends the second act content for the first time in ages.

Act III: The Final Frontier

Act III begins around page 90 and runs for 20 to 30 minutes, although because of its fast pace, it often seems like less. At this point, you've raised the central question, "Will my protagonist succeed?" several times. Why? Your entire film revolves around the quest for an answer. Act III provides that answer.

At the beginning of Act III, your protagonist either faces the upward hike or the downward sprint to the most gripping moment in the script. To push him toward this last lap, one of the following things generally happens:

- **The protagonist abandons hope and must be inspired back to action.** In **The Untouchables,** Elliot Ness must be reminded of why he started to fight in the first place. Both his friends and Capone's behavior accomplish this task.

- **The protagonist makes a breakthrough discovery.** The kids in **Goonies** discover the pirate ship and a way to get out of the cave.

- **The protagonist acquires a final necessary skill.** Ralph Macchio's character gains the life lessons necessary to encourage his newfound karate skills in **The Karate Kid.**

- **The villain forces the hero into combat.** In **Rear Window,** the villain discovers that he's being watched and brings the fight to Jimmy Steward's character.

- **The protagonist overcomes an internal obstacle that enables him to fight a physical antagonist.** In **Erin Brockovich,** the heroine harnesses her temper and uses it to her advantage.

Shortly after Act III begins, the protagonist has to make the choice to continue forward. It may be a reluctant choice, but it nevertheless pushes him to pursue one last chance for success.

The climax

The *climax* is your script's final battlefield. It represents the most intense and, generally, the largest scene of the film in which the protagonist makes one last attempt at achieving his or her goal.

There's a subtle irony surrounding your story's climax. Your entire plot moves toward this point in one sense or another. It's the most shocking, devastating, hysterical, or frightening scene in the film. And how long does it last? A few minutes at most. The climax, which begins around page 110 or 115, usually lasts about five pages and is followed by an even faster resolution. Why build 100 pages to such a short burst of action? There's a saying, "Life's a journey, not a destination." That saying's true of film life as well. *You've* been working toward this final battle, but your film is really about how you got there.

Keep these points in mind when crafting your climax:

- ✔ Your character should be an active participant.
- ✔ Your villain should be equally formidable.
- ✔ Something personal is now at stake.
- ✔ There should be little time to think.
- ✔ Something unexpected should occur.
- ✔ Your character should use some acquired skill in his or her attempt to succeed.
- ✔ You should answer the central question, which for most stories is, "Will your protagonist succeed in achieving his or her goal?"

Don't let things happen to your protagonist; let her happen to things. Keep the pace fast, allowing the audience less time to ponder than your characters. Create a few surprises, impediments, turnarounds, or miscalculations — anything to force the characters to think on their feet. And please, answer the central question. If your character succeeds, marvelous. If she fails, so be it. But don't make me wonder which outcome occurred. Give an audience its well-deserved conclusion.

The resolution

The key words for the final one to five pages are fast, fast, and fast. You've illustrated the most dramatic scene, and your character has solved the problem or been defeated by it. Don't linger too long thereafter. A slick resolution offers just enough time for an audience to absorb the final outcome. In those few pages, the action may

- ✔ Suggest a future life for the protagonist.
- ✔ Illustrate the repercussions of the climax.
- ✔ Establish any changes in the protagonist.
- ✔ Suggest a just or an unjust world.

The resolution tackles the question, "So what?" What sort of world have you led your audience to, and was it worth the journey? Find a way for the final answer to be yes, it was well worth the journey.

A Note on Subplots

Often, writers will pitch an idea based on some theme that they're enamored with only to realize that there's little in the idea to generate an action-based plot. In fact, themes don't make great foundations for a story; they tend to produce long-winded, theoretical discussions in place of goal-oriented inter-action. Yet every story needs one. For this reason, most screenwriters rely on subplots to carry their theme.

Subplots are usually plots involving secondary characters included to provide depth and dimension. Movies without them tend to be dull and self-indulgent. After all, no world revolves around just one person. Secondary characters provide new outlooks, differing opinions and advice, and alternate ways of life. They often bolster the main character's confidence, provide necessary tutelage, or sharpen his personal beliefs by downright disagreeing with him. In some cases, subplots arise between protagonists.

In structuring your subplot, follow the three-act structure of the main story-line. In the following list, I provide a series of questions for you to answer, and I use the subplot from *When Harry Met Sally* as an example of each:

- **What setup does your subplot require?** In *When Harry Met Sally,* the audience needs to meet the protagonists' respective best friends and assess their personal views on relationships.

- **What is your subplot's central question?** In this case, the subplot shares a central question with the main plot: Will the characters find a love that they can maintain?

- **What is the inciting incident that starts the action?** Sally is set up with Harry's best friend, and Harry is set up with Sally's best friend on a rather awkward double date. The two best friends end up having more in common with each other than with Harry or Sally, and they leave the evening as a pair.

- **What obstacles do the subplot characters endure?** The new couple moves in together, surviving fight after fight over decor and living arrange-ments. They're also constantly counseling their still-single best friends.

- **How do they answer the central question?** This is a romantic comedy, so they get married, of course.

However you choose to craft your subplots, make sure that they do the following:

- Require their own setup, turning points, climax, and resolution
- Offer the protagonists a chance to breathe, confess, love, rage, dream, and so on
- Criss-cross the main plotline at pivotal moments
- Express the story's theme
- Offer opportunities to witness changes in the protagonist

Allow the subplot characters to be as strong and vibrant as possible, but make sure that the protagonists match that vitality in some way.

TRY IT

Structuring a fairy tale

Because restructuring an existing story is less intimidating than structuring your own from the ground up, I've included a project here that let's you do just that. See if you can pinpoint the three-act elements in some of your favorite fairy tales. The following elements lie somewhere between "once upon a time" and "happily ever after": the setup, the inciting incident, the central question, plot point one, the midpoint, plot point two, the climax, and the resolution.

I've broken down *Jack and the Beanstalk* as an example.

Act I

The setup: Jack and his mother are so poor that she instructs him to sell their last cow for money or food.

The inciting incident: Jack meets a man who claims he has magic beans, and Jack trades the cow for those beans instead of money or food.

The central question: Will Jack find a way to provide for his family?

Plot point one: Enraged that Jack has returned empty-handed, his mother tosses the beans out the window. They grow into a beanstalk overnight.

Act II

Midpoint: After successfully stealing the giant's golden egg, Jack returns to the castle to go after the bag of gold.

Plot point two: Jack tries to steal the magic harp, but it sings a warning, and the giant wakes up.

Act III

The climax: The giant chases Jack down the beanstalk. Jack chops the beanstalk down with an ax.

The resolution: The giant perishes in the fall. Jack and his mother live a prosperous life thereafter, and (hopefully) Jack has learned a life lesson about theft.

Now, you try it with a fairy tale you're familiar with. I recommend *Hansel and Gretel*, *Rumpelstiltskin*, or *The Princess and the Pea*, but if you don't know these stories well, just pick whatever fairy tale you like best.

Finally, remember that your secondary characters don't know that they're part of a subplot — and it's a good thing they don't. Craft them as if they were main characters, and allow them to be unwilling, skeptical, brutally honest, and unkind should the situation call for it. Otherwise, they become pawns, fulfilling a role that you've contrived for them. They become punching bags or sounding boards for the main characters, both of which are dull and unrealistic options. They're an integral part of the story. Let them be cruel or supportive, but above all, let them be real.

Chapter 16

Take Two: Rewriting Your Script

*E*rnest Hemingway once said that the first draft of anything is garbage. I'm paraphrasing, of course — his language was a bit more colorful than that — but the sentiment remains the same. Everyone's first draft requires a revision or two, or four, or ten. If your first draft is perfect, stop reading; you don't need this book. And don't tell any writers. Trust me: They don't want to know. For most of us, the second draft is where the real writing gets done.

Like many artists, writers have two modes in which they work: the right-brain mode and the left-brain mode. Consider them the wild animal and the rider, or the creator and the critic, or the free-form essay and the giant red pen. However you envision them, one mode colors outside the lines while the other erases until a recognizable form appears. The right brain dreams, and the left brain outlines. The right brain produces the first draft, and the left brain manages the revision. So get ready to switch gears and pick up that giant red pen because this chapter explores the rewriting process.

Downshifting between Drafts

Many writers tackle the first draft at a feverish pitch behind closed doors, churning it out in record time. Why so fast? They know that the first draft is about total immersion, about pinning down the story without thought to spelling, grammar, and possibly even format. The first draft is the story-only draft. If you worry about perfection, you'll lose time, momentum, and much-needed sleep. You may even drop the project before completing a draft at all.

Perfection isn't possible yet. You don't know what the story's about, not really. At the pace you're going, you won't know where you've been until you get to the finish line and look back.

When you throw the door open and stride into the room exhausted and flushed, with a stack of pages in one hand and a glass of champagne in the other — then and only then can you worry about perfection. And even then, you'll hold off because the first thing that you're going to do is rest.

How to work when you're not working

How long should you stay away from your work? The time frame varies, but I always advise a two-week hiatus at the very least. If you're on a deadline, two weeks may be all you get, but if not, take more. Lock the manuscript away somewhere or save it on your computer and forget about it. You have other things to do.

Some writers can't abide the thought of leaving their scripts. After all, it consumes your life for anywhere from two months to a year, possibly more. And now I'm telling you to forget about it? Impossible. Nevertheless, you really do need to ignore that voice screaming at you to rework the draft right away. Here's why:

- ✔ Your imagination needs time to replenish itself.

- ✔ You need time to absorb the story's conclusion.

- ✔ Time away provides the distance necessary to see the story as a whole.

- ✔ You're going to slash it eventually. The less consumed you are with the project, the less personal it will seem when you do.

- ✔ Now's your chance to return to visual research.

Writing an original piece, as opposed to a commissioned work, is like raising a child. By the time you complete a draft, you know it intimately, you respect what it has become, and you're likely to protect it at all costs. You need that sensitivity to fade. It's difficult to protect a work and tear it apart at the same time.

What do you do in the interim? You continue working, of course. But you work minus the computer, the desk, the late nights, and the aching wrists — minus everything but the awareness. You're going to be visually employed now. Here are a few suggestions for keeping your mind on your story while you're keeping your hands off:

- ✔ **Immerse yourself in the time frame.** Now's your opportunity to revisit and refresh past research. Read novels written at the time in which your film takes place; track down newspaper clippings, including classified ads and obituaries. Peruse the poetry and music of the era. Do anything to keep the views and language of the time frame alive. If your story takes place in a futuristic or fabricated era, see if you can dig up articles or stories that suggest what you envision. Or the opposite of what you envision. Other writers and filmmakers have presented fictional worlds — are they similar or different from your own? Try to verbalize those distinctions in detail.

✔ **Return to other visual mediums.** Photographs, paintings, sculptures — all these mediums helped craft your original backstory, so return to them now. Different images will catch your eye, or you'll discover new details in an illustration you previously visited. Visual art may speak to themes and motifs in your script as well. Playwrights surround themselves with images that express details in a play, ranging from costumes to mechanical devices to color schemes. See what happens if you do the same. You immersed yourself in your writing; now, immerse yourself in art. You'll be surprised what catches your eye after completing a first draft.

✔ **Visit appropriate locations.** Does much of your script take place in an office? Find one and spend some time in the lobby. Do any of your friends work for a corporation? Bring them lunch and meet their colleagues. With this kind of research, you're seeking out an environmental rhythm. The pace, the sounds, and the patterns of movement in Grand Central Station, for example, are considerably different from those in a park. How so exactly?

If you can't visit a similar location, if your settings are obscure or fictional, find places with a similar essence. Perhaps I can't visit a circus or an amusement park with ease, but I can sit at a McDonald's play area for a while or drive past a grade school at recess. If the location doesn't match, perhaps the soundscape and the atmosphere will.

✔ **Observe human behavior.** Does your protagonist fall in love? Is he particularly disgruntled or cynical on a regular basis? What does that mood look like? Observe a few people who share tendencies with your main characters. Which exact set of gestures, postures, and choices seem to match? Watch duos or groups of people and search for status. This search isn't about being right or wrong; it's about perception. If you perceive that the woman in the park controls her romantic relationship, for all intents and purposes, she does. You made that assumption for a reason. Perhaps she said or did something to tip you off. Think about what caused you to perceive that woman's status the way you did and how you might translate that assumption to the page.

✔ **See lots and lots of films.** Now that you're aware of cinematic elements, such as character, action, turning points, language, and resolutions, other films may help you to clarify and further define your sense of structure. Strong films can provide positive examples, but even weak films do their part. Hopefully, you'll be able to pinpoint what you believe makes a stronger and a weaker script for when you finally revisit your own story.

Generally, I advise writers to avoid films with premises comparable to their own. If the other film's great, you'll worry that your own doesn't match up. If it's wretched, you'll worry that your own premise is, too. Either way, you worry. And who needs that when you're trying to write?

So, you're probably wondering when you actually *will* revisit your story and get started on the revision process. That depends, of course, on you, but I generally suggest that you're prepared to rewrite when one of the following three things occurs:

- ✔ You consider or begin another project.
- ✔ You stop worrying about your script every day.
- ✔ You've forgotten exact details of character or plot development.

When one or all of these scenarios occur, you're ready to revisit the piece.

Your first time back: Read-through #1

Your first glance through a beginning draft may feel like a punch in the gut. You may find so many awkward paragraphs and glaring improbabilities that you decide to leave the writing profession altogether. However, if you've allowed yourself enough time away from the work, and if you prepare yourself for the encounter in advance, revisiting your first draft needn't be traumatic. It may actually feel like coming home.

Reserve a stretch of time for this first read. In order to assess the story as a whole, you need to be able to read the story as a whole, which means reading it in one sitting. If you absolutely must divide the reading time up, I suggest skimming the first act, stopping, and then skimming the second and third acts together. The second act is traditionally where your problems arise, so it's important to read that as a unit. Oh, and as soon as you're in a room with your draft, unplug the phone and close the door.

The first thing that you'll need is a pen of some distinguishing color. I prefer red or green because they stand out against the page. If you prefer to revise on the computer screen itself, use the revision marks feature or simply change the color of the type, so that you can see your edits. I always advise printing out a hard copy, though. Flipping between actual pages is less cumbersome than scrolling up and down the screen, trying to find the right place in the text. You may eventually want to rearrange the order of scenes or read scenes side by side, and you're going to hand the draft to another reader fairly soon. How are you going to do all that without a hard copy?

After you've chosen a pen, consider how you're going to use it. Every writer devises a set of revision symbols, those chicken scratches in the margins that scream, "Hey you! Come back to this section later." This first read is technical, so the symbols that you choose will delineate the following details:

- ✔ Misspellings
- ✔ Grammatical errors
- ✔ Formatting trouble
- ✔ Awkward description or exposition
- ✔ Unanswered plot questions
- ✔ Character inconsistencies
- ✔ Implausibility

Of that list, misspellings, grammar, and formatting are obviously the easiest to correct. If you can fix them quickly as you go, be my guest. The last four items on the list require a rewrite, and I advise you to simply mark those paragraphs and move on. This first read is your chance to sense the story as a complete entity, to determine where it picks up momentum and where it falls flat. Pausing that process to rework a scene defeats the purpose. You'll have time for that later.

Some writers keep separate lists as they read. When they stumble upon clumsy dialogue or a bland character voice, they mark the page number on one list. On another list, they keep track of pivotal questions that the draft raises and double-check later to see whether those questions find answers. And the final list, which is often the most important, is reserved for consistency and plausibility concerns.

When you realize that your main character spends the first act afraid of heights and the second act leaping across the tops of buildings, you have a consistency problem. If Brody runs into the waters of *Jaws* right away, this action would be inconsistent with his fear of water. When your main character, who's never left her house, drives the getaway car in scene five, you have a scene implausibility.

Here's a quick way to determine the difference between consistency and plausibility problems:

- ✔ If your character *would* never do something that she does, you have a consistency problem.
- ✔ If your character *could* never do something that she does, you have a plausibility problem.

The final symbol that you need is a silent pat on the back for clear, well-written drama. Even the worst drafts harbor cinematic gems. Odds are that you've done something right. Circle it, star it, photocopy the page, whatever. If there's something that you want to keep, find a way to remind yourself later or you're likely to rewrite it along with everything else. You'll enjoy the comfort that those triumphs provide when you're wading through all the other not-quite-so-brilliant scenes ahead.

A second glance: Read-through #2

You probably don't know this (we've never met, after all), but I have Aristotle's *Poetics* taped to my computer screen as well as to the inside flap of my personal journal. They're that important to me and to my writing. I outline Aristotle's *Poetics* in Chapter 5. You can refer to that chapter to get the full scoop on each of them, but in a nutshell, they're the building blocks of a story. Aristotle's *Poetics* can help you devise backstory, prioritize exposition, generate action, and, yes, even help you revise. I've listed each Poetic here as well, so you copy them down and carry them with you, too. They are:

- Plot
- Character
- Thought
- Spectacle
- Diction
- Music

In the rewriting process, each element on the *Poetics* list becomes a lens through which to view the draft. One lens enables you to isolate plot and plot action, another lens highlights character shifts, still another focuses your attention on language, and so on. The first revision is technical and should move quickly. In medical terms, it's like noting the symptoms of a mysterious illness. The second revision takes longer. In this stage, you trace the movement of each dramatic component through the entire text. Consider these to be the preliminary tests you run before offering a diagnosis.

Deconstructing plot

Most first drafts suffer from flashes of plot frailty. I say flashes of frailty, not frailty in general, and therein lies the problem. If your entire plot is weak, the solution is simple — start over. But chances are your whole plot isn't weak; moments of it are. Certain portions of the script feel unsubstantiated or episodic. Something's missing from the final scene. You can sense these problems. You can feel the story falter, but do you know *why* it falters? Can you locate the source of the trouble?

You can't fix a script unless you know exactly what's broken. For this reason, I usually begin my second round of revisions by tracking the action. Remember that plot is a series of actions, and actions spark other actions. That cause and effect relationship can be traced, and more often than not, the resulting outline reveals over half of what needs to be changed. Here's how you begin:

1. **Number your scenes.**

   Don't bother adding these numbers to your format; a director will do that in a later draft. Number them in pencil for revision purposes.

2. **Move from beginning to end, hunting for actions.**

3. **Jot each action down in a few sentences under the appropriate scene number.**

4. **Find the result of each action in ensuing scenes. Record those results below the original action.**

5. **Also below the action, write the number of the scene where its response arises.**

For instance, suppose that your main character robs a local business in scene one. This robbery results in the closing of that store, the death of its owner, and another robbery years later. Your outline for that action will look like this:

Scene 1

Action: Dennis robs the local five-and-dime store. A young boy witnesses the crime.

Result: The store is forced to close. (Scene 3)
The owner passes away. (Scene 6)
The young boy robs a bank years later. (Scene 22)

These results will probably spur other actions. When that happens, rerecord them as action in the appropriate scene and then track their results below. For example, if Dennis realizes that he's partially responsible for the second robbery and decides to end his wicked ways, that action will look like this:

Scene 22

Action: The young boy robs a bank.

Result: Dennis realizes that this robbery is partially his fault, and he seeks out a job in law enforcement. (Scene 24)

This process may seem tedious, but after a few scenes, it moves more quickly. And take the time you need; it's important to be precise. If you plant an action that never pays off, this outline can tell you that. If your plot has a hole, this outline can tell you where. You may know what the result of an action should be but find that it never occurs. You'll need to add a payoff scene later. Or perhaps an action occurs for seemingly no reason. In that case, you'll support it with a prior scene. The action outline is invaluable. It's like the red arrow on the map that says, "You are here," and then proceeds to mark all locations that you need to hit before you leave. The outline is your revision roadmap.

Character makeovers

Dull or inconsistent characters are the next most common script ailment. In the first-draft dash to capture the plot of a story, many writers neglect the players. That's to be expected. Fix them now. Here's how:

1. **List your main and supporting characters on a separate sheet of paper.**

2. **Reread the first act and the third act, assessing one character at a time**

3. **Make a list of all the character's physical and emotional qualities prior to Plot Point I.**

4. **Make a list of all the character's physical and emotional qualities after Plot Point II.**

5. **Compare the lists.**

These inventories represent the beginning and the end of your character's *arc,* or her transformation. Act II takes her from one point to the other. If you compare the lists and find that your character changes in a plausible way, congratulations. That's one less rewrite. However, most writers discover one of the following complications:

- ✔ The character doesn't change.
- ✔ The character changes completely.
- ✔ The character hasn't learned anything new.
- ✔ The character is inconsistent.

Your action outline may help troubleshoot some of these character complications. Characters often seem inconsistent because scenes supporting their transformation from one type of a person to another are missing. The fact that Brody (in *Jaws*) is deathly afraid of water in Act I but battles a shark in Act III seems inconsistent. However, scenes in Act II justify the change. Characters are only inconsistent if they change without explanation. In other words, I have to see it to believe it. Use the outline to check Act II for those crucial transition scenes. If your character doesn't change at all, restructure her arc. Something about her should flourish, and something should fade away.

Alas, an action outline can't fix everything. You know the phrase "Some things don't change"? That's true of people and, therefore, of characters. People don't reshape their entire lives; it's unrealistic. A timid person may perform a courageous act, but he's probably not ready to become the next superhero. The traits that a character most wants to change in herself are often what make her a unique individual. In *Kissing Jessica Stein,* Jessica becomes more open-minded and approachable after dating women, but she's still stubborn, overly organized, and neurotic. These traits make her Jessica Stein. Character changes are essential, but don't kill the good stuff in your quest to revamp the bad.

Here are some final techniques for identifying character rewrites. Again, these are areas that usually require help; they may or may not apply to you and your story.

- ✔ **Revisit your backstory.** Backstory refers to details and events you imagine took place prior to your story's first scene. Backstory includes all the research and dream time that made it possible to write your story. Although revealing all these details to an audience isn't necessary, these details often add flavor and dimension to a script's characters. For instance, the fact that Captain Quint has hundreds of shark jaws hanging in his shop is an exciting but unnecessary detail. The writers include it to further illustrate his obsession with the hunt. It's not necessary, but it makes his character more interesting. You may have such details in your backstory that are waiting to be incorporated into the action. Now is a good time to revisit the information that you came up with prior to writing a draft.

✔ **Trace your character's skills and opportunities.** Two things commonly result in contrived action. First, a character suddenly exhibits skills that just happen to push the plot forward. Second, a character's original skills just happen to solve every conflict that she encounters. Notice the repetition of the phrase "just happen to"? When things "just happen to" work out in a script, the conflict slips away. It's too convenient, it's unrealistic, and it's too darn easy. Here's how you fix it:

  • Create a conflict that requires a new skill or a new plan.

  • Make sure that your character begins the journey with a reasonable list of skills. (They may be superhero skills, but limit the list.)

  • Create scenes that require the skills of another individual.

Try not to give your character talents simply to solve a plot problem, or change an event based on your character's current abilities. Real people in real trouble — that's your goal.

✔ **Strengthen your antagonist.** If your character feels flat or simplistic, reinvestigate what she's up against. In theory, the obstacles that a character faces should exceed her ability to overcome them. I say "in theory," because the theory is generally incorrect. Audiences want your character to survive in spite of the odds against her. If your villain is too easily defeated, your action will seem unimportant.

✔ **Mix and match your characters.** Look at your cast of characters. Have you placed each character together in scene? Introducing your villain to your protagonist's best friend may not make sense, but then again, maybe it does. Even if you decide against a pairing, it never hurts to consider it.

Giving it a thought

Thought is the theme or the argument of your script. What do you think about the proceedings? What are you trying to communicate? Why did you write this story in place of others? Many films are thoughtless, and I don't mean inconsiderate. Action-adventures are often written for entertainment purposes alone. The ***Mission Impossible*** films are fast-paced and fun, but what do they really communicate? Many of the James Bond movies are written to raise the collective pulse of an audience and little else. Comedies often fall into this category as well. Look at ***Airplane*** and the ***Naked Gun*** series.

What's the point? Entertainment is the point.

Nothing's wrong with this type of movie, but most first-time screenwriters have a point, thank goodness. They have a theme, an opinion, a belief, and, most importantly, a question that they want to explore on the screen. If you want your movie to have a point, glance through your draft with the following questions in mind:

- ✔ Which characters share your beliefs?
- ✔ Which characters oppose your beliefs?
- ✔ Have you given them opportunities to share their views?
- ✔ Are their arguments clear?
- ✔ Have you portrayed both sides of the argument?

Every smart lawyer knows that, in order to win a case, you have to understand the opposing counsel's argument. You have to put yourself in his or her shoes. The same is true with thematic structure. You have something you want to say — fantastic. You have something you fervently believe — better yet. However, a script shouldn't become a vehicle to brainwash an audience into agreeing with you. A script allows you the opportunity to craft scenes in such a way that an audience understands your point of view. They get it. Whether they believe it or not is always up to them. Great drama doesn't preach — it persuades, it seduces, it explores, and most importantly, it asks. Nobody likes to be told what to think.

If you want to write about substance abuse, you should understand substance abusers. If you despise politicians, you nevertheless have to understand the crazy world of politics. In other words, you have to know why you feel the way you do. You have to know the opposing arguments in order to refute them. Check your work. Are you asking a question or pushing a belief? Have you crafted people who believe differently than yourself and, more importantly, have you crafted them with equal vigor? If you don't at least hint at a choice between points of view, you're not crafting drama. You're writing a public service announcement.

Re-envisioning your visuals

Spectacle refers to the visual images in your piece that elicit a palpable response from your audience. They shock, they arouse, they frighten, they delight, and the strongest examples help an audience to better understand the story. Because all cinematic scenes rely on moving pictures, you can easily forget that some images are more compelling than others. As you revise, look for the two kinds of spectacle that may enhance your action:

- ✔ **One-time spectacle:** These images crop up once in a film to liven it up, to cap an action, or to provide work for the special effects department. The helicopter chase in *Outbreak,* the first kiss in *When Harry Met*

Sally, the giant fires in *Gone with the Wind* — these are prime examples of one-time spectacle. They catch your eye and then your breath.

- **Recurring spectacle:** These images crop up periodically as thematic reminders of some inherent idea. The film *Chocolat* is about two people who move from town to town, leaving when the winds return. As a result, they have no home. When they finally settle into one, the writers craft images to remind them of life on the road. A band of gypsies comes to town in a boat that's always ready to leave port. The winds return periodically. Shots of the woman's suitcase suggests that she could leave any minute. These images vary in form and dramatic weight, but they're linked by a common theme. You may want to craft a thematic language for your own script.

Recomposing the score

Music and diction problems generally result in awkward dialogue, flat character voice, and generic locations. The good news is that they're easy to find and fun to fix. A few simple tests reveal the moments that need help.

- **Compare the length and look of character dialogue.** If you glance through a scene and discover that every character speaks in three-line sentences, you've got a problem. If every character ends his or her sentences with an exclamation point, you've got a problem. If I can't identify the speaker by the words that he uses, you've got a problem. These are indications that your characters suffer from similar voice. Rework their diction, so that they sound distinct.

- **Reconsider location.** Scenic location shouldn't be an arbitrary choice; it's too important. A location affects the way a character speaks and behaves, as well as how the audience views that character's actions. Suppose that your character is incredibly loud and crude. Imagine that character in a church or a library. Your scene suddenly becomes incredibly awkward or incredibly funny. If someone tells a character to grow up while standing in the middle of a kindergarten classroom, the scene is suddenly ironic. Make sure that you've chosen all your locations for a reason, and then double-check that they affect the characters in the scene.

- **Consider character intent and emotion.** Sometimes, dialogue falters because the characters forget their goals. Characters base their tactics on what they want from the other person. Those tactics, in turn, affect dialogue and behavior. Also, consider how your character feels about the situation she's in. Those emotions might also underscore the action. If your character is frightened, make sure that the rhythm of the scene (dialogue included) suggests this fright.

The best writers aren't necessarily those who craft the finest first drafts. They're the writers who know instinctively what to rewrite. They've adapted an ear for awkward and an eye for excessive. The more you write, the better you become at sensing which portions of your first draft require attention and how you might administer help. For now, consider the preceding revision tips as places to begin when you don't know where to begin.

Back in the Saddle Again: Rewrites

You've read through your script once, twice, perhaps many times over, and you have a list of things to fix. What's that? You have an entire scroll of things to fix? That's all right. Think of this time as an opportunity to make your script better. Yeah, that's it. It's an *opportunity*.

Rewrites are daunting — that's all there is to it. You have to be critical, you have to be cruel, and you have to memorize phrases like "It's for the good of the script" because the first thing you have to do is cut. If you have more than 120 pages of script, cut one-fourth of it. That means cutting 30 pages or so. If you have fewer than 120 pages, cut 10 percent. Be strict about this cutting; 30 pages is 30 pages. You can reach that goal by cutting lines here and there, or you can eliminate entire scenes. It's up to you. You may want to keep the cuts in a separate pile in case you want to reinstate them later, but cut them for now.

Cutting poorly written text is a breeze; you'll hum as you hold down the delete key. However, you're also going to come across magnificent speeches, witty repartee, and images that dazzle the eye. And guess what? You're going to have to kill some of them, too, or put them aside for a future script. Good isn't the same as necessary.

How do you know what should stay and what should go? Ask yourself why you want to keep it. The following arguments are *not* convincing:

- ✔ I like it.
- ✔ It sounds good.
- ✔ My friends like it.
- ✔ It worked in that other film.

If any or all of these excuses serve as your only reasoning, the section should probably go. However, the next arguments may suggest otherwise:

- ✔ It sets up crucial information.
- ✔ It expresses character.
- ✔ It supports another scene.
- ✔ I know that it means something.

If any of these arguments apply to the section in question, consider carefully before you hit delete, especially the last phrase. Your first instinct on a rewrite is often correct. If you know that a selection means something, don't cut it just because you can't verbalize what that something is. Live with it for a bit until you know.

After you cut, tackle the problems that you discovered in your first and second read-throughs. Generally, writers move scene by scene, so I include a final list of questions that can help guide you through those revisions.

✔ Where did the characters just come from? Where are they going next?

✔ How much time has elapsed since the last scene? What's happened in that time, and how does an audience know?

✔ What do your characters want in the scene? Is that clear?

✔ What tactics do they use to obtain that goal?

✔ What is your character's relationship to other people in the scene?

✔ Who's in control of the scene? When does that change?

✔ What's the obstacle in the scene?

✔ Could this scene really occur this way?

✔ What changes between the beginning and end of the scene?

✔ What does the audience discover in the scene?

✔ What happens as a result of this scene?

✔ If you had to cut one element, what would it be?

✔ What's your argument for keeping that element in?

✔ Can you combine this scene with another one and get the same effect?

Hopefully, one or two of these questions can help you. You may discover that you have several scenes left to write. If you've cut the necessary pages prior to the revision, you'll have room to accommodate those new moments. Rewrites have no set time frame. Some writers locate all the problematic text and rewrite quickly thereafter. Others move chronologically, testing and rewriting each scene as a unit before moving on to the next. How you do it is up to you. Take the time that you need to get it right because the next step is out of your hands.

Finding a Reader

Some writers write with a specific reader in mind. This reader is your first target audience. You want that person to laugh, cry, or gasp in certain spots, so you craft scenes that (hopefully) elicit that response. This system is an intelligent one, and it tends to produce reliable drama because it keeps you focused on an audience. If you have such a person in mind, great. Hand that person a copy of your script right now. If you don't, start scanning your relationships in search of a reader.

Honesty is your top priority in this search. Your readers must care enough about you and/or your script to give you an honest critique. Therefore, try to avoid the following readers:

✔ Anyone who's afraid of hurting your feelings

✔ Anyone who believes that you can do no wrong

✔ Anyone whom you consider to be direct competition

✔ Anyone whom you indiscreetly based a character on

These people have a personal bias that may get in the way of an honest read. You can show it to them after you've crafted a polished draft. Or send them tickets to opening night. The following people, however, make excellent second-draft readers:

✔ **Someone who's supportive of your craft:** Family members and friends make strong readers if — and this is a big if — they are capable of mixing piercing criticism with glowing commentary. Also, family members are notorious for recognizing themselves in the work. If you're even slightly worried that this may be the case, hand the script to someone else.

✔ **Someone who's brutally honest:** The truth is often hard to take, but truth couched in false praise is worse. Find someone who will tell you what he thinks about your script without pause or ornamentation. Then, force yourself to listen.

✔ **The perfect target audience:** Film companies poll their target audiences by screening the film prior to the final cut. If you find a reader who exemplifies your target audience, you can do the same thing in advance.

✔ **The antithesis of your target audience:** Find someone who you think would never go see your film. Your instinct may be right; that person may hate it. But that person also may surprise you. And his or her commentary may prepare you for future reviews.

✔ **A film virgin:** People who know nothing about movies let alone the writing craft are the best readers. They'll be the first to tell you when something doesn't make sense, and they'll pick up on technicalities directing their attention away from the story. If you know someone like this, enlist them at all costs.

✔ **A film buff:** Film aficionados are fun readers. They'll tell you if your film's already been made, and they're familiar with your lingo and your form. Better yet, they have high expectations. If your film doesn't match up, they'll be sure to tell you why.

As you can see, the credentials of these readers vary, and so, therefore, will their feedback. It's important to enlist several readers at once, so print out three or four copies of your new draft and pick up the phone.

Your Critique: Surviving the Aftermath

Your readers are done, the jury is back, and the verdict is here. As you listen to the feedback, at some point, you'll want to scream. You may also want to run, crawl under the couch, or melt into the floor. Don't do any of these things. Nod and smile and listen. Remember, this critique hurts you more than it hurts them, but it will help you develop a critical tool — the writer's filter.

Every writer needs an internal filter to help sift through all the criticism that she receives. The filter works two ways: It listens for criticism that seems to make sense for one reason or another, and it filters out the rest. How does it know what to take seriously? It uses the following criteria.

It remembers

- ✔ Any criticism that it hears more than once
- ✔ Anything deemed confusing or unclear
- ✔ Anything that you suspected was problematic prior to the reading
- ✔ Anything that elicited a surprising or unintentional response
- ✔ Anything that supports your original intention

It forgets

- ✔ Anything deemed "bad" or "good" without explanation
- ✔ Any comments that differ among the majority of readers
- ✔ Pretty much everything else

The best criticism reflects the script back to you. Sometimes, the comments "I liked it" or "I hated it" are important, but they rarely help you revise. You need to know what the reader saw, what he heard, what he took away from the script in as much detail as he can muster. Those comments help you determine what to change completely and what to bolster. Remember that you're the one sitting at a computer or a notebook every day. You sit with these characters for hours at a stretch. You're the only person who really knows the script and what it wants to explore. Although criticism is usually given with the best intentions, that doesn't mean that it's all worthwhile.

Chapter 17

Adaptation and Collaboration: Two Alternate Ways to Work

So you've found a story; it just landed in your lap. It has well-developed characters, plot twists galore, style, wit, emotion, and a theme to pull them all together. You only have one problem — your story already exists in a different form. It's a novel, a stage play, a poem, an article, a song — the point is, it's not your story, and it's not your form. Or is it?

If you're at this crossroads, now is the time to consider *adaptation*. By adaptation, I mean taking that story from its original medium and transforming it into a film. Some writers find this process exhilarating and infinitely simpler than devising a script from the ground up. However, adaptation requires a knowledge of and a respect for many different kinds of writing, and this sensibility often takes years to develop. For this reason, many people choose to collaborate with a writing partner, dividing the tasks and bouncing ideas back and forth.

This chapter illustrates the challenges and advantages of the adaptation process and provides tips for how to proceed after you've found the story of your dreams. It also offers suggestions for writing with another artist, should the need or the desire arise.

Navigating between Forms

I'm a firm believer that stories seek the form that best expresses their narrative content. In other words, if *The Cider House Rules* had wanted to be a film first, it would've been a film first. It didn't. It wanted to be the novel that John Irving composed. Does that mean that crafting a screenplay from a work of fiction is wrong? No. It means that you'll have to change that work of fiction into a different kind of story, a kind of story that's best expressed cinematically. Let me repeat that first bit — you'll have to *change* the work.

Every literary form is structurally unique and has its own advantages and limitations. Fiction and prose invite scenic description where plays and film invite physical action, for example. Poetry and songs often facilitate shorter, more compact subjects than would sustain a novel or a screenplay. In order to write the film version of a poem then, you have to know what makes a poem structurally different from a film and change the story accordingly. (For details on the specific elements of different literary and artistic forms, refer to Chapter 2.) Now's the time to consider how the structural elements of the original source might help or hinder your eventual screenplay.

From fiction to film

Fiction is the medium most often adapted into film. *The Cider House Rules, Gone with the Wind, Jaws, Lord of the Rings, Silence of the Lambs,* and virtually every John Grisham piece are just a few examples on the weighty list of adapted novels. Several writers have successfully converted short stories as well. The movie **Stand By Me,** for example, is based on a short piece by Stephen King called "The Body."

With such a long list, you may think that jumping between these forms is simple, and in some ways, it can be. After all, characters, events, and dialogue bits are already in place for you to sift through and select. However, more often than not, the success of a film adaptation is a result of how the writer chooses to work around cinematically troubling aspects of the original form. What follows are some techniques specific to fiction along with potential ways to approach them in film.

Description

Novelists are able to describe everything in detail, from the location to the characters' physical conditions to their thoughts. Henry James spends more than 20 pages depicting Isabel Archer's daydream in **Portrait of a Lady,** for goodness sake. The sheer amount of physical and psychological detail can be both a benefit and a boon to the visually oriented screenwriter, who must capture the essence of important description through image, dialogue, or action. I include a list of both the pros and cons of fictional description to further prepare you for the adaptation process.

Pros: Description clearly conveys

✔ A detailed sense of location, atmosphere, and person.

✔ A complete *backstory* (everything that you imagine takes place prior to your story's beginning).

✔ The composition of key images.

✔ Metaphors and allegories that link scenes together.

Cons: Description may be challenging because

✔ What occurs in a chapter can take seconds of screen time.

✔ What fiction depicts in a sentence may require several scenes on-screen.

✔ Details in abundance may quickly become overwhelming.

Adapt description on-screen by

✔ Condensing several characters into one.

✔ Choosing one or two protagonists to follow, eliminating characters that don't support their journey.

✔ Suggesting metaphor by revisiting an image several times.

Internal and external worlds

Novels can move between physical and psychological action in a sentence or two. In other words, fiction takes place equally inside and outside a character's mind. Thoughts, fears, and emotions quickly become another landscape. Fiction writers call this technique *narrative movement,* and again, it can be both a help and a hindrance to a screenwriter. Because cinema relies on what a writer can translate into image and action, narrative movement poses the following pros and cons to the world of screenwriting:

Pros: Narrative movement provides

✔ A complete psychological and physical profile of each character.

✔ Each character's opinion or take on what they witness.

✔ A sense of how, when, and why characters move into and out of thought.

Cons: Narrative movement may be challenging because

✔ Films primarily dwell in the external world of action.

✔ The number of memories and daydreams may become overwhelming.

✔ Characters usually harbor thoughts and beliefs that they wouldn't readily discuss with another character or the audience.

Adapt narrative movement on-screen by

- Condensing and eliminating reveries.
- Creating active scenes that suggest a character's thoughts and fears.
- Dramatizing key moments in the backstory that suggest what a character might be feeling in the present.
- Creating a pace between scenes that mimics the pace between internal and external worlds in the novel.

Narrative voice

Fiction relies as much on the story's speaker as it does on the characters themselves. The narrator may or may not have a personal investment in the events. He may be omniscient or restricted to certain knowledge. He may be trustworthy or unreliable. The narrator sometimes changes from section to section, as different people tell the same story. Unless a screenwriter allows a character to directly address the audience, as in *Ferris Bueller's Day Off,* she'll have to find alternate ways to convey the narrative voice.

Pros: Narrative voice provides

- An opinion or judgment of specific events.
- A suggestion of events in the future.
- A context and/or reason for telling the story.
- A sense of several events taking place simultaneously.

Cons: Narrative voice may be problematic because

- The narrator's information may be difficult to dramatize.
- Without a narrator, the tone of the piece may be lost.
- The narrative voice provides texture that general scenes may not.

Adapt narrative voice on-screen by

- Eliminating the narrator altogether.
- Distributing the voice among other characters.
- Creating a new character to embody that voice.
- Transferring the feeling of the narrator to the film's atmosphere and style.

From stage to screen

Marvin's Room, Steel Magnolias, On Golden Pond, Glengarry Glen Ross, Mousetrap, and *Who's Afraid of Virginia Woolf?* are just a few stage plays to make it onto the big screen. In film adaptation, stage plays present their own set of benefits and complications. The following list touches upon key aspects of a play and how you may work with or against them in your movie script.

Dialogue

In the past, stage plays relied on carefully crafted dialogue to convey everything from backstory to character motivation to mood. Nowadays, plays are becoming more physical in nature, but they still place great importance on language. Screenwriters may transfer some of the dialogue directly into their scripts, but many of the dramatist's words must become moving pictures. How do you know which words to keep and which to transform into visual bits? Consider these dialogue suggestions.

Pros: Stage dialogue provides

- Strong sense of character voice.
- Rhythm for each character and the piece overall.
- Suggested backstory and metaphor.

Cons: Stage dialogue often

- Impedes the screenwriter's ability to concentrate on image.
- Suggests too many or too few events to convey on film.

Adapt stage dialogue by

- Turning references of past events into visual scenes.
- Transferring the character's vocal pattern into a physical pattern.
- Restructuring events, so that they take place in a new chronology.
- Maintaining key dialogue moments and crafting visual scenes around them.

Character and location limitations

Unlike film, which jumps between any number of places and times within seconds, most plays concentrate on a handful of locations, if not on one alone. The same rule applies to the number of characters in each medium. Films use extras to create the most realistic environment possible; plays rely on lights, sound, and their main characters to provide that environment. These limitations often stem from budgetary concerns, but they tend to have artistic reasons as well. In film, location is usually a backdrop. In theater, it's a competing force. And more characters in a play means less time spent on any one journey. The detailed locations of a play will certainly help a screenwriter, but the limited number explored will not. Consider the following suggestions when transferring locations from stage to screen.

Pros: Location and character restrictions provide

- ✔ A strong sense of protagonist and the protagonist's journey.
- ✔ Clearly defined goals for all the characters involved.
- ✔ Enough time to detail an environment and its ensuing mood.

Cons: Location and character restrictions

- ✔ Do not often suggest the realistic setting a screenwriter desires.
- ✔ Limit a screenwriter to a few settings, which can become static on-screen.
- ✔ Limit the drama to the scope of a few characters.

Adapt these limitations to film by

- ✔ Discovering other places and/or times for the scenes to occur.
- ✔ Considering all characters referenced in the play as possible characters to dramatize on-screen.
- ✔ Creating characters that aren't suggested but might exist in this world.
- ✔ Using all parts of the primary locations, especially those referenced in a play but never explored — script scenes in all rooms of the main house, for example.

Poetry and music

These last two mediums are strong launching points for a story, but they rarely provide an entire structure to work from. Some writers revel in the creative freedom that these sources allow; some are daunted by the lack of detail that they provide. In this section, I include cinematic strengths and weaknesses for both forms as well as possible ways to adapt them into a film.

If poetry and music share anything in common with film, it's a fondness for image and mood. Poetry is, by its nature, condensed into several strong pictures or metaphors that drive the rest of the piece. Music creates an entire sensual world through rhythm and melody. These structural components can be a great source of inspiration for a filmmaker. They differ from the other mediums in brevity of form.

Pros: Music and poetry provide

- ✔ A set of clearly composed images to work from.
- ✔ Universal metaphors that may speak to a film's theme.
- ✔ A suggested rhythm and style for the eventual piece.

Cons: Music and poetry are

- ✔ Fleeting in nature.
- ✔ Often highly allegorical and, therefore, subjective.
- ✔ Driven by emotion instead of event.

Adapt music and poetry to film by

- ✔ Finding possible narratives hidden within the piece and work from there.
- ✔ Uncovering the historical background of the piece and dramatizing that story.
- ✔ Using the mood that each piece creates as a backdrop for a different film.
- ✔ Using one or two choice phrases as a starting point for an original piece.

In any adaptation, you're searching for the essence of the original form. Remaining true to every aspect of the account is neither necessary nor required. In fact, screenplays that try to maintain every aspect of a story tend to fail. Why? You're not re-creating a work of fiction or stagecraft or poetry — you're creating a film, which is a new story with a language of its own. What caught your fancy? How did it make you feel? What about the story is unique? What aspects of the piece are vital to understanding the narrative? If you can answer those questions, you're ready to begin.

The Process of Adaptation

Much of this book details the creation of an original piece. So how does the process of adaptation compare? I often tell students that adapting a work is like a different kind of magic with roughly the same spell. You're creating an original piece — this one just happens to be based on something else. The work you're adapting is your *source* and nothing else. It may suggest a setting, unique characters, or a theme; it may give you an entire blueprint for the action. But it's still just a source. You may have heard the old saying that you should never let facts get in the way of a good story. Take that to heart. You're crafting this piece in the same way that you'd craft any piece — you just have more to work with at the onset.

How to approach an original work

With any adaptation, writers are scanning the original piece for two things: character and plot. Occasionally, a theme becomes the backbone of your work, but generally, the *who* and the *what* take precedence. You can move from one form to another in three primary ways:

- **Follow the form.** Take everything that you can from the original piece — characters and character transformations; the beginning, middle, and end of the work; the style and the pace. Turn them all into action or image and begin. You're an architect. The original piece provides the structure; you layer the cinematic moments upon it.

- **Work from key scenes.** The scenes that strike your fancy may or may not be pivotal moments in the text. Pinpoint the five or six moments that speak to you, rearrange them as necessary, and write what comes in between.

- **Use the story as a launching point.** Often, a single character, line, or action jumps out at you. If this is the case, take that one piece and spin your drama upon it.

You may always gravitate toward the same method. If you enjoy complete creative freedom, you'll probably always choose method number three. If you crave structure, the first method will be a better match. However, don't be surprised if the original source suggests the method.

After you determine which method to follow, the creation process is very similar to that of an original piece. I encourage you to continue dreaming and researching and demanding more of the work. Don't assume that the information you start with is all there is. It's really only a beginning.

Here's a basic set of steps to follow in order to proceed with your adaptation:

1. **Read the original piece *at least* three times.**

   You first encounter a work in a state of naiveté. Everything is new; nothing is certain. You're left with a series of impressions and a general sense of the piece. You notice details on a second read as the structure becomes apparent, and the by the third read, you should know what grabs you about the piece and what you could do without. By the third read, the original piece is in your bones.

2. **Write an outline of pivotal scenes and actions.**

Follow the original piece on this first outline. Include moments as they happen, even if you're certain that you won't use them. You're searching for a base structure from which to work. Pay particular attention to where this version of the story begins and ends.

3. **Make a list of all the characters.**

Again, list all the characters, whether or not you intend to use them in your film. You may need to layer their attributes onto someone else later on. Take special note of which characters are primary, secondary, and incidental.

4. **Reduce the story to a three- or four-line premise.**

How would you pitch this story? What's the main storyline? What makes this piece exciting? If you can reduce the story to a nutshell description, you have a stronger sense of what the story is ultimately about.

5. **Determine the question, concept, or point of view.**

Why was this story written? What does it ask or demand of a reader? The answers to these questions help to you keep the integrity of the original piece intact.

6. **Find the holes.**

What is not dramatized is often as important as what is dramatized. You may discover that the story not told is the one worth pursuing. Imagine around the original piece; you may be surprised at what you discover.

7. **Choose several key moments, put them in order, and begin.**

Now's the time to choose what you want to dramatize and arrange those elements in some chronology that makes sense to your piece. After you have two or three key moments in place, build scenes that bridge them together.

By the time you start writing, the characters may seem quite different from the ones that you discovered in that first read. Your entire plot may hinge on events that were merely suggested in the first piece. If this is the case, congratulations. You've hit upon the balance between someone else's work and your own. Best of all, if you become frustrated along the way, you can always return to the source.

What to do when you're stuck

Adaptation is a challenging and often cumbersome process. You have to find a balance between remaining true to a source and writing your own piece. If you find yourself leaning too heavily on one side, try one or all of the following suggestions:

✔ **Imagine the story in a different time period or location.** Sometimes, taking the action out of the world of the piece helps to clarify what it's really about. What adjustments would you have to make if *Gone with the Wind,* for example, took place in 1950s Manhattan instead of in the Civil War–torn South?

✔ **Imagine the work from a different point of view.** The original piece may clearly delineate a main character, but what if you chose someone else to lead the story? What if the new protagonist was the rarely seen neighbor or the old protagonist's arch rival?

✔ **Eliminate flashbacks or memories.** Flashbacks aren't forward moving; they pause the action in order to recall an event. Novels and short stories are riddled with flashbacks. If you find yourself unsure of how to include them, try reorganizing the plot sequence so that the events occur in sequence. You may also allude to them in a scene or even eliminate them entirely.

✔ **Condense and expand.** If your original source is 500 pages, you're going to have to pick and choose your events. Similarly, if you're taken with one line or paragraph, you'll have to imagine around it. Sometimes, the sheer act of narrowing the action down or expanding it sparks a cinematic idea.

✔ **Determine your main characters and their goals.** Primary source material often has more characters than you know what to do with. Choose one or two protagonists and give them very specific goals. The rest of the action should revolve around helping or hindering those people in achieving their goals.

The Art of Collaboration

Screenwriting, like playwriting, relies on collaboration. If you continue working in the field, you'll most likely collaborate with agents who sell your work, producers who buy it, and directors and actors who give voice to it on the screen. Screenwriters collaborate with everyone, including other screenwriters. A student once commented that my workshop on literary collaboration felt very much like a workshop on marriage. Well, collaboration is a marriage. It's a marriage of talent and imagination, and you should approach it with the seriousness that a marriage requires. Writers collaborate for various reasons, but the collaboration usually begins when someone decides that it takes more than one person to write a particular story. That person then goes in search of another writer whose talents complement her own, whose knowledge and skill seem appropriate to the project, and whose schedule and connections will help the work to get done. Sound simple? Think again. Finding someone who fits this description is easier said than done.

What to look for in a writing partner

Here's where the marriage metaphor really kicks in. If you substitute artistic chemistry for sexual chemistry, searching for a writing partner is almost exactly like searching for a spouse. Here are a few things to look for:

- ✔ **Someone responsible whom you can trust:** Both you and your partner have your work cut out for you. Find someone who will keep her deadlines, pull her weight, and keep the project between the two of you.

- ✔ **Someone who knows and respects your work, and someone whose work you know and respect:** If you don't know what your partner has written, how will you know if he's right for the project? Make sure that both of you are comfortable with the other one's interests, style, and vision.

- ✔ **Someone who has a similar concept of the project, if different reasons for pursuing it.** Eventually, you and your partner will have to agree upon a premise and a purpose for the work. Start that conversation now. If your thoughts of the work differ greatly, you may end up with two films instead of one.

Share this list with your potential partner early on and demand that each of you meet it for the other. Start the line of communication now. You may feel bad if that person doesn't care to work with you, but you'll feel worse if you discover it halfway through the first draft.

How to approach collaboration

After you find someone to work with, the two of you need to have two discussions right off the bat. One involves the work itself, and one involves the writing process.

Sharing the work: Part 1

Ask and answer the following questions with your partner: What interests you about the project? What does not? Who do you believe the script is about? What do those characters want? What is the general premise of the piece? Why does this piece have to be written?

This discussion and its outcome form the foundation upon which the screenplay can be written. You both should agree upon why the script needs to be written and around whom it revolves. I ask students to pound out a mission statement of sorts, depicting what the project wants to achieve. Should egos arise later on — and they *will* arise later on — the writers have something to go back to.

After you've spoken for a bit, take a stab at character biographies. Write them together or on your own and then compare. Do the same with an outline for the piece. The beginning, middle, and end may change as you write, but at least you're starting from a point of agreement. After an outline and a premise are in place, you're ready to discuss process.

Sharing the work: Part II

You've spoken about the work as a story, now talk about the work as work. In other words, discuss the division of labor. Within any writer's job are several tasks: research, interviews, outlines, draft work, typing, revision, the pitch, and so on. Who's going to take on what task? Be clear, and divide the tasks according to your strengths and your interests. After you determine who's doing what and when, consider the following suggestions:

- ✔ **Decide on a schedule.** When do you like to write? When will you write on your own, and when will you write as a team? Give yourselves assignments and goals for each meeting. Finding a schedule that works for both of you will take a least a week, maybe longer.

- ✔ **Kill the ego.** This project is not about you. It's not about whether you're right or wrong. It's about the piece. When you feel the ego taking over, when you or your partner becomes overly sensitive, return to that mission statement.

- ✔ **Divide the work evenly.** Problems arise when one person takes the lead. Bitterness and resentment inevitably follow. If one person wants the dominant role, discuss what dominant entails and devise some kind of an agreement. Remember that there was a reason you chose to collaborate in the first place.

- ✔ **Discuss problems as they arise.** Most creative problems occur because one partner forgets to communicate with the other.

If you've had these discussions, you're ready to start writing. As with any process, this one presents unique challenges. You and your partner *will* make mistakes. Acknowledge them and move on. You *will* become angry at each other, perhaps even irate. Talk about it and move on. You *will* reach a point where you'll want to write the script yourself. Return to your mission statement and move on. As with any marriage, the key is to keep talking and keep working. The challenges don't stop, but the eventual rewards make it all worthwhile.

Part IV
Selling Your Script to Show Business

The 5th Wave   By Rich Tennant

Bigö   WST

"I'm pretty confident about selling my screenplay.
I already have an agent, a manager, and a lawyer.
It's my barber, my mechanic, and my dry cleaner."

In this part . . .

Ah, Hollywood. The producers, the directors, the agents, the studios, the stars and, well, you. Placing yourself in the show business scene is a juggling act unto itself, and making an entrance is a step in the right direction. This part is all about equipping yourself for the market — assembling a network, what to prepare in advance and how to package the product of you. Armed with that information, you should be able to launch yourself into the industry full speed ahead. But just in case, the last half of the section details what to do when you get there.

Chapter 18

Before You Send It Out: Pre-Marketing Considerations

In This Chapter

▶ Hollywood's main players

▶ Keeping personal records

▶ How networking works

▶ Preparing your script for submission

▶ Protecting your work in advance

Completing a revised draft is cause for celebration. Take a vacation, do something mindless, and by all means, spend as much time away from your office as possible. After all, your work is half done.

Wait a second, did I just say "half done"? But you've survived research, interviews, plot development, treatments, months of writing and revisions — is that really just *half* of the journey? Possibly. If you wrote the script for yourself, to enjoy the craft for craft's sake, you're finished right now. Put that script on a shelf and start another one; there's infinitely more to learn. However, if you wrote the screenplay for an audience, then yes, you're only half done. The second half of the journey involves getting your screenplay ready for that audience, be it reader, agent, producer, or studio executive. The time's come to consider the business.

Unlike creative work, which may begin haphazardly and fly you down several paths on your way to an idea, the next stage of the game involves immediate and thorough preparation. One of the worst things that a writer can do — to her career, to her script, and to her self-esteem — is to enter the market prematurely. In Hollywood, time is always of the essence — meetings are brief, openings limited, and attention spans short. Show business is not a business to approach ill-equipped. This chapter helps to make the marketing process less intimidating and arms you with information and organizational skills for the crazy road ahead.

Understanding the "Biz" in Showbiz

You only have to glance at the opening and closing credits of any film to appreciate the sheer number of people that it takes to complete a project. You have literary agents and their assistants, directors and assistant directors, actors, their agents, their managers, producers, production companies, and studios heads. The list reads like an Oscar acceptance speech. How on earth will you navigate between all these roles? Well, you probably won't until you know what each person is responsible for and what each person wants. So for starters, familiarize yourself with the players.

Getting to know the players: The Hollywood hierarchy

Many people in Hollywood do various jobs at various times. Actors own production companies, actors are also directors, producers may be directors, and so on. That information changes on a yearly, if not a monthly, basis. So keep your eye out for new developments. The following list is designed as an overview of the kinds of roles you'll run into when selling a script:

- ✔ **Producers — the wallet:** Producers manage and financially back the production elements of your work. They oversee anything and everything from marketing and publicity to hiring a staff for the project. Some producers find ways to fund the project themselves; others (independent producers) may be looking for a studio to provide financial support. In terms of the writer, producers are looking for two things: the strength of your finished screenplay and your ability to write for other projects they have in mind.

- ✔ **Directors — the eye:** Directors are in charge of completing the screenplay. By completing, I mean bringing it to life on the screen and giving it dimension. Directors make the script camera-ready, breaking each scene into specific shots with the aid of a cinematographer. They also work with the actors, sound designers, camera crew, and so on to create a unified vision for the piece.

- ✔ **Actors — the true players:** These are obviously the people who star in the films. However, many actors also own production companies and may seek out new work, most often scripts with a large role for them. Though showing an actor your work is often difficult, attaching an actor to your project is always a good thing. At best, that actor pitches it for you and it gets made; at worst, the script gains recognition.

- ✔ **Agents — your ticket in:** These men and women represent new talent. They send scripts to various executives, seek writing assignments for their clients, arrange the meetings, and negotiate contracts on the writer's behalf. They may act as final reader for the piece and step in should legal problems arise. They're looking for writers with talent, with a good attitude, with innovative ideas, and with staying power.

- ✔ **Studios — the big guns:** Studios, such as Warner Brothers, DreamWorks, Paramount, and so on, finance projects and provide space and materials. In many cases, they attach producers and directors to projects they've purchased. They're interested in a worthwhile investment and scripts that fit their audience. They keep a close eye on the budget proposal and marketability of each film they approach.

Each film has countless people on board. The list extends far beyond the first five roles that I mentioned. To name just a few more, cinematographers help design and shoot each scene, editors cut the film for pace and momentum, and sound designers do exactly what their title suggests — design your sound. But you won't meet these people until your film is in production, well after the script has been purchased. People in the first five roles are the ones who may help get you in the door.

Getting a "grip": Hollywood jargon

Do you know what a *grip* is? How about a *dolly* or a *super* or a *wipe* or a *zip pan*? It's okay if you don't; that's the biz talking. The credo "walk the walk and talk the talk" may be alive and well in Hollywood, but talking the talk is often more difficult than it sounds. Business jargon or *lingo* changes annually, and it would be difficult to record every new phrase out there. So instead, I've compiled a brief list of terms that predominantly affect writers. Some you'll hear quite often, some are reserved for production, and some are just plain fun.

- ✔ **ADR:** This term, which stands for *additional dialogue replacement,* refers to any material added to a film after production. It may be atmosphere additions, such as crowd noises or responses to action sequences, or it may be phrases that were simply replaced.

- ✔ **The buzz:** The buzz is the "hype" around a project, or what people are saying about it. The buzz is usually a positive expression, signifying excitement over the work.

- ✔ **Coverage:** The report that a professional reader gives a new screenplay is referred to as coverage. It includes the vital stats as well as a synopsis and/or commentary on the work. It rates the strength of dialogue, characterization, plot structure, and so on. I cover coverage more thoroughly in the next few sections of this chapter.

✔ **The hook:** I've mentioned this one before, but it's so important that it bears repeating. The hook is that unique aspect of your story that immediately grabs a reader's attention. You use your hook with producers, agents, in query letters, and in marketing. It may be the major selling point of your story.

✔ **On-the-nose:** This phrase is used to describe dialogue that too plainly reveals the characters' or the author's intentions. On-the-nose dialogue tells the audience what the story is about instead of allowing that discovery to arise through situation.

✔ **Pinks:** Printing shooting-script changes on multicolored paper is a common practice. Those pages are traditionally pink, blue, and yellow — generally in that order. Pinks refers to those rewrites, as in "It was switched in the pinks." You'll probably hear them referred to as "the pinks" regardless of what color the rewrites really are.

✔ **The pitch:** The pitch is a concise and exciting story synopsis that you verbally sell to agents and producers. Like a movie trailer, it grabs attention, suggests a tone, and provides enough character and plot information to indicate a feature film. For more on how to pitch, see Chapter 19.

✔ **The polish:** A highly revised draft of your script is called the polish. It's been through several readers, workshops, and/or script analysts. It's tight, efficient, and ready for you to send out.

✔ **Script doctor:** A script doctor is someone who's hired to revise part or all of an existing screenplay. These jobs often pay well, though you may not get credit for them.

✔ **Second-act curtain:** In a three-act screenplay, this is the moment of greatest conflict. It generally precedes or becomes the script's climax.

✔ **A sleeper:** A sleeper is surprise box office success. No one expects it to do as well as it does, despite a strong story or interesting concept. *My Big Fat Greek Wedding, The Blair Witch Project,* and *The Sixth Sense* are recent examples of sleeper hits.

✔ **Spec script:** This term is used to refer to the script you prepare for submission. It emphasizes the story, so it doesn't include camera directions, explanation of action, or personal commentary. Those items are reserved for a *shooting script,* which is generally composed by the director and cinematographer before production. The spec script is the script that sells your idea.

Preparing Yourself for the Biz

Writing a screenplay involves concentrating all your efforts on the story. How do the events transpire? Are you accurately depicting the characters? Is the situation plausible and clear? These are the questions that consume countless days.

With all the attention on product, you may easily assume that your foremost goal in Hollywood is to sell that particular script. Luckily, that assumption's incorrect. Selling the screenplay is always an objective, but your first priority is selling yourself as a competent, competitive writer. You are the commodity here. The script may not sell for reasons that defy explanation — the story has too many characters, it's not the "right time" for a screwball comedy, another studio just purchased a talking donkey film — you can't foresee everything. But if studio executives like your work, they'll hire you for other projects. They may even ask for a second script, who knows? Because you're the commodity, you need to prepare yourself for the market now.

Putting on a happy face: The art of attitude

Regardless of how you behave in your private life, you're going to have to don a few traits to get through the Hollywood maze. Here are a few characteristics to foster in yourself as you proceed:

- **A professional air:** There's a fine line between confident and cocky, pride and arrogance, and savvy and dishonest. Master the art of presenting your work with poise and assurance while remaining open to critique.

- **Enthusiasm:** You love this project, and you love this profession. Even when it drives you insane, you love it. If this isn't the case, find a way to convince yourself that it is. Enthusiasm is contagious, and nothing's more enticing than someone passionate about his work. Find a way to communicate that zeal to others.

- **Intelligence:** Knowledge is power. The more you know about your script, about the business, and about the world, the more willing people will be to hire you. You may be a novice in the business, but you certainly don't have to sound like one.

- **Patience:** Every writer wants to be read and read now. It usually takes a long time to introduce your script, let alone your name, to Hollywood and its various agents. Now may not be the right time to pitch your script, either. Frustration is understandable, but don't let it affect the quality of your work or your work ethic.

- **Persistence:** Rejection is a given in this profession. Disregard it and keep working. Many mediocre writers are produced because they're persistent enough to push their work through. Screenwriters quickly build up an immunity to rejection. Instead of letting it stop your process, just keep forging ahead. Eventually, you'll catch a break.

Producers, like agents, are looking for a team player. Before you approach them, make a list of your strengths as a writer and as a person. Be specific. If you write historical dramas, call yourself a historian and list which eras you're familiar with. If you're opinionated, find a positive way to phrase that. You have a unique vision of the world or a different spin on politics, for example. Don't underestimate punctuality and organization; studios look for both. And a sense of humor never hurts, either, so let yourself laugh.

You might think that maintaining a positive attitude is the easy part of the process. However, after eight or nine rejections, even the most confident people start to doubt their abilities. Should you experience this dejection, repeat the following facts diligently to yourself. They're inspirational and better yet — they're true.

- ✔ Every writer begins without an agent.
- ✔ Every writer works for little or no pay at some point.
- ✔ There's a lot of bad writing out there; there's a need for great material.
- ✔ Only you can tell your stories.

Everything worth anything in life involves risk, fear, and struggle. This is where persistence comes in. Keep writing; success can strike at any time.

Organizing your records

Do you know which studios are looking for romantic comedies or which agent represents your favorite writer? Do you know how many thrillers were purchased last year, and, of those, how many made it into production? Do you know who to contact about submitting work to independent producers? By the time you're through with this chapter, you should be keeping several lists. Those lists are meant to help answer these questions and countless others. They serve as your network in written form and as a marketing progress report, so keep the following records updated and close by.

Your contact list

Everyone in your life is a potential contact. Don't be too picky when you begin this list. You never know when someone's expertise will prove invaluable. Think about who you already know. Record the person's name, her relationship to you, any pertinent or personal details you want to include, and her contact information. You might divide this list into two sections — those contacts who work in the film industry and those who do not. You'll consult the first section when you need help revising, marketing, or selling your script. Contacts in the second section may help you generate ideas or research a project.

The marketing list

This list includes studios, producers, directors, agents, actors, and managers, the companies they work for, and what kind of movies they purchase or accept. When you discover who represents your favorite screenwriters, include that information here. When Matt Damon and Ben Affleck request submissions for their next new film contest, include that information here. When producers switch studios or actors launch their own companies, include that information here. Consider this list to be your personal screenwriter's sourcebook. Each new entry should include the following:

- ✔ The person's name and position (if applicable)
- ✔ The organization he works for or represents
- ✔ Previous projects he has commissioned or purchased
- ✔ The kind of work he's recently requested
- ✔ The contact information (if you have it)

After maintaining this list for a while, patterns begin to emerge. You'll notice what sort of story sells quickly, which screenwriters generate interest at any given moment, and which genre might be ripe for revival. Pay attention to this list and record all fluctuations. You can't join the market without first knowing what it looks like and how it works.

Meetings and phone calls

This list begins the moment that you start calling people for information or script help. Anyone whom you speak to regarding your story, in an official capacity or otherwise, should be logged in your records. This log might include

- ✔ Anyone who helped you with initial research
- ✔ Anyone whom you've interviewed as part of the process
- ✔ Anyone reading and/or critiquing your work.
- ✔ Any calls you make or replies you send out
- ✔ The agencies copyrighting your work and the date of official copyright
- ✔ Anyone in the business whom you meet with or speak to on the phone, and the outcome of that exchange

This log tracks your history with various studios and individuals. It offers a quick summation of meetings, should you need to recall people quickly. It also reminds you to follow up with anyone kind enough to inquire about your work. The list should include the person's or agency's name, the date of the meeting or submission, a brief description of what transpired, and a notation of any further or impending exchange.

Transfer anyone on this record to your contact list as well.

Submissions and results

Some people include this information in the previous list, but I find it helpful to reserve a separate record for submissions and results. After all, meeting with someone is a different process than submitting your work. You may wait months to hear from a studio, and you'll want a place to keep any rejections or positive feedback.

Writers usually send scripts to several places at once, and they may have two or more works circulating at any given time. This is not to suggest that you want the same script passing through various studios at once. You don't. But it's not uncommon for a writer to circulate one script to several agencies or contests at the same time, and if you have more than one polished script, you might market both simultaneously, albeit to different venues. Multiple submissions have the potential to become confusing. So when you submit a work, record the following:

- ✔ The title of the script
- ✔ The organization or person you sent it to
- ✔ Their contact information
- ✔ The date it was sent
- ✔ A line about the nature of the submission — a request, a referral, something else

Leave room below each item to add follow-up reports that arise later. You should *always* send a thank-you note to anyone interested in your work, so log that information below the submission date to make sure that you've sent one. This list ensures that you don't submit the same work to a studio twice, and after a while, it also reveals patterns. If no one is interested in a script, the time may have come to launch a new one. If a script generates mass curiosity but doesn't sell, a rewrite might be necessary. If the script sparks a meeting or a phone call, well, you have a whole other list for that info, don't you?

Acquiring the right information

"But I'm new to this business," you say. "How do I discover what to include on all these lists?" That's a good question. When you first enter the business, your contact list may be short, your marketing list limited, and the other two records may be nonexistent. That's okay. Everyone starts somewhere. Luckily, a variety of resources are available to help expand that network.

The media

An array of publications report on the Hollywood marketing scene. The trade publications (also known simply as *trades*), which include *Daily Variety* (www. variety.com) and *The Hollywood Reporter* (www.hollywoodreporter.com), announce which screenplays are bought and sold, what their premises are, who's doing the purchasing, when their slated for production, and when to expect a release. Articles and weekly focus sections include studio progress reports, information on promotions and position shifts within organizations, and updates on television programming and acquisitions. The trades are available in daily and weekly editions.

Other publications include *Script* (www.scriptmag.com), a magazine focusing on writing and marketing scripts of all kinds; *Premiere* (www.premiere.com) and *Entertainment Weekly* (www.ew.com), which focus on the players, their bios, and up-and-coming projects; *The Hollywood Scriptwriter* (www.holly woodscriptwriter.com), another trade publication with an emphasis on feature films; and *The New York Screenwriter* (www.nyscreenwriter.com) for writers positioned near the East Coast market.

An important set of directories for Hollywood is *The Hollywood Creative Directory* (www.hcdonline.com). These directories contain regularly updated booklets: for producers, distribution, agents, and so on. They are invaluable when looking for sources to submit your screenplay to.

A quick computer search reveals many more publications that you may subscribe to, online and otherwise. I suggest subscribing to at least one trade paper and one magazine. You can follow the others as your budget allows. The updated information that you glean from them is invaluable.

Conferences and symposiums

Most metropolitan areas sponsor annual screenwriting conferences and symposiums. If your city doesn't, you can probably find one nearby. They range in price anywhere from $50 to $500, depending on who's attending and how long the forum lasts. Many are daylong or weekend events, but a few stretch into a week. What do these functions provide? Among other things, conferences offer

- ✔ A panel of established writers, directors, and studio executives
- ✔ Literary agents and script analysts
- ✔ Marketing tips and strategies
- ✔ Discounted books and software
- ✔ Possible contacts with other fledgling writers and established agencies

Longer symposiums may schedule workshops with writers or marketing gurus. Some may also have script analysts available to look over a synopsis or a treatment of your work (for an additional fee, of course.) You can find complete listings of conferences online as well as through advertisements in trade papers and Hollywood publications. Should one jump to your attention, do some research to see who might be attending. Surrounding yourself with professional or would-be professional writers may just be the jumpstart that you need.

Courses and Contests

Writing classes, workshops, and contests are other great ways to network. If you live near a university or an institution that provides adult or continuing education, inquire about creative-writing courses. Some courses require that you pay on the spot to reserve a space in the class, but others allow you to sit in on a class before you decide to join. Artistic workshops are also advertised in writing publications or at your local bookstores and/or library, so keep an eye out.

Workshops certainly aren't for everyone. Some writers fear that their ideas may be stolen by other participants, or that the criticism might affect their work. However, in addition to constant feedback, classes and workshops provide contacts with writers who may well make it in the industry. You might learn the process through example, and any support group has its emotional advantages.

You can also research contests online. New competitions sprout up every day. If you're considering this route, pay attention to the following items:

- **The submission request:** What kind of material do they want? Are they looking for full-length features, short films, or adaptations? Do they support work by any writer, or do they specialize in films written by minorities? In other words, do you fit the bill?

- **The cost:** Most contests have a nonrefundable submission cost. They're often less than $50, but watch out — some cost more.

- **The deadline date:** Most contests are annual, but some are biannual and even monthly. Also, deadlines change every year, so make sure that your information is current.

- **The award:** Some contests award cash prizes, some introduce you to Hollywood executives, and some offer winners a one-on-one meeting with agencies and script analysts. Know what you're getting into in advance.

- **Past award winners:** Some contests publicize any winners now working in the business. If the names sound familiar, it may be a good contest to enter.

Send a SASE (self-addressed stamped envelope) unless the contest rules specifically state that scripts will not be returned. You might as well get that copy back, and sometimes, the judges send written comments to the runners-up.

Contests are also listed in publications and periodicals. University callboards are another great source of information; local competitions may be posted there.

Setting personal expectations

Selling yourself as a writer is a big commitment that requires an immense amount of preparation, especially at the beginning. You can easily become overwhelmed with the sheer number of calls, records, and follow-up letters that fill up your week. Keeping a weekly list of goals is one way to manage the madness.

A typical weekly plan might include the following information:

- ✔ The dates of the week in question
- ✔ One primary goal for the week
- ✔ At least three secondary goals
- ✔ The amount of time you have available to tackle those goals
- ✔ A list of ways that you might achieve those goals
- ✔ A log of any phone calls, meetings, or follow-up responses
- ✔ A log of any information that you discover during the week
- ✔ A quick summation of how each week went, what you accomplished, and what still needs to be done

Weekly plans clarify and prioritize the tasks, so that you can manage them with greater ease. Better yet, you're putting those commitments in writing, which always makes them feel more official. You're making a silent but visible promise to continue forging ahead.

Polishing the Copy You Send Out

In Chapter 14, I mention the adage, "You never get another chance to make a first impression." If there was ever a time to take that phrase to heart, it's now, when you're considering sending work to producers and agents. Hollywood has thousands of writers, and many of them are newcomers. Organizations are looking for reasons to reject your script, and although a strong script's progress may not be hampered by one misspelling, why risk it?

A last-minute checklist

Agents and studios don't mind working with new writers, but they bolt at the thought of an amateur. If they see a clean, well-formatted script, they assume that the writing is strong. If the script looks messy and ill-prepared, they assume that the same holds true for the writer. The script's appearance is one thing that you have control over, so take the time you need to get it right.

Here are a few things to double-check before you submit work:

- **Spelling and grammatical errors:** If you're not strong in these areas, consider having a friend who is look over your script one last time.

- **Word usage:** Are you using the correct version of a word? For instance, "you're" or "your," "tale" or "tail," "desert" or "dessert," "meat" or "meet," "it's" or "its," and so on.

- **Margins:** Don't make margins smaller in an attempt to cram the story in. Keep the margins at the desired width (see Chapter 14).

- **Dangling names:** This happens when a name hangs at the bottom of the page, and the ensuing dialogue is floating on top of the next page. Space the text so that this doesn't occur.

- **All your writing is meant to be seen:** Make sure that your script contains no editorials or character thoughts hidden in the scene description.

- **Page numbers are accurate and in order:** Many producers give a script the "five-and-dime treatment," meaning that they read the first five pages and the last ten to assess the story. They're primarily looking for scripts that are between 90 and 120 pages. If your page numbers are incorrect, they may assume that your story is longer or shorter than it really is.

- **No missing pages:** You want your readers immersed in your story. Imagine their frustration if part of that story is missing.

- **No quote marks around dialogue:** Dialogue is only quoted in your treatment, never in a script. It has its own placement on the page that makes quotes unnecessary.

- **No camera angles:** Camera angles fall into the director and cinematographer's domains. They also clutter up your page and distract a reader from your story.

- **Scenes are not numbered:** A director will number your scenes later, in a shooting draft of the script. This is your story draft; numbers and technical notations quickly become distracting.

- **Font is 12-point Courier:** This is the standard screenwriting font utilized for timing purposes. In Courier, each page of script equates to around a minute of screen time.

- **No treatments or synopsis included unless requested:** If they've requested your script, send your script. You want them reading the whole story if possible, so don't send a synopsis or they're likely to read that instead.

✔ **Work is undated (unless registered with a copyright office):** It's always a good idea to offer the illusion that your story is a new one. If executives see that your script was written ten years ago, they may assume it has been rejected for ten years and will shy away from purchasing it themselves.

✔ **No use of bold print or italics:** Bold print tends to distract a reader, and italics are barely discernable in Courier. If you want to emphasize a certain line, write the scene that suggests that emphasis, or direct the reader with a line of description.

After you scan through the script twice yourself, I suggest handing the script off to at least two other people. One might read for form and spelling; the other for content. A distanced eye might catch what you've missed. Paying a script analyst to read your work is another option. In addition to proofreading, script analysts often provide commentary on the strength of your story and its components. Fees can range from $75 to $200 or more, but the feedback may be well worth the cost.

Front-page news

Your script's appearance should scream that it's professional and direct, and nothing conveys that more clearly than the title page. The number-one rule here is no cover art, please. Draw attention to your ability as a writer, not to an initial illustration. The title page includes your working title, centered and spaced one-fourth of the way down. Some writers put the title in quotes. Just below that, include your name. Put your contact information in the bottom-right corner. Include your address, phone number, and e-mail, if desired. Agencies should be able to reach you if they like your script. Scripts without return addresses are generally thrown out. If you have an agent, she'll include her information on the cover as well. Only date your work if you've registered it with the copyright office, and perhaps not even then. Dating your play, well, dates your play. No agency wants to read a seven-year-old script, so try not to alert them to its age. You needn't include anything else on the title page. Figure 18-1 shows a sample page.

Screenplays are printed on 8.5 x 11-inch (standard letter size) white paper, then three-hole punched and bound with 1¼ to 1½-inch brass brads. You can purchase both the paper and the brads at any local office supply store, and if you're planning on writing a lot, I suggest buying in bulk. Brads traditionally go through the top and bottom holes, leaving the middle hole empty. That's the current trend, but it's not a requirement. I suggest buying them in bulk because you'll bind every script this way. Choose a cover of some kind. I prefer the clear plastic covers, something to shield your work from the numerous hands that you hope it will pass through. Anything simple will do.

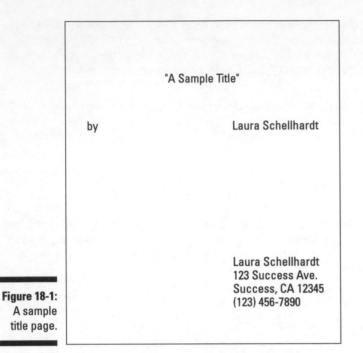

"A Sample Title"

by   Laura Schellhardt

Laura Schellhardt
123 Success Ave.
Success, CA 12345
(123) 456-7890

Figure 18-1:
A sample
title page.

Protecting Your Work

Eventually, after the script's been through readers, proofreaders, and revisions, you'll be ready to send it out. The only thing left to do beforehand is to register it. Bear in mind that you can't protect everything. Titles, names, short phrases, slogans, historical data, ideas, concepts, and anything within public domain are up for grabs. You can and should protect your polished draft, though. Here are a few ways to do it.

The Library of Congress

The current law states that works are automatically copyrighted from the moment of conception. In other words, you own the material as you write it. The following procedure then involves registering that copyright, or making it official. The traditional way to register works is with the U.S. Copyright office. To do so, you need only send a completed application, a $30 payment, and a non-returnable copy of your script to the following address:

The Library of Congress
Copyright Office
101 Independence Ave., SE
Washington, DC. 20559-6000

You may download an application from their Web site (`www.copyright.gov`), or you can call their offices, and they'll mail you a form. You'll receive a notice of registration after four to five months. Under the law, your work is protected from the moment that they receive your application to 70 years after your death. The law used to state that after you'd registered a work with the Library of Congress, you were required to place the copyright date on the script. That's no longer the case, although they still recommend it. Again, however, you may not want to alert studios to the age of your work.

The Writer's Guild of America

Most established writers register their work with the *Writer's Guild of America* (WGA). There are two Guild offices, one on the East Coast and one on the West. Writers living east of the Mississippi River register with the New York office, and writers living west of the river register in Los Angeles. The addresses of both offices are as follows:

The Writer's Guild of America, West
7000 West Third St.
Los Angeles, CA 90048
(323) 951-4000 (within S. California)
(800) 548-4532 (outside S. California)

The Writer's Guild of America, East
555 West 57th St., Suite 1230
New York, NY 10019
(212) 767-7800

The current registration fee is $20 for WGA West, and $22 for WGA East, but prices change annually, so be sure to check their Web site at `www.wga.org` for updated information. You can also register your script on-line by sending an e-mail with your credit card information and your script attachment. The WGA offers other services to nonmembers as well. In addition to holding your script for five years, the WGA will

✔ Register treatments, outlines, and a synopsis

✔ Provide a list of agencies that participate with the Guild

✔ Provide a script library open for perusal

✔ Arbitrate artistic disputes over credit and ownership

✔ Provide standard contracts if your script is optioned by a studio or producer who participates with the Guild

After five years' time, you may retrieve your work or register it again. If you choose only one method of registering your copyright, I recommend this one. The contacts and aid that the Guild provides are more than helpful, especially for beginning writers in search of representation.

The "poor-man's copyright"

Writers have used this method as an initial protection against theft. After you have a draft, either mail one to yourself or visit the post office and ask them to stamp and register it for you there. Whatever you do, don't break the seal once it's registered. The idea is that if you suspect that your work has been stolen, you have a script postmarked on the date that you completed the work. I don't recommend this method as your primary protection, but it certainly doesn't hurt. Because you officially copyright only polished or published works, you might try this method with a first or second draft.

Whatever you do, register your material in some fashion prior to sending work out. Although most of Hollywood is more interested in purchasing your story than stealing it, you can never be too careful.

Chapter 19

Getting Your Screenplay Noticed

● ●

In This Chapter

▶ Creating the package deal

▶ Pitching your script like a pro

▶ Finding an agent

▶ Approaching production companies

▶ Knowing what happens after you get their attention

● ●

Congratulations, you're ready to launch yourself into the industry. You have a polished script and a steadily growing contact log, and you're fairly market savvy. Now, all you need is what I call a "willing and able" — someone who's *willing* to read your script and *able* to generate work based on its prowess. This person may be an agent, a producer, a director, or a star — you don't know yet. But you're about to find out.

Steel yourself for a bumpy but enlightening ride. This part of the process involves risk and rejection. Behind every "yes" lies at least ten "nos," and not every "yes" will land you a job. However, you're also armed with a positive attitude and an unflagging determination, right? Make the promise to yourself now: You will do all that you can, and you will not give up.

Oh, and you can add information to that arsenal. This chapter helps you strengthen your marketing design and commercialize your product. It also guides you through the letters, phone calls, and meetings that stand between you and your "willing and able." Finally, this chapter also touches upon what to expect when (not if) you do sell a script.

Designing Your Own Package

A film's package includes anything and everything that makes it commercially (which means financially) attractive to agents, producers, and the audience. Some of these elements may be

- A high-concept story with low-budget needs.

- Any director or actors already attached to the project.

- Star potential. (Does the film have a great role for Tom Hanks or Julia Roberts?)

- Possible advertising spin-offs. (What products might it inspire?)

- Universal appeal.

- Current Hollywood interest. (Is there a buzz on the project?)

- A resemblance to other financially successful films.

The producer and the director usually assemble the package, but you should consider it as well. It will affect how you pitch your story to executives when you land a meeting, and if you can attach people to your project in advance, your story is more likely to sell right away. So consider whether you know of a specific director who might match the material. Perhaps you were writing with actors in mind — are they stars who would appeal to a mass audience? Can you come up with at least two other films that yours resembles? Answer these questions now before producers surprise you with them mid-meeting. The game of selling your story is about predicting what the buyers are after and convincing them that you can provide it. Knowing the package is a step in that direction.

Before you begin the process — and this is important — you must be clear on what is sacred in your script. By *sacred,* I mean what components of your story do you hope to protect above all? The characters? The theme? The outcome? Film is a collaborative medium, and during collaboration, your script will undoubtedly change. Directors will add shots as necessary, editors will condense sequences, and actors may request dialogue changes. The time may come, heaven forbid, when they even hire another writer to tweak the whole story. You're going to lose something along the way.

However, you can certainly highlight elements you want to preserve in your pitch, in your query letters, and in any synopsis you hand in. So know what's sacred now, and plan your marketing strategies accordingly.

Highlighting the universal

Agents and studio executives want the same thing — a writer with universal appeal. You need to convince them that you're just such a writer. What does that mean? It means that your work will sell to a mass audience. It entices the 20-year-old college student as well as her 50-year-old parents. It speaks to the human condition. Executives look for that ability in your sales pitch and in your spec script, should they decide to read it. So glance through the script before they do with the following thoughts in mind. Universal stories:

- Have a hero or heroes worth rooting for
- Provide a goal or a dream for the hero to pursue
- Evoke passions, such as fear, envy, joy, hatred, hope, awe, lust, and so on
- Include formidable obstacles and opponents
- Offer something familiar: a location, a theme, character relationships
- Suggest elements at risk or at stake

Pay particular attention to that last item. You're likely to be asked what's at stake in your film, and that answer may very well be the selling point. So what will be lost in your story if the protagonist doesn't succeed? It's most likely one or the following things:

- Someone's life (*Titanic*)
- Someone's reputation or integrity (*Unforgiven*)
- Another character's love or admiration (*When Harry Met Sally*)
- A sense of order or harmony (*Lord of the Rings*)
- An understanding of the world (*Nell*)
- Precious objects or information (*Raiders of the Lost Ark*)

Hopefully, your story combines several of these elements. They almost always ensure you an audience larger then one socio-economic group of people.

When you discover and record the universal elements, you can then summarize them in a catchy phrase or two. This phrase may later become your pitch. Is your film

- A coming of age story?
- A family reunion?
- A fight to preserve integrity, reputation, or personal freedom?
- A story of revenge or betrayal?
- A quest for redemption?
- A story of love in the face of hate?
- A triumph of human will and ingenuity?
- A "from rags to riches" adventure?

If these phrases sound like clichés, it's because they are. Most films fit into one of these categories, so they're incredibly familiar to audiences. Yet each grouping includes hundreds of stories that differ in tone, content, and scope. ***Billy Elliot*** and ***Back to the Future*** are both triumphs of the human spirit. ***West Side Story*** and ***Life is Beautiful*** both champion love in the face of hate. Your film isn't less unique if it falls into one of these groups; it's simply marketable.

Gaining the competitive edge

In order to push ahead of the competition, you have to concentrate your efforts on portions of the market that your work seems to match. I'm speaking both about the public market and the industry market here. Imagine the ideal audience for your script. What do you know about that person? How old is he? What stories excite him? Does he like small- or large-scale films? What has he seen or bought in the past? What hasn't he seen in a long time? Where do his values seem to lie? How should you approach him?

If you give the public something that it wants, it'll advertise your work. If you give a producer something that he wants, he'll buy your work. Either way, you win.

At the same time you're choosing a market for your work, consider the competition therein. Other writers want the same job; other writers pitch to that market. What makes you unique? Is it your professional background? Former police officers, federal agents, and journalists intrigue studio executives, for instance. These jobs require a person to track down people and stories, often from unlikely sources. So if you once held this kind of a position, executives assume that you can do the same on the page. Perhaps it's your cultural background. ***My Big Fat Greek Wedding*** is successful, in part, because the writer is able to poke fun at the Greek culture in an educated manner. Maybe it's who you know. Referrals are the number-one reason that new writers are read. Whatever it is, find something that distinguishes you from other writers in your market.

Another way to fine-tune your salesmanship is to imply both economical and emotional benefits. If your film has a great female role, make that a selling point. A great female role draws box-office revenue (an economical benefit for the company) and makes the film easier to market (an emotional benefit for the producer.) The same strategy applies when courting an agent. A positive attitude means that you'll be more likely to work in the industry (an economical benefit for the agency) and you'll be easier to work with in general (an emotional benefit for the agent.) If you advertise both qualities in yourself and the script, you're more likely to land the job.

Considering the reader

Very few agents or producers actually read the work that comes in. Most scripts are handed to professional readers who then type up a *coverage* (a brief synopsis and artistic evaluation) of the story and pass that up for consideration. If the story earns good coverage, the agent might skim the script or read the first ten pages.

You can't control everything about how the reader receives your script. The reader may be in a bad mood when she reads it, or despise screwball comedies, or be writing a script of her own based on a similar premise. You can't do anything about that. However, knowing what readers are trained to look for in a script can be helpful. If you know what might make good coverage, you can work on emphasizing those elements in advance. Figure 19-1 presents the first page of a standard coverage form.

Other examples vary in format, but they generally include the same information.

The reader follows the front page of the form that's shown in Figure 19-1 with a detailed synopsis of the story and a commentary on the overall content.

As a writer, your goal is to catch the reader's attention and give a him or her a favorable impression of the story. In order to do that, your *logline* — that all important one-line premise — should be exciting (or in this case gory), and the general elements of your story should be clear. You can see, though, that coverage forms like these are highly subjective. Readers are coached to put their personal preference aside, but this doesn't always happen. The response may hinge on a reader's taste in cinema. Nine times out of ten, the best and only defense is a strong script. The quality of the writing will then impress a reader who might not otherwise favor the genre.

Success Films
Coverage Sheet

Title: The Coverage Sheet

Author: Jane Doe

Time:1965

Location: Rhode Island

Genre: Drama/Coming-of-age

Form: Spec

Page: 110

Draft/ Date: 1-11-01

Represented by:

Submitted by

Submitted to: John Doe

Date Received: 2-2-02

Date Covered: 3-3-02

Log Line: a young and rather high-strung screenwriter rises to stardom by slaughtering the competition, literally.

Comment Summary: An edge-of-your-seat thriller with a surprising turn of events. There might be a story here if the writer spends more time on character and less on gory detail.

	Excellent	Good	Fair	Poor
Concept				
Characterization				
Dialogue				
Cinematic Structure				
Story Line				
Setting/ Prod Values				

Pass for Features _____   Consider for Features ___X___

Figure 19-1: The first page of a standard coverage form.

Preparing to Pitch

Pitching a script is an art form, and although it can be stressful, it's something every writer has to perfect before approaching executives or agents. So what is pitching exactly?

A *pitch* is an animated summation of a script with emphasis on the main characters, the conflict, and the genre. When pitching a script, you use this summation to persuade industry professionals to *option* the work (purchase it for consideration).

Pitches come in two forms: the two-minute pitch, also known as the *teaser,* and the *story pitch,* which is traditionally 10 to 20 minutes in length, though the shorter the better. You absolutely must have both types of pitches prepared *before* you contact industry personnel. You never know when you'll be called upon to sell your story or how you'll be asked to sell it.

The teaser pitch

The teaser pitch is a short pitch, and when I say short, I mean *short.* Traditionally, you get three sentences to hook listeners into the premise, the genre, and the scope of your film. When crafting this pitch, pay particular attention to what you think they might be listening for. Producers probably want to know the following details:

- ✔ How the film might be cast
- ✔ How much it will cost to make
- ✔ How they'll market it
- ✔ What films it resembles

If you follow those requests, your first sentence introduces the characters, the next sentence illustrates their conflict, and the final sentence leaves listeners wanting more. The conflict generally suggests the film's genre, but if not, consider alluding to that in the final sentence as well.

Here are some examples:

> Europe, 1912. Jack Dawson and Rose DeWitt Bukater enjoy a secret and passionate romance after they meet on a ship chartered toward New York. That ships happens to be the *Titanic.*

> Jessica Stein has met and refused virtually every man in New York City. Maybe it's time she looked for a woman. (***Kissing Jessica Stein***)

> Northern England, 1984. Young Billy Elliot, the son of a poor local miner, decides to start training for a career. In ballet. (***Billy Elliot***)

These examples suggest the skeleton of a short pitch. You might use them at the onset of a meeting to rope listeners into a more detailed explanation, or perhaps insert more details in between these sentences. In any case, practice your pitch at home with a stopwatch. Never exceed two minutes — try to do it in one, if you can. If you maintain the three to five page limitation, timing shouldn't be a problem; you'll finish in well under two minutes. If executives want to know more, they'll ask. Be animated, enthusiastic, and concise. Movie trailers are good examples of this kind of pitch; so are the blurbs on the back of video and DVD boxes. Some writers craft a teaser pitch for stories that they haven't written yet, in case they're asked what other material they're working on. It never hurts to have two or three teasers on hand, in case you're asked to do the same.

The story pitch

The story pitch is much longer than the teaser pitch, but try to keep it under ten minutes, if possible. People in the industry keep long and frantic hours, which naturally affects their attention spans. If you ramble on or get off-track, they're likely to start planning their next meeting before you're done. Some writers use note cards to help them through this pitch. That's perfectly acceptable, but don't rely on them. Reference the notes occasionally, but keep your focus up and on your listeners. If you practice pitching your story several times before the session, you should have it pretty well burned into your memory, so keeping your eyes on your listeners and off your notes won't be hard.

The story pitch follows the basic pattern of a *treatment* (see Chapter 18). You start with your hook or your logline, and then you run down the rest of the story. Be sure to illustrate those universal elements — the heroes, their goals, the conflict, what's at risk and why they're fighting to save it, any pivotal events or emotional turning points, and the conclusion.

Because you're giving a longer pitch, you have more chances to go astray. Here are a few things to avoid right away:

- ✔ Don't compare your film to others too much. It used to be common practice to depict a script through a combination of two existing films. (It's **When Harry Met Sally** in **Waterworld,** or it's **Goonies** meets **The Field of Dreams.**) Know what your film shares with others, but keep the comparisons brief.

- ✔ Don't ever compare your script to box-office disasters. No one wants to make another **Ishtar.**

- ✔ Avoid listing action in chronological order — tell them a story instead.

- ✔ Avoid depicting too many subplots or details. Concentrate on two or three characters and pivotal events, or the pitch will quickly become convoluted.

- ✔ Don't keep pitching if they express disinterest, and (on the bright side) don't keep pitching after they agree to consider it.

✔ Don't mention actors that you have in mind. Describe the characters, so that your listeners will envision them.

✔ Never lie about the story or its hype. Producers discover false information quickly.

As with any sale, personality is paramount. If you're enthusiastic, they will be, too. If you're charming and witty, they'll remember you even if they can't accept the script. And never express desperation. There's always some other way to generate interest. Pitching scares some writers to death. If you're one of those frightened few, do something about it. Acting classes are a great way to build confidence in your presentation, as are courses in public speaking. Or, if you'd rather, practice in front of friends and family. See whether they'd want to purchase the script based on your description.

After you've typed up both pitches and are comfortable delivering them, you're ready to search for an agent and/or a producer.

Finding an Agent

You've heard the contradiction: You can't find work without an agent, and you can't find an agent until you've worked. There's a grain of truth here. Unsolicited writers do have a hard time finding representation. It takes careful planning, meticulous organization, and luck — lots and lots of luck.

An *unsolicited* writer is one who doesn't yet have representation. Many studios and agents refuse to look at unsolicited work, fearing that it hasn't been through an initial screening process. As soon as you sell a script or find an agent, that dubious title disappears.

So how does one go about finding an agent in the first place? The following list gives the four primary ways to track agencies down:

✔ **Your personal contacts:** Call anyone on your contact list who works in the business. Tell them about the script (maybe use that teaser pitch?) and ask if they're willing to read the script, or if they know any agencies that might. If they enjoy the piece, they might refer it themselves. At the very least, you can use that person's name to help pave the way at whatever agency they recommend. Never underestimate the power of a referral.

✔ **The WGA:** For a nominal fee, the Writer's Guild of America (www.wga.org) can provide a list of agencies that work with them. They can also tell you who represents writers you admire, although they limit you to three answers per phone call. So make a list of movies that you adore, keep track of those writers, and find out who's making their careers possible. If your work is similar, an agent might be more apt to pick you and your story up.

✔ **Trade papers:** If a deal's being made, *Daily Variety* or *The Hollywood Reporter* will announce it. They usually highlight the script that was bought, who wrote it, and who picked it up. If the agency's large enough, they might name the agent. If not, you have the writer's name, so get on the phone and find out who represents him or her.

✔ **Reference books:** Several reference books list literary agents and script analysts. *The Writer's Guide to Hollywood Producers, Directors & Screenwriter's Agents* is one of the most well known, but new ones crop up every year. Purchase one of these books only after trying one of the other methods, or as a supplement.

Scour through the resulting list of potential "hits." Highlight any agency that represents artists you admire, any you've heard good things about (or simply heard of), and a few smaller to midsize agencies as well. Don't bother prioritizing them. Writers never contact just one agent at a time; they'd be 90 years old before they made a sale. You're going to approach them all at once.

Approaching an Agent

Before pounding on doors, polishing off letters, or picking up the phone, you may be interested to know what an agent's looking for, and what you should be looking for in an agent.

An agent wants

✔ **Someone whose work they can sell.** Typically, agents make 10 percent of whatever sale or option they negotiate. If your works seems particularly marketable, they'll be more likely to take you on.

✔ **Someone who understands the business.** Yes, an agent's job is to find work for you. However, your work won't end when an agent accepts you. Most writers continue to hunt down work for themselves even after they find representation. So, if you're willing to work, your agent will be, too.

✔ **Someone pursuing a career.** Agents know that markets are fickle and that selling a script sometimes takes a long time. They need writers who will keep producing despite the dry spells. They need writers who are passionate about the craft and determined to maintain a career.

✔ **Someone who won't make his or her job more difficult.** Attitude is everything. If you seem like a high-maintenance writer who requires daily calls and compliments, agents will pass on your work regardless of its potential.

Take these items as silent requests on the part of each agent you approach. Try to be an agent's ideal writer. Doing so can separate you from hundreds of other less savvy petitioners.

On the flip side, you want

 ✔ **Someone who enjoys your work.** An agent may hate your work but recognize selling potential. If he or she is willing to take you on for that reason, so be it. However, you may find it difficult to accept criticism or support from someone who's uncomfortable with what you produce. On the other hand, if your agent's enthusiastic about a piece, that enthusiasm will wear off on whomever they call about purchasing it.

 ✔ **Someone influential.** It helps immensely if your agent has connections all over the business. If they can't reach producers directly, they should know someone who *can* reach them. Don't shy away from small agencies because you fear that they lack contacts. New agents have often worked for the most powerful people in the business.

 ✔ **Someone committed.** You want an agent dedicated to getting you work or selling your scripts. It helps if this commitment arises from interest in your writing and not simply financial gain, but really, either one will do just fine.

 ✔ **Someone professional.** If you gain representation, you should expect to hear from your agent once or twice a week while he's finding you work, and at least once a month while you're on a project. You should be updated on what's being done to help your career and what the response has been so far. He should also return your phone calls within 48 hours or have a secretary tell you when to expect a call. If your agent can't or doesn't provide this service, you may need to look for more-professional representation.

Let me say in advance that you don't need to have an agent to sell a script. You have at least three other ways to get your script through the Hollywood maze (sending the script yourself to independent producers, actors, or directors), and I detail those options later in this chapter. So don't despair if finding an agent doesn't work out in the first round. However, you go through the same process with anyone you approach, so make sure that you know what's required for agencies before you try someone else.

The query letter

Most writers approach agents through a query letter. You can also call or drop into an agency unannounced, but you'll be saying pretty much the same thing that you'd include in a letter.

A *query* is a pitch in letter form. It's your attempt to convince a producer, agent, or star to take a look at your work or meet you in person.

Never submit a script without a request to do so. Agents and other executives will simply return it unopened or recycle it altogether. You can't afford to lose all those scripts. Send a query first.

Taking your first step

First, call the agency and find out who to address the query to. Always be polite. The secretary can often get you in the door faster than the letter itself, and you never know — today's secretary may be tomorrow's agent. So be nice, explain what you need, and thank him or her profusely.

Putting the letter together

Now, construct the letter. Queries are no more than one page in length. Longer letters won't be read. Use plain white paper — no fancy letterhead, please. Single-space within each paragraph and double-space between them. Your layout should be clean, clear, and concise. You may remember from high school the mind-numbing effect that long blocks of uninterrupted prose can have on a reader.

On the top right-hand side of the page, type the date, the agent's name, the agency, and its address. Double-check the spelling of any name before you send the letter. The man you're calling "John Smith" might really be "Jon Smyth." If you spell an agent's name wrong, you're just asking him to not read your work.

Queries usually consist of three paragraphs. The first one may alter slightly, depending on who you're writing to; the second and third remain the same. In the first paragraph, introduce yourself and mention why you're writing. The first paragraph is where you should include any of the following information:

- A personal reference or mutual friend
- Writing programs or educational institutions you're affiliated with
- Previous work as a playwright or as a reporter, on television or radio (basically, past writing experience)
- Any contests you've placed in or writing awards you've received
- A compliment on one of the agent's deals or on a writer he or she represents (only include this if it is sincere)

The second paragraph introduces the title of the screenplay you're pitching and your teaser. Be sure to emphasize the hook, your protagonists, the conflict, and the genre in this section.

The third paragraph lets the person know how he can contact you should he wish to read the script or see other examples of your work. Let him how you want him to respond — if, for example, you've sent an SASE or a stamped postcard, tell him that here. If you don't live near the West Coast, you might tell the agent that you're also interested in assignments and would be happy to travel as necessary.

Write "Sincerely" or however you prefer to sign off a business letter, sign your name, and print it below.

You may rearrange the order in which you provide this information, but I suggest starting with the three-paragraph method. It organizes your pitch and naturally restricts the length of correspondence.

You want to pitch the strong points of your package in a query. If your script has a great concept or hook, begin with that. If you were referred by someone with clout, by all means, say that up front. Agents are most interested in the work and in any detail that suggests you'd be someone they could generate work for. Give them what they want.

A sample query

Here's a generic version of what you might send to an agency. *Don't* send a script or an outline with this letter. Wait for someone to express interest.

> 2/2/02
>
> Ms. Successful Agent
> Success Agency
> 1234 Lucky Ave.
> Prosperous Springs, CA 12345
>
> Dear Ms. Agent,
>
> I am currently seeking representation for my original film script, **Luck of the Draw.** The script won the New Screenplay Contest in Grandstand, New York, last year, and it has received two awards since then. The story originated during my stint as a journalist for the *Grandstand Times.*
>
> In **Luck of the Draw,** energetic young reporter, Ace Dobson, finds evidence linking a prominent New Yorker to a string of bank robberies. It's a first-time journalist's dream come true, except for one minor detail. The thief in question happens to be his father, and his boss. **Luck of the Draw** is a compelling look at one man's struggle to choose between family loyalty and justice.
>
> I'd like to send the complete script for your review. I've enclosed a postcard for your reply, or you may call me at (123) 456-7890. Thank you for your time and consideration.
>
> Sincerely,
>
> (your signature here)
>
> Jane Doe

Sending the letter

Try to send out letters so that they'll arrive Tuesday through Thursday. Very few agents have time at the beginning or end of the week to look at new queries. Wait at least a week before your follow-up phone call. When you do phone, politely ask to speak with the agent. If the secretary asks what it's about, let him know that you want to make sure that the letter arrived and ask if you should send a script. More often than not, you'll hear that the agency doesn't accept unsolicited work. If your salesmanship can't bypass this answer, don't fret. Tell them that you may try back again in a few months, thank them for their time, and move on to the next call.

Query aftermath: What to expect

The best news that you can get is a "Yes, send me a copy of the screenplay, please." If and when that occurs, type up a brief cover letter reminding the agent of the phone call or the written response, and include it with your script. Be sure to send an SASE (self-addressed stamped envelope) or a postcard with the script as well. Follow up in a few days to make sure that the package arrived, and wait at least a month to call again. You'll have other projects to keep you busy in the interim.

At the beginning, you're likely to receive three responses:

- ✔ The query is returned unopened.
- ✔ The query is rejected.
- ✔ You receive no correspondence at all.

As disheartening as these reactions are, try not to let it affect your work or your determination to succeed. Every writer goes through this at one point in his or her career. And remember that agents aren't the only way to sell a script in Hollywood. You have other options, which I discuss in the section, "Pitching Your Script without an Agent," later in this chapter.

The "cold call" and the "drop in"

For those of you who are slightly more direct and/or brave, you may want to try calling an agency directly or dropping by. This approach saves time and money on postage, but it's also more nerve-wracking. After all, you have infinite time to compose and edit a letter. When you're talking to someone directly, you have one shot to get it right.

Cold calls work in much the same way as a letter does. Ask for the agent directly; tell the secretary what the call is about. If he says that the agent is too busy to speak to you now (which is probably true), ask if there's a better time to call back. He might let you leave contact information. If he says that they don't accept unsolicited work, tell him what the work is about and ask if there's any place he might suggest calling instead. You never know what's going to work. Whatever the outcome, be courteous and kind.

If you do get an agent on the phone, go through the steps of a query letter. Tell them who you are, pitch the film, and ask the agent's permission to send it. If the agent asks where you're located, be sure to emphasize that you'd be happy to travel as necessary. If the agent says that she's not interested, ask if she'd like to hear about the other film you're writing (if you have one). If she refuses the script, ask for suggestions on where else to send it and then thank her for her time. Do you see that pattern here? Always thank agents for their time. You may be calling them again later.

You're less likely to get a response by dropping by an agency, but then again, you never know. Several writers have convinced someone to at least glance at their script simply because they had it with them. Others have received permission to send a query letter. As long as you're not embarrassing yourself or anyone else, it's certainly worth a shot.

Pitching Your Script without an Agent

Waiting to hear from an agent doesn't mean that your career is on hold. Quite the contrary, querying an agent is just the beginning. Many scripts are sold without representation, so you should also be pursuing at least one of the following options:

- **Independent producers (Indies):** Independent producers either run small companies of their own, work for larger studios on a project to project basis, or are able to find financial backers for projects that they option.

- **Actors or directors:** These individuals may read a script and shop it around for you, or they may have production companies of their own.

- **Private financiers:** This group includes grant committees, state commission departments, film festivals, and wealthy individuals who are willing to finance a film.

Executives in these groups are more likely to consider unsolicited scripts, though referrals never hurt. The primary difference between them lies in what they're after. Producers are looking for films to boost their production companies or writers who match projects they have in mind. Actors and directors want scripts that will boost their careers or that offer an exciting change of pace. Private financiers are looking for worthwhile projects and sound investments. Note these different needs in advance and plan your marketing strategies accordingly.

Here's what you need to pitch on your own:

- At least one polished feature-length script, preferably two or three.

- A teaser or story pitch for any script you have. You'll want copies of these taped to your phone in case you receive an impromptu call.

- Your nutshell synopsis (See Chapter 5), and a detailed treatment (Chapter 18). You may be asked to submit them in place of a script.

- A query letter tailored to the individual buyer. Mention other work the production company has done, and make sure that actors and directors know that you believe the project is well suited to their talents. This technique may feel phony, but you're approaching them for a reason. Let them know what it is.

- A standard release form that you feel comfortable signing.

What's a release form? Industry executives are wary of unsolicited material, in part, because they fear lawsuits. If you submit material and their company produces something later with a similar theme, you could sue them for theft. A release form, or a "submission agreement," absolves them of responsibility should such a scenario occur. It's not the best agreement for a writer. If you sign an agreement and they do steal your work, there may be little you can do. However, few studios will even look at your work without a release, so more often than not, you'll have to comply. Most executives will accept a standard form that you draw up with an entertainment attorney. Some may try to take advantage of you, though not usually.

Avoid signing anything that asks you to agree on a selling price before they agree to purchase the script. In fact, avoid signing anything without consulting an attorney. The pain it may save you later is well worth the cost of consultation.

After your paperwork's in order, you approach these backers in the same way that you approach an agent:

- Call or send a query letter.

- Send the script, outline, or synopsis when they request it.

- Make follow-up calls to make sure that your letter/script arrived, and after a month, call for a progress report.

- Send a written thank-you note to anyone who agrees to read your work.

Your script will probably go to a reader for coverage. If the backers want to meet you, you'll receive a call. If they can't use your material at the moment, you may or may not receive word back. Remember to still write during this process. Writing helps the wait and produces more material to shop around. Don't let rejection affect your work.

What to Do When They Say Yes

If you're persistent enough and continue honing your craft, eventually, you'll land a meeting with someone. Arrange a time with that person's secretary, thank him or her again, and celebrate. You're one step closer to a career in film. Meetings with agents vary slightly from meetings with executives. After all, these individuals want different things. Luckily, you'll be prepared for both.

Meeting with an agent

If an agent agrees to meet with you, she's already interested in something. It may be your current script, it may be your writing potential, and it may be something in your query letter. Either way, she'll need more information before signing you up. Be prepared to discuss the following items:

- ✔ What else you're working on. You should have one or two more pitches ready when this comes up.

- ✔ What genres or markets interest you the most. Are you drawn to thrillers or romantic comedies? Would you be interested in writing for sitcoms or cable television? Is there anything you're uncomfortable writing?

- ✔ Your willingness to relocate. You certainly don't have to move to L.A. to write, but an agent will ask. If you're willing to relocate for the perfect job, tell them that. If not, make sure that they know you'd be happy to commute.

- ✔ Your career potential. Why are you writing? How long have you been at it? What are your personal career goals and why? Who else do you know, and what is your business experience thus far?

- ✔ How well do you pitch? (You probably demonstrated this ability already, but you may be asked to do it again.)

- ✔ Are you willing to accept writing assignments?

If you're lucky, the agent will also mention a contract. Most agents receive 10 percent of any sale they negotiate, and contracts are usually binding for at least 90 days. If your agent doesn't find you anything after 90 days, you can leave, although you'll probably want to give them more time than that at the beginning. If your agent is affiliated with the WGA, you'll receive a standard contact of some sort. If not, it never hurts to run the contract by an attorney.

Even though the desire to secure representation is overwhelming, never feel that you *have* to sign with an agency. You should make inquiries during this meeting as well. Two things that you might ask are:

✔ Who else does the agent represent? What sales is she most proud of?

✔ What does the agent think of your work? (Don't be alarmed if she offers constructive criticism. She may be right.)

Always be honest. If your script has not generated any interest, that's fine. Tell the agent that you've just begun shopping it around. Let her know immediately where else you've submitted the work. Doing so saves her the embarrassment of pitching it to a studio that may have rejected it in the past. The agent will understand if you're unable to relocate or if you're hesitant about certain projects, although I wouldn't emphasize the negative. You're looking for someone you're comfortable with. The agent's looking for an enthusiastic and prolific new writer. Make sure that you both win in the deal.

Meeting with executives

You might find yourself pitching to producers for three reasons:

✔ Someone (probably a reader) read your work and recommended a meeting.

✔ The query letter or script teaser caught their attention. They may or may not want to discuss the script, but something interests them about your work.

✔ Your agent submitted a spec script, and though they rejected the piece, they're interested in you as a rising talent.

These meetings are nerve-wracking, especially because more than one person may be involved. Dress comfortably, but look professional. You don't need to worry about wearing a fancy dress or even a business suit if doing so makes you feel out of place, but choose something with clean lines — nothing frumpy. On a first meeting, I'd avoid jeans and a T-shirt, for instance, and opt instead for a skirt, dress pants, or khakis and a nice shirt or sweater.

Arrive at least 15 minutes early and sign in with the secretary. Let her know you have an appointment, but it's not for another ten minutes or so (in other words, let HER know you're early). Be kind to whomever you meet out front; these people work hard and are often executives in training. Eventually, someone will lead you into the room.

The first portion of the meeting will most likely involve informal chit-chat. Keep your energy up and try to relax. Inquire after a project you know they're working on or mention an interesting object in the room. If they ask you about yourself, be careful. They're not looking for your biography or even a short summation of your work thus far. They're just breaking the ice. Tell them something interesting, possibly make a joke, and keep what ever you say brief.

Eventually, they'll ask what projects you're working on. Pitch an idea; if possible, pitch two or three. If they like one of these ideas, they may offer you a deal to develop material. If not, they're most likely interested in your creative ability. Ask if they're looking for any projects in particular and listen carefully to what they suggest. They probably have a writing assignment open. They may ask you to come up with a pitch for one of their ideas. Be aware that you aren't the only writer they've asked. Eventually, they'll sift through all the results and assign one writer to the project. However, the fact that they've even extended a request is a step in the right direction.

When the meeting is over, they'll thank you and say that they'll be in touch. Maybe you've landed a job, maybe not. Either way, send a thank-you note and congratulate yourself. You're moving up.

Looking Ahead: Upon Achieving Success

Success always has two parts — the financial and the personal. Your financial success will be based on acquiring one of the following deals:

- ✔ **The sale of a spec script.** This deal is rare, but fantastic when it occurs. If you have an agent, she'll contact as many potential buyers as she can. The ensuing auction may mean a six-figure check, more if your script is produced. Again, this event is rare, but you can always dream!

- ✔ **A development deal.** This deal occurs when a studio or producer likes a pitch and hires you to develop it. It might be a pitch you brought in or one they asked you to design. You agree on a purchase price and are paid in installments.

- ✔ **An option.** Here, the producer or studio options the rights to a script for a smaller sum and maintains them for a specified length of time. During that time, the producer or studio attempts to attach talent to the project and generate a buzz. At the end of the time, the producer or studio will either purchase the script or pass on the deal altogether.

- ✔ **Staff position.** This option is for writers interested in television. If a producer likes your work, he may hire you for the writing staff of a new show. This is steady pay, but the hours are long, and you have to relocate if you're not a California local. This position may or may not help your film career.

Should you be offered any of these deals, your agent will handle the contract negotiations. If you don't have an agent at the time, you can try to use the interest in your script to secure one. Otherwise, negotiate the contract through an entertainment attorney.

The Hollywood market is all about highs and lows, ups and downs. One moment, you'll be in a meeting, pitching like a pro; the next minute, you're back to sending query letters and collecting rejections. Yet throughout the roller coaster ride, one thing remains constant: You're still writing, which leads me to the second definition of success — artistic success. Because I consider your artistic success more important than financial success, I've crafted it into a final note to send you off.

A Final Note

If I have one final message for you, it's this: Writing is an ancient art form and a noble profession. When people ask what you do for a living, practice saying, "I'm an artist," and leave it at that. Take pride in what you do. Write for reasons unconnected with development deals, options, or beach-front property. Write because you love the process. Write because there are things that you want to know. Write because you can't imagine life without writing. If you maintain this passion for the craft, the rest will fall into place.

Part V
The Part of Tens

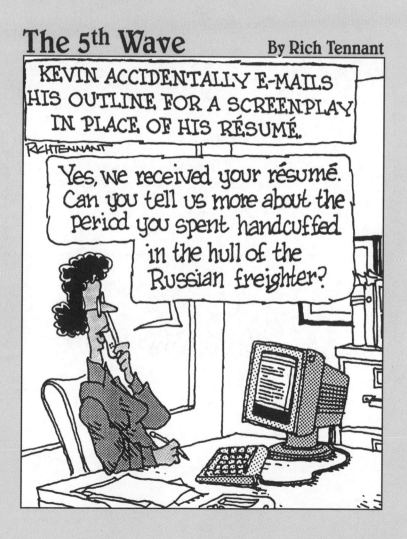

In this part . . .

So who's writing all these great scripts? Who has been doing it for years and who, like yourself, is up-and-coming? This part is a sampler of sorts. It details a few writers to watch, a few scripts to read, and a few screenwriting myths you may encounter and feel free to ignore.

Chapter 20

Ten Screenwriters You Should Know

So who's behind all this writing for Hollywood? That's a good question — and one that's rarely asked outside the confines of studios. By the time a film comes out, the all-star cast is usually what's drawing the crowds, or perhaps the director's reputation is causing a stir. It might also be the film's premise, but ask movie-goers who came up with that premise. They're likely to cite the director or simply shake their heads and admit defeat. You can't really fault them for not knowing who wrote the epic adventure, piercing drama, or romantic comedy they're about to enjoy. Hollywood is an actor-centric industry. Writers own their script up until the sale, at which point it becomes a vehicle for celebrities. The story becomes one small part of a package deal. Most writers spend their whole careers in general anonymity. And yet, without writers, where would we be?

This section celebrates ten of those artists and the words they've brought to the screen. I've chosen these ten writers because, together, they present an eclectic and diverse body of work. Some of them adapt fiction, some dabble in sci-fi, some in comedy, and many of them work in several genres. I also chose writers who arrived in Hollywood via different paths. Two sold spec scripts immediately, one worked in television first, another began onstage. Some of these writers have been in the industry for years, and some are up-and-comers. I tried to provide as wide a range of expertise as possible. So here's the question: You've probably seen their work, but do you know their names?

William Goldman

Occupations: screenwriter, novelist

Industry credits:

- *Masquerade* (1965)
- *Harper* (1966)
- *Butch Cassidy and the Sundance Kid* (1969)
- *The Hot Rock* (1972)
- *The Stepford Wives* (1975)
- *The Great Waldo Pepper* (1975)
- *All the President's Men* (1976)
- *The Princess Bride* (1987)
- *Misery* (1990)
- *Chaplin* (1992)
- *Maverick* (1994)
- *The General's Daughter*(1999)
- *Jurassic Park III* (2001)
- *Hearts In Atlantis* (2001)
- And many more . . .

William Goldman is a virtual icon in the screenwriting world. Born in Chicago, Illinois, in 1931, he spent much of his childhood watching movies in the Alcyon. This theater and his experiences therein may well have sparked his interest in storytelling. He started writing novels after the war, the second of which he adapted into a screenplay (*Soldier in the Rain*). Shortly thereafter, he wrote *Butch Cassidy and the Sundance Kid.* It won him an Oscar, a Golden Globe, and a WGA screen award. It also launched his career in film.

Over the years, Goldman has worked steadily with various studios and stars. He's known for his gift of dialogue, his tendency to approach difficult subjects with humor and humorous subjects with depth, and the ability to craft multifaceted characters in fast-paced plots. He's increasingly excited by the advances in film technology. He believes that now screenwriters will be able to see a finished product that may match the one in their heads. He also encourages any new writer to study his or her craft. All people want is a well-told story, but there are fewer and fewer storytellers around. He suspects that many new writers become frustrated too easily, and he wants to rid them of the notion that professional screenwriters have some secret stash of information or technique. "They don't," he says. "We're all just tearing our hair out together."

Ruth Prawer Jhabvala

Occupations: screenwriter, novelist

Industry credits:

- *The Householder* (1960)
- *Bombay Talkie* (1970)
- *Autobiography of a Princess* (1975)
- *A Room With a View* (1985)
- *Slaves of New York* (1989)
- *Mr. and Mrs. Bridge* (1990)
- *Howards End* (1992)
- *The Remains of the Day* (1993)
- And many more . . .

Ruth Prawer Jhabvala (pronounced JAHB'-va-la) has been writing for more than 50 years, and her life reads very much like one of her Merchant-Ivory collaborations. Born in Berlin, Germany, in 1923, Jhabvala immigrated to England where she entered school and eventually received a degree in English Literature from London University. She moved to India in 1951 with her husband, and there, her writing career began. Like William Goldman, she started writing novels, and her work eventually caught the attention of producer Ismail Merchant and director James Ivory. They asked her to adapt her novel *The Householder* for the screen, and the collaboration of a lifetime began. Since that time, the three have produced more than a dozen films, with two of them receiving screenwriting Oscars (*A Room With a View, Howards End*) and one of them earning a nomination (*The Remains of the Day*). Not bad for a woman who wasn't particularly interested in film.

Jhabvala suggests writing fiction as a precursor to film. She believes that you can discover a lot by spending concentrated time on a project by yourself, and fiction writing demands that prolonged solitude. When adapting novels, she reads the source two or three times, writing a general synopsis of each scene. Then, she pushes the work aside and writes a first draft from those notes. Her scripts lack direction as a rule — she thinks that too much direction hampers actors and directors who need that room to maneuver. Instead, she fills her work with rich prose that's full of possibility. She encourages writers to select projects that impress them or touch them in some way and to never select a project simply for financial gain. She believes that if you're true to the work and to yourself, you'll inspire the same sentiment in others.

Alan Ball

Occupations: screenwriter, actor, writer, producer

Industry credits:

Television:

- ✔ *Oh Grow Up*
- ✔ *Cybill*
- ✔ *Grace Under Fire*
- ✔ *Six Feet Under*

Film:

- ✔ *American Beauty* (1999)

Alan Ball may be one of the few writers on his way to becoming a household name. His film, *American Beauty,* swept the Oscars in 1999, earning him the award for Best Original Screenplay, after which many critics called him the new rising talent in Hollywood. Yet, truth be told, Ball is anything but new to the world of writing. He began his career as a noted New York playwright, a profession that helped sharpen his craft but ill-prepared him for the actor-driven world of television. His four years as a sitcom writer and producer were frustrating. As a playwright, he was encouraged to maintain a firm enthusiasm and connection to his work. As a sitcom writer, the opposite seemed true. Most of what he wrote was altered or rewritten entirely before being taped, and Ball discovered that he had to detach himself from the writing more often than not — a difficult task for a writer with such grand vision.

Ultimately, though, that frustration became the foundation for *American Beauty.* The film, which follows a man struggling to change his mundane life, is a piercing look at what it means to be spiritually awake. Its tenor, at once nihilistic, romantic, and exceedingly funny, seems to pervade much of Ball's writing, including his new HBO series, *Six Feet Under,* which is about a family that runs a funeral home. Although he does extensive research prior to writing each project, Ball calls himself an instinctive writer, rarely mapping projects out in advance. He trusts his instincts to get him to the next event.

Nora Ephron

Occupations: screenwriter, director, producer, novelist

Industry credits:

- *Silkwood* (1983)
- *Heartburn* (1986)
- *When Harry Met Sally* (1989)
- *This Is My Life* (1992)
- *Sleepless in Seattle* (1993)
- *Michael* (1997)
- *You've Got Mail* (1998)
- *Hanging Up* (2000)
- And many more . . .

Nora Ephron's professional resume scrolls well past the page that most screenwriters are encouraged to maintain. Film credits aside, Ephron is also a successful novelist and essay writer, who penned *Heartburn, Crazy Salad,* and *Scribble Scribble* prior to becoming a successful screenwriter. Her prolific bent makes sense, however, when you consider her upbringing. Ephron is the child of screenwriting team Phoebe and Henry Ephron, noted for scripts like *There's No Business Like Show Business,* and *Desk Set.* Her childhood included many bouts of verbal repartee, and one of her sisters has compared family dinners to "the Algonquin Round Table."

Ephron quickly determined to become a writer, though she originally sought work as a reporter. After graduating from Wellesley with a journalism degree, she went on to write for the *New York Post, Esquire,* and the *New York Times Magazine.* So when did the screenwriting bug kick in? Her first movie assignment was *Silkwood.* It was nominated for an Oscar, and the rest, as they say, is history — or herstory as the case may be. Twenty years later, Ephron is one of the few women *always* working in Hollywood. In several interviews, she speaks very candidly about the industry. She notes that good books are generally published, but much of what is written in Hollywood goes unproduced. Her advice? Keep writing. Don't worry about the final product or if there's even going to be one. Just keep writing.

John Logan

Occupations: screenwriter, playwright, executive producer, teacher

Industry credits:

- *Tornado* (1996)
- *RKO 281* (1999)
- *Bats* (1999)

- *Any Given Sunday* (2000)
- *Gladiator* (2001)
- *Time Machine* (2002)
- *Star Trek: Nemesis* (2002)
- *The Last Samurai* (2003)

John Logan doesn't live in Hollywood; he lives in Chicago. But these days, he travels quite a bit. Although he entered Northwestern University to pursue acting, he left school very much a writer. While at NU, his play *Never the Sinner* won the Agnes Nixon Playwriting Festival and later received a production in Chicago. He stuck with that script, rewriting and removing characters between other projects, and 13 years later, it went on to win the New York Outer Critics Circle award for an off-Broadway play. That same dogged determination won him an Oscar nomination for the HBO film **RKO 281,** the story of the making of **Citizen Kane.** It's release was the result of seven years of research on Logan's part. He received his second Oscar nod for **Gladiator,** a film that he cowrote with David Franzoni and William Nicholson. Since that time, he's had his pick of projects. **Star Trek: Nemesis,** for instance, was a "dream come true" for Logan, who's been a self-proclaimed Trekkie since he was a boy.

One of John Logan's most inspiring qualities (if you have to select one), is his unwavering passion for his craft. He advocates a fierce regimen of reading, writing, and being "multitentacled" (as he puts it), or having a hand in as many pockets of history as possible. And does he practice what he preaches? Absolutely. His writing routine includes rising at 6 a.m. and working well through the day, stopping only to eat, sleep, and to walk the dogs occasionally. When crafting a first draft, Logan commits to "total immersion." He researches the era, reads literature, and listens to music of the time; he looks at the story from every angle. He tends to juggle several projects at once, although each one is in a different stage of development, and without fail, he finds something to celebrate in each one. It's difficult, if not impossible, to speak with John Logan and leave uninspired. He's the perfect salesman for the screenwriting craft — because he means what he says.

Amy Holden Jones

Occupations: screenwriter, director, documentary filmmaker

Industry credits:

- *Slumber Party Massacre* (1982)
- *Love Letters* (1984)
- *Maid to Order* (1987)

✔ *Mystic Pizza* (1988)

✔ *Beethoven* (1992)

✔ *Indecent Proposal* (1993)

✔ *The Rich Man's Wife* (1996)

✔ *The Relic* (1997)

Amy Holden Jones had no intention of becoming a screenwriter. A director, maybe, but not a writer. She graduated with an art history degree from Wellesley College, went on to study still photography at MIT, and branched into documentaries. However, her writing was what brought her acclaim. Her short film, "A Weekend Home," won the Western National Student Film Award, which was one of the country's largest festivals at the time. Martin Scorsese was one of the judges. She wrote to him later, and he offered her a job as his assistant on *Taxi Driver.* From there, she was able to rewrite and direct *Slumber Party Massacre,* which was enough of a surprise hit to gain her attention from the film community. Yet she still wanted to direct, and found herself writing vehicles that would allow her to do so. That goal changed after the success of *Mystic Pizza.* Jones decided that she was more successful when she wrote scripts for other directors and big-name stars. And that's what she proceeded to do with *Indecent Proposal.* Since that time, she's worked regularly on assignment, as both a writer and an editor. She occasionally directs.

Her advice to screenwriters? Hone your marketing strategies. If you're writing for a studio, expect your work to change. Remember that it's a collaborative effort; other people help make that script work as a film. The trick is finding a way to fit your vision into the new ideas. She also encourages writers to take acting classes. An actor's approach to a character isn't so different from a writer's.

M. Night Shyamalan

Occupations: screenwriter, director, producer, actor

Industry credits:

✔ *Praying With Anger* (1992)

✔ *Wide Awake* (1998)

✔ *Stuart Little* (1999)

✔ *The Sixth Sense* (1999)

✔ *Unbreakable* (2000)

✔ *Signs* (2002)

M. Night Shyamalan's dreams of becoming a filmmaker began at the age of 8, when he was given his first super 8 camera. By the time that he was 17, he'd made 45 home movies. All this from a man who was supposed to be a doctor. Both Shyamalan's parents are doctors, as are 12 of his aunts and uncles. He might have been a medical student at Penn State, but at the last minute, he applied to New York University's Tisch School for the arts in filmmaking. Thank goodness he did.

Shyamalan's passion for the screenwriting craft is apparent in every interview and in every project he takes on. He selects projects with which he feels an emotional and spiritual connection, even on assignment. He asks his agents to send him everything offered, just in case. This practice brought him *Stuart Little,* a film about a talking mouse. He chose to write it because he wanted, as he puts it "to do a very lyrical piece" and "find a rhythm to dialogue." The project, which most critics passed off initially as just another family film, won him praise for its concise, clever script. He has little need to work on assignments these days. His film *The Sixth Sense* sold for 3 million dollars and went on to become one of the top-grossing films of 1999. He wrote, directed, and produced the film, which seems to be his bill of fare these days. He did the same with *Signs.*

Shyamalan believes whole-heartedly in the screenwriter's responsibility to the work. He scrutinizes every flawed scene, every awkward bit of dialogue, and every scathing review for hints on what he might do better next time. He has said on numerous occasions that writers are trying first and foremost to emotionally engage the audience. He won't commit to projects that he feels fail in this regard. Fortunately, he hasn't had to.

Callie Khouri

Occupations: screenwriter, actress

Industry credits:

- ✔ *Thelma and Louise* (1991)
- ✔ *Something to Talk About* (1995)

Callie Khouri started out as an actress. She went to drama school at Purdue University and then dropped out and moved to Nashville, Tennessee, where she took classes and tried her hand at theater. While at the Strasberg Institute, Khouri realized that she was no longer enamored with the craft, and she wasn't reading any exciting material for women her age — for women in general, actually. She was irritated by the fact that most of the roles she encountered were for abuse victims, prostitutes, or eye candy. This frustration sparked the idea for *Thelma and Louise.* It took six months to write and virtually no time to sell, and it eventually won an Academy Award for Best Original Screenplay. Khouri is one of three women to earn this award for a solo credit. Her second film took four years to make, in part because she was overwhelmed by the overnight success of her first endeavor. She has said on numerous occasions that her fear over a second film failure was paralyzing at times. *Something to Talk About* is also a character-driven piece, and it took a while to put the various plot pieces that Khouri envisioned into some type of an order.

Her advice to new writers seems to be the same advice that she gives herself daily. Don't worry about what other people think of you; they're probably worrying about the same thing. Don't be afraid to have a dream; it's the only thing that will keep you going. Always do what you love, and keep writing, despite the inner voices talking about failure, writer's block, and end result. The best way to kill that fear, it seems, is to turn on the computer or pick up the pen.

Christopher Nolan

Occupations: screenwriter, director, producer

Industry credits:

- *Following* (1998)
- *Memento* (2001)
- *Insomnia* (2002)

Like M. Night Shyamalan, Christopher Nolan began making films at an early age. In his case, he began his career as a 7-year-old, when he picked up his father's super 8 camera. He went on to make 16mm films while he was a student of English Literature at University College in London. He divided his time between reading books and working at the college film society, though it was hardly an equal division of labor. The result of this training was a black and white film noir of sorts titled *Following.* Like most film noirs, *Following* relies heavily on shadow, suspense, and a pervading mood to hold it together. The title stems from the protagonist's primary action in the film — following strangers on the street. The film was highly acclaimed in several festivals, but it never reached the mainstream audiences. His second film, however, did.

Memento is another film noir that's told entirely in reverse. It's based on a short story written by Christopher's brother, Jonathan Nolan, and it earned a nomination for Best Screenwriting at the 2001 Academy Awards. As if this sophomore effort weren't exciting enough, Nolan's third film, *Insomnia,* roped him a celebrity cast. The film stars Robin Williams, Al Pacino, and Hillary Swank, and is a remake of the 1997 Norwegian effort. It's an understatement to say that the past three years have been exciting ones for Mr. Nolan.

Nia Vardalos

Occupations: screenwriter, playwright, comedienne, actress

Industry credits:

▌✔ *My Big Fat Greek Wedding* (2002)

Nia Vardalos landed her first writing job in a way that reads like a scene from one of her comedy routines. She was working in the box office of Second City, a job she took in her desire to become part of the ensemble. When one of the performers called in sick, Nia took advantage of the situation and offered to fill in for her. After all, she knew the show. She was hired the next day, and quickly began writing sketches for the group and performing in them as well.

Since then, Nia has been writing and performing her own material for the stage. She moved to L.A. in 1994 and found herself auditioning for primarily ethnic roles. It soon became clear that although material existed for Latino, Jewish, and Italian women, there was no voice for anyone Greek. And so *My Big Fat Greek Wedding* was born. The project began as a one-woman show based on her own wedding. Her creative process was simple: Call all your relatives, ask them to send family stories, and cram them all into one script. The first draft only took two weeks to write. It was during a sold-out performance that Nia decided to turn it into a screenplay.

The script went through many hands on its way to final production. Several studio executives wanted it to portray a Latino family that would star Marisa Tomei. Another studio suggested it be about an Italian family. Nia rejected these offers, many of them potentially lucrative. Several years later, Rita Wilson and Tom Hanks provided the support necessary to produce the work. To everyone's astonishment, it was the box-office hit of the summer, netting over 35 million dollars in the months after its release. (Not bad for a film that only took 3 million to produce.) The success isn't surprising though, for someone as tenacious as Vardalos. She encourages new writers to nurture that tenacity in themselves, refusing to take no for an answer or compromise the script for a quick sale. After all, look where it got her.

Chapter 21

Ten Movies You Should See and/or Read

Ten movies I should see and/or read? But wait, you cry, haven't several lists already been compiled over the past few decades on just this topic? Yes, in fact, there have. The American Film Institute, individual critics, and other periodicals have all issued lists of several kinds, including "The 100 Greatest American Movies," "The 100 Greatest Films of All Times," "The Top 100 Comedies, Romances, Suspense Films," and so on. Every film seems to fit on a list somewhere according to genre, cinematic era, or style. And here's one more grouping for you to consider, though it was assembled in a slightly different way.

The films in this section may or may not have made previous rankings. I've chosen them on the strength of their scripts first and their impact as a film second, though all became successful final products. Of course, films I've already mentioned in detail still lurk around the considerably frayed edges of this list. You should still run, not walk, to see *American Beauty, Jaws,* and *The Untouchables,* but I thought it best to include scripts that I haven't featured prominently elsewhere. Notice that this chapter isn't called "The *Top* Ten films you should see and/or read." That list would've been an impossible one to compile, and this one was hard enough. For all my ranting and raving over dramatically paltry material, I find that excellent writing still abounds. For every one selection here, I reluctantly pushed three possibilities aside — a fact that should strike hope in the hearts of screenwriters everywhere, aspiring or otherwise.

A Note on Criteria

I've selected the scripts here based on the clarity, precision, and integrity of the following textual elements:

- ✔ Character portrayal
- ✔ Character development
- ✔ Plot structure and execution
- ✔ Stylistic components
- ✔ Pervading atmosphere or mood
- ✔ The film's theme and intent

Beyond those factors, I've tried to include a film from every genre and provide examples from several time frames. I've also selected a few films based on the way they were made. I include the vital statistics of each film, as well as a synopsis (I hope I don't give too much away), a historical background, and a list of awards that the film has received. Please note that the films here aren't listed in order of personal preference, but rather, in the order in which they were released. I enjoy the first film in the list as much as I enjoy the last.

Citizen Kane

Released: 1941 by RKO Pictures
Director: Orson Welles
Producer: John Houseman
Writers: Herman J. Mankiewicz and Orson Welles
Genre: classic/drama/film noir

Citizen Kane ranks in the top ten of virtually every film listing, and well it should. It's one of the world's most famous films, in part because of its innovative cinematic techniques, in part because of its script, and in large part because of its scandalous history.

The film is an epic rags-to-riches tale of a young boy who inherits a fortune and is removed from his modest surroundings to be raised by a prominent banker. The boy becomes Charles Foster Kane, a tremendously wealthy newspaper magnate, who claims to champion the lower-class masses but is secretly out only for himself. The story chronicles his shoddy attempt at a political career, his public affair with a talentless singer, and his eventual demise. One of the script's strongest components is its plot structure. The story isn't told from

Kane's perspective but is narrated instead by a variety of unreliable and often contradictory sources. As a result, the audience receives an enigmatic portrayal of Kane, fueled by speculation and hearsay. This sense of unease is emphasized by sophisticated camera movements, fast-paced and overlapping dialogue, and the use of unconventional lighting.

Though widely acclaimed now, *Citizen Kane* almost wasn't released, and it took 25 years from the time it was conceived to be completed. Orson Welles was known as a boy genius who made a career off of scandal. When the project began, he was only 24 years old and fresh from the infamous success of the radio broadcast "War of the Worlds." He met his match in William Randolph Hearst, the newspaperman upon whose life Welles based his script. Hearst tried valiantly to have the film shut down; he waged newspaper campaigns, blackmailed Hollywood executives, and called in the FBI at one point. It was a war neither man fully recovered from. Though the film finally did open, it was booed at the Academy Awards where it only took one of the nine awards that it was nominated for. Ironically, it was an award for best script. Since that time, the film has sparked several other projects, most notably the Oscar-nominated documentary *The Battle over Citizen Kane* by Thomas Lennon and Michael Epstein, and the HBO film *RKO 281* by John Logan.

The African Queen

Released: 1951 by United Artists
Director: John Huston
Producer: Sam Spiegel
Writers: James Agee and John Huston (based on a novel by C. S. Forester)
Genre: classic/romance

The African Queen takes place in central Africa during World War I and remains one of the best examples of character-driven drama today. It tells the story of Rose Sayer, a British missionary who's come to Africa with her brother, Reverend Sayer, to tend the sick and provide religious comfort. She's a spinster in every sense of the word at the beginning of the film, convinced that Africa is merely an extension of British civilization, or that she can make it so through her work. By contrast, Charlie Alnutt is an unkempt, gin-guzzling riverman who panders to several neighboring villages. It's not your typical match, but in the tradition of romantic comedies, a match it becomes. When German troops destroy the village, killing Rose's brother in the process, Charlie offers to take her downriver on his steamboat, *The African Queen*. Rose is convinced that it's her duty to sink a German cruiser downstream, and her attempts to convince Charlie comprise the bulk of the film's delightful escapades.

The African Queen is a fine example of adaptation at its best. Though the location rarely moves beyond the steamboat, the action provides enough suspense and surprises to hold your attention. The characters undergo startling changes as a result of their interaction; they learn and they instruct along the way. The film also stars Katharine Hepburn and Humphrey Bogart, which never hurts. The film was nominated for four Academy Awards, one of which went to Humphrey Bogart for Best Actor in 1951.

Rear Window

Released: 1954 by Paramount Pictures
Director: Alfred Hitchcock
Producer: Alfred Hitchcock
Writer: John Michael Hayes
Genre: suspense/thriller

Here's a classic suspense film from the master himself. Like *The African Queen,* this movie is also an adaptation, though I'd deem *Rear Window* "loosely based" on the short story "It Had to Be Murder" by William Irish (aka Cornell Woolrich.) In true Hitchcockian tradition, it tosses a well-intentioned albeit voyeuristic protagonist into a potentially deadly situation and lets him wiggle his way out. I mean "wiggle" literally here because the protagonist, L.B. Jefferies, is confined to a wheelchair for most of the action. He amuses himself by peering in at his neighbors day and night through binoculars. Lucky for him, his windows overlook the entire apartment complex. So what happens next? Well, *Rear Window*'s a thriller, so eventually, Jefferies sees something that he's not supposed to see. He witnesses his neighbor, Lars Thorwald, murder his wife. Or at least he thinks he does, but how can he be sure? The remainder of the film hinges upon what Jefferies truly saw, how he's going to prove it, and what happens when the accused murderer discovers that he's being watched.

The film also stars Grace Kelly as Jefferies's would-be fiancée and Raymond Burr as the suggested villain. It was nominated for four Academy Awards, including Best Screenplay and Best Director. When you rent this film or grab the screenplay, pay close attention to how Hitchcock and Hayes craft suspense. The first portion of the movie lulls an audience into a routine, acquainting you with the neighbors through the voyeuristic eyes of the protagonist. The main event, therefore, creeps in unannounced. Notice the camera's role here as well. It never leaves the confines of the apartment, and on one occasion, the audience witnesses an event that the protagonist misses because — well because he's asleep at the time. The result is an efficient example of edge-of-your-seat suspense. How's that for a pitch?

Guess Who's Coming to Dinner

Released: 1967 by Columbia Pictures
Director: Stanley Kramer
Writer: William Rose
Genre: classic/drama

Given the subject matter and the time of its release, it's amazing that ***Guess Who's Coming to Dinner*** was well-received — let alone that it took the Oscar for Best Screenplay. The story centers on Matt and Christina Drayton (played by Spencer Tracy and Katharine Hepburn). Both are self-proclaimed liberals who have raised their daughter to think progressively like themselves. They are *not*, however, prepared for her new fiancé — African-American doctor John Prentice (Sidney Poitier) — whom she brings home with her to announce the engagement. John eventually surprises his family with the news as well. The remaining plot explores the prejudice that everyone does, in fact, harbor, as both families struggle to understand and accept the new union.

This film was released during the racially charged 1960s. It made quite a few people uncomfortable, yet it received critical acclaim almost instantly. Its success is a direct result of well-rounded characters who are given time and room to change considerably. The differences in race and the questions of interracial marriage are treated with respect and care. This film tackles theme from all sides of the table.

E.T. the Extra Terrestrial

Released: 1982 by Universal Pictures
Director: Steven Spielberg
Producer: Kathleen Kennedy
Writer: Melissa Matheson
Genre: sci-fi/family

Here's an example of a film that defies classification. It's both funny and poignant, it satisfies children and adults alike, and it has, therefore, become one of the top-grossing films of all time. So what's the secret to all this success? Look at the script, and then look at the director.

E.T. tells the story of a friendship that defies the laws of physics. It's a variation on that continually successful formula: a relationship that defies the impossible. Young Elliot lives with his newly single mother, his older brother Michael, and his younger sister Gertie. He's a quiet kid, still emotionally bruised from an absentee father, and he's often by himself. Aren't you just waiting for the phrase "until one day"? Well, here it comes: until one day, he discovers something strange in the woods — an alien. The charming extra-terrestrial (aka E.T.) has been left behind accidentally and has no idea how to get home. What follows is a comic and touching portrayal of the family's attempts to hide and eventually rescue E.T. from an increasingly threatening adult world.

You've probably already seen this movie, but seek out the script regardless. It's an original screenplay, nothing adapted here, and a unique mixture of a character-driven story inside a plot-driven script. Notice how it draws an audience. Fantasy lovers enjoy the science-fiction bent, children enjoy the childcentric story (a well-directed one at that), and parents can appreciate how it hints at a family coming to terms with a painful divorce. With all this going for it, the question is: "Who doesn't it reach?"

Ghost

Released: 1990 by Paramount Pictures
Director: Jerry Zucker
Producer: Lisa Weinstein
Writer: Peter Barsocchini
Genre: drama/romance

Ghost was another surprise box-office hit, in part because of its all-star cast, and in part because of its unusual script. The film is a hybrid, at once a drama, romance, and a science-fiction story. Its primary plot resembles an Alfred Hitchcock film: Promising young businessman Sam Wheat (played by Patrick Swayze) is killed by a mugger one night while walking home with his wife Molly (Demi Moore). The audience slowly discovers that Sam's death was no accident but a premeditated murder arranged by his close friend and co-worker Carl Brunner. Carl was afraid that Sam would discover his embezzlement plans, and now, he has designs on Sam's wife. Here's the catch: When Sam is shot, his spirit lingers behind. He's not dead, he's not alive, and he can follow people freely but is unable to communicate with them. When he discovers Carl's plan, his rage leads him to amateur psychic Oda Mae Brown, whom he torments into communicating to Molly and helping him enact revenge.

Want to learn from this script? Look at the classic plot construction. The lines between good and evil are clearly drawn, yet the characters are not types. Oda Mae is a reluctant hero, as is Sam Wheat, who would much rather be alive with his wife than chasing his betrayer. The stakes are life and death, literally, and the audience wants the protagonist to succeed. A palpable theme underscores throughout — your actions have consequences. If they don't catch up with you now, they will later.

Sling Blade

Released: 1996 by Miramax Films/Shooting Gallery
Director: Billy Bob Thorton
Producer: Brandon Rosser
Writer: Billy Bob Thorton
Genre: independent/drama

Sling Blade was a noteworthy debut for Billy Bob Thorton, who wrote and directed the film, and also starred as protagonist Karl Childers. The film earned him Academy Awards for Best Actor and Best Adapted Screenplay in 1996.

The film is a simple and chilling look at Karl Childers, a mentally handicapped man who was institutionalized at the age of 12 for murdering his mother. As the story goes, he witnessed his mother sleeping with a strange man and killed them both in a fit of rage. He is released years later as a result of budget cuts and finds himself befriending a young boy named Frank, who sees Karl not as a damaged adult but as a kind man and a potential ally. Frank's mother dates a cruel, bigoted alcoholic who continually abuses both mother and son. The violence soon becomes more than Karl can take.

Sling Blade was produced on a shoestring budget, and its success is almost entirely due to the strength of the script and several outstanding performances. Note how Thorton slowly constructs Karl, piece by piece throughout. His character has very simple goals: He wants to survive, he wants to find a job, and he wants to maintain his friendship with Frank. Yet even these basic needs seem impossible to achieve in the world Thorton creates. Karl is plagued both by the people he encounters and his own quiet rage. You're never sure exactly what he's capable of, and you hope that he succeeds. *Sling Blade* is an example of a small, quiet story with universal appeal.

Life Is Beautiful

Released: 1997 by Miramax
Director: Roberto Benigni
Producers: Gianlugi Braschi and Elda Ferri
Writers: Roberto Benigni and Vincenzo Cerami
Genre: foreign/tragicomedy

Life Is Beautiful also blurs the lines between drama and comedy, though drama eventually wins out. The script fuses two plots together. In one storyline, Guido (played by Benigni) courts Tuscan schoolteacher Dora. Dora is taken with his comic charm, but she remains faithful to her pompous and prominent fiancé. In a parallel plot, anti-Semitism is sweeping Europe, and both Guido and his uncle come under attack. Though Guido finally convinces Dora to marry him, though they have a child and start a small business, Hitler's reign proves overwhelming. They're transported to concentration camps halfway through the film. From this point forward, the two plots collide, and Guido struggles to maintain humor in a humorless environment, and to create a beautiful life for his son in a world where less and less beauty can be found.

You may not be able to find an English translation of this script, but translated sections have been posted on the Internet. If you rent the film, note how Benigni and Cerami weave comedy and tragedy together throughout. Just when Guido's antics invite you to forget the war, they slap you in the face with another reminder. The result is a multilayered drama nominated for eight Academy Awards, including Best Actor, Best Foreign Language Film, and Best Score, which it won.

Shakespeare in Love

Released: 1998 by Miramax and Universal Pictures
Director: John Madden
Producers: Donna Gigliotti, Harvey Weinstein, and Edward Zwick
Writers: Tom Stoppard and Marc Norman
Genre: comedy/romance

Shakespeare in Love swept the Oscars in 1998. Of the 13 awards that it was nominated for, it took 7, including Best Actress for Gwyneth Paltrow, Best Supporting Actress for Judi Dench, Best Screenplay, and Best Picture — not too shabby for a film many critics passed off as an entertaining farce of a film. Its success may be due to a stellar cast and an experienced production team, but I suspect that it had much to do with a clever script as well. Tom Stoppard is a playwright known for his ability as a wordsmith. The film is full of puns, witty repartee, and Shakespeare quotations all delivered in the lightening pace of British comedy.

The story takes a look at William Shakespeare not as the genius of modern day but as a young writer, struggling to pay the rent and compete with the ever-popular Christopher Marlowe. When the show opens, young Will is trying to complete a draft of "Romeo and Ethel, the Pirate's Daughter." As you can imagine, he's not having much luck. In a parallel plot, Lady Viola, an ardent theatregoer despite her gender and grooming, is about to be sold into a loveless marriage. In her longing to be free of all things upper-class, she disguises herself as a boy and secures the lead role in Shakespeare's new play. Love blossoms between the two when Will finally realizes the plot, and so the play "Romeo and Juliet" is born.

This script, like *Citizen Kane,* was many years in the making. What started as a suggestion from Norman's son went down several paths on its way to becoming an award-winning film. This script is a particularly good example of an original piece created by borrowing lightly from several sources, namely Shakespeare's own plays. It's full of internal rhyme and multiple plots, and cleverly drawn characters abound.

Signs

Released: 2002 by Buena Vista/Touchstone Pictures
Director: M. Night Shyamalan
Producers: M. Night Shyamalan, Frank Marshall, and Sam Mercer
Writer: M. Night Shyamalan
Genre: sci-fi/suspense

M. Night Shyamalan is forging quite a name for himself. The movie *Signs* follows the success of *The Sixth Sense,* which won him Oscar nods three years earlier. *Signs* is another paranormal adventure, this time set in rural Pennsylvania on the farm of former minister Graham Hess. Graham gave up the ministry when his wife was killed in a freak car accident and has concentrated on raising his children, Morgan and Bo, with the help of his brother Merrill. Their small world is shattered again when strange signs begin showing up in fields across the country, signs that many reporters feel might be extraterrestrial. One of those signs shows up in their field at the onset of the film.

Shyamalan is a master of leaving no detail unused. Every aspect of his scripts is reincorporated several times, until you begin to feel that every event in the world really is the direct result of something that occurred in the past. This connection is part of what he's attempting to explore in *Signs.* Watch this script for the "how" of the story. Because Shyamalan directs his own work, he's able to fashion a complete cinematic atmosphere around the text. His scripts have a distinct style. He's also a master of dialogue. Long stretches pass where nothing is said, but when characters finally do speak, pay attention. The film, starring Mel Gibson, Joaquin Phoenix, and Cherry Jones, also sports an all-star cast.

My Big Fat Greek Wedding

Released: 2002 by Gold Star Films
Director: Joel Zwick
Producers: Tom Hanks and Rita Wilson
Writer: Nia Vardalos (adapted from her play)
Genre: independent/romantic comedy

Okay, if you've paid attention, you may have noticed that this is actually the eleventh movie discussed in this chapter, but I wanted to include it because it's funny, efficient, and a surprise box-office hit. I also include it as inspiration for aspiring screenwriters because it's the first movie for Nia Vardalos, a California comedienne who also stars in the film. Drawing from reallife experience, the story whirls around Toula, a 30-year-old woman who is still single, which, to her parents, is something of a crime. Frightened at the prospect of a life spent taking care of her parents' restaurant, Toula determines to redirect her future by signing up for college courses, another potential crime in the orthodox Greek household. Soon, she has a new job, a new look, and a new beau who is perfect but for one minor detail — he's not Greek. What follows is a hilarious romp towards the altar, though who knows if she'll ever get there.

Although some critics called the script fun but frivolous, many consider its overnight success proof of how very much the world needs strong, inoffensive material. This film is about sex, without high sexual content, it's about race, without slurs and overt cursing, and it's a film in which Vardalos can poke fun at her heritage without insulting her past. This film was also produced on a small budget, which is more proof that a smart marketing campaign and a strong script can still take the world by storm.

Chapter 22

Ten Screenwriting Myths

In This Chapter

▶ Encouragement to be a writer

▶ Advice for making it in the business

Any profession that's been around long enough, or as my grandfather would say "any profession worth its salt," is riddled with myths. As you may imagine, screenwriting is no exception. This chapter challenges ten of those myths — the top offenders, if you will. I encourage you to begin trouncing them now so that they don't hinder your progress later.

I have to live in Los Angeles to write screenplays.

"No, you don't" is the fastest and most complete response for this myth, especially for anybody writing a first screenplay. Producers and agents don't care where you live. If you can write a strong story and mail them a draft, they're satisfied. If your screenplays are produced, you'll probably spend time in California or other parts of the country. The more films you sell, the more traveling you will do, but with the advent of electronic communication, fax machines, and priority mail, you should be able to write from virtually anywhere. Remember also that film companies are cropping up all over the country. New York and Chicago are adding their names to the list of cinematically thriving cities as well, and smaller production companies are launching new work all the time.

"Do I *want* to live in Los Angeles?" is really the question to ask. How immediately connected would you like to be with the Hollywood scene? If you thrive on hustle and bustle, if you're an inherent salesman and your own best agent, if you can't stand the thought of missing an opportunity to slip some producer your script, you might love L.A. life. However, don't think that you'll miss out if you live in the opposite direction. Many writers feel that life outside L.A. keeps them grounded and focused on the work instead of the image. John Logan, whose list of screenwriting credits includes *Any Given Sunday,* *Time Machine,* and *Gladiator,* lives in Chicago. He frequently travels from coast to coast, but California is not his home base. M. Night Shyamalan, writer of *Sixth Sense* and *Signs,* lives and works in Philadelphia. Your story is the key. Write a good story, and the world will come to you.

You have to go to school to learn how to write.

If this myth were true, half the screenwriters of today wouldn't be writing. If your aim is to teach screenwriting eventually, then yes, a degree in writing or film will probably help. If your aim is purely artistic, your career depends on your ability to tell a story. If the script is exciting, innovative, and marketable, it's going to generate interest. If the story is flat or cliché-ridden, a degree from the best film school on the planet can't help you. A writer should be curious, passionate, alert, and determined. In many ways, determination gets you farther than raw talent can. You may dream up the next *Casablanca* or *American Beauty,* but if you don't sit down every day and pound it out, who will know? Screenwriting is a difficult job. It requires hours of writing, a capacity to meet deadlines, a mind that can juggle many tasks at once, and constant collaboration. Getting through all that is more than half the battle.

Will a film school or a creative-writing program help you? It depends on what you're looking for. Educational settings offer perks that may be worth investigating. Some of those include:

- ✓ **A network:** The students, mentors, and visiting artists you meet may turn out to be invaluable when you're trying to sell your work later.

- ✓ **A workshop:** Film schools and writing departments generally provide a critical forum for your work. You'll have to bounce your work between readers later on — why not do it here?

- ✓ **Deadlines:** Schools require you to write at least one screenplay during your stint, sometimes three or four. You may generate an entire portfolio by the time you leave.

- ✓ **Classes, classes, classes:** Anything and everything that you learn strengthens your writing. Educational institutions provide an array of subjects for you to explore.

If you want some of these perks but would rather not commit to an entire program, see if the educational institutions near you offer writing courses or seminars. Colleges, libraries, and community centers tend to schedule creative-writing classes or workshops after school hours, at night, and in the summer. I encourage you to consider the educational route, but don't place undue importance on it. In order to write, you must have a story and a will to write. If you have those things, a diploma's just icing.

Screenwriting is entertainment; it's not a real profession.

I would argue that storytelling is one of the few professions that has stood the test of time. Throughout the ages, cultures of all kinds have crafted stories to preserve their heritage, to chronicle historical events, to explore what it means to be human, and to make sense of a nonsensical world. Why do people continue to flock to theaters? Some people might say as a means of escape, and that may be true. But I argue that, more often, people go in search of something. Is it inspiration? Hope? An education? A better understanding of themselves or some part of their world? If they go for even one of these reasons, screenwriting's a noble profession. If the question you're trying to answer is "But does it save lives?" stop trying. It probably doesn't, but then how would you ever know? At its best, screenwriting asks questions, challenges tradition, inspires action, sparks debate, and makes people think and feel on a potentially grand level. Now, how many professions do all that?

If you've never written before, it's too late to start now.

It's never too late to start writing. The older you are, the more stories you've encountered, the more wisdom you can impart, and (hopefully) the more questions you have to ask. Margaret Mitchell completed her first and only novel when she was 36. It won the Pulitzer. Perhaps you've heard of it — it's called *Gone with the Wind.* Frank McCourt wrote his first novel, *Angela's Ashes,* when he was 66. It was a best-seller and also won a Pulitzer. Ray Krok founded McDonalds in his 50s, Grandma Moses began painting at 78; the list goes on and on. If you don't start writing now, the only regret you'll have in five years is that you didn't start writing five years ago. As an older student of mine once said, "You're going to be 72 anyway. Why not be 72 and a writer?"

Writing is a lonely profession.

I'm not going to lie to you: Writing involves many mornings, afternoons, and/or evenings alone. When crafting a first draft, you will (hopefully) spend three or four hours a day, four to five times a week, in a room with your computer, your characters, and your plot, which is really just another way of saying "by yourself."

On the flip side, screenwriting is a highly social profession. A screenplay, like a stage play, isn't really complete until you've handed it to a production team. You craft the story, and they transform it into a three-dimensional piece. Want a metaphor for that relationship? You build the boat and the sails, and the production team provides the wind. Research for each project will undoubtedly require interaction of all sorts, as will revisions. Frankly, you can't do this job without collaborating at least 60 percent of the time. You may become *more* social as a result of the craft.

Screenwriting also differs from many professions in that the kind of work you do varies in form. Working means spending time alone, but it also means taking long walks, conversing with friends, or cooking dinner for six. Writers work everywhere. So keep writing, or start writing. When cabin fever sets in, and it will set in, go work somewhere else.

Hollywood has no ethics; it'll ruin the integrity of my script.

I think that the underlining question here is "Can I work in Hollywood and remain an artist?". The answer is yes, you can. Commercial success doesn't negate artistry. As in any profession, you have to know what you're getting into and you have to have savvy. Do your research. Know the answers to the following questions:

- What movies are current box-office hits?
- What are the major production companies, and what kind of work are they producing?
- What are the smaller production companies, and what kind of work are they producing?
- Who's writing scripts you enjoy? Who represents them?
- What are the artistic strengths of your piece? What are the commercial strengths?
- What parts of your piece are you the most interested in protecting? What parts of your piece are you flexible on?
- How can you sell someone on *your* story?

Answering these questions in advance enables you to plan an appropriate marketing campaign. You'll know which studios and executives are more likely to champion your story and keep it intact. If you prioritize the elements of your story prior to meeting with those executives, you'll also know how to respond should they propose changes. You'll know what elements you want to safeguard at all costs, and you can entertain suggestions on the rest. This strategy allows you to be both protective and flexible.

Hollywood has a lot of money, and like any business, it has a lot of people interested in that money. Hollywood also has many champions of strong work. Finding them may take a while, but they're there. If you go into the profession with your eyes open, if you know your story backwards and forwards, if you know the market in advance — those supporters will eventually find you.

It's not what you know; it's who you know that matters.

I'm going to address this myth in two parts. First, does it help to know someone in Hollywood? Probably, depending on your relationship with that person. Approaching the business isn't unlike going to a new school or your first day on a job; if you know people there in advance, the transition is usually less frightening. A Hollywood contact can do the following:

- ✔ Introduce you to agents, producers, directors, actors, and so on
- ✔ Help you find temporary work that may further your career
- ✔ Show you the town
- ✔ Pass your work onto readers
- ✔ Fill you in on what kind of work various companies are doing

Knowing someone in L.A. also considerably cuts down on the fear factor and, if you're moving to the West Coast, on the loneliness.

However, is it who you know that really matters? No, the story is what matters. If your story is compelling, it will make the introductions for you. If you're passionate about what you know, someone will respond. So, to the beginning screenwriter I say, get out there. It's a social profession, so meet as many people as you can. But worry about your script first. In the end, everything comes back to the story.

I have too many obligations to be a writer.

The first thing to do when you encounter this myth is to list those obligations — all of them. That list might start with any or all of the following: a family to support, a job (or two or three), classes to take, social functions to run, and a household to maintain

These obligations are just the top ones in most of our lives; there are infinitely more. Think about it for a while. Jot down anything that takes time out of your day. If you're responsible for walking the dog or looking after the neighbor's flowers, include those tasks on the list, and when you're through, add one more item. At the bottom of the page (or the scroll as the case may be) write "Work on screenplay." Now, it's on the list of obligations.

If you want to write a screenplay, you need time. You need concentrated chunks of time, at least an hour for each session, and any schedule can be managed. Anton Chekhov wrote his short stories between seeing patients in the hospital and supporting a family. J. K. Rowling was a single mother trying to make ends meet when she wrote *Harry Potter and the Sorcerer's Stone*. You have time if you *make* time. Face it, any one of the top items on the obligation list can take up your whole week, if you allow that to happen. You simply can't allow that to happen.

You're only as successful as the last screenplay you sold.

What if you've never sold a screenplay? Does that mean that you're not successful? What if your screenplay was purchased but never produced? Or if it was produced, yet it bombed at the box office? Or if it was commercially successful and critically panned? Or if it was critically successful and socially panned? Are you successful then?

The real questions to ask are: Why are you writing, and how do you define success? If you're writing to make money, you're writing for the wrong reasons. You may never make money. If you're writing to seek critical acclaim, you're writing for the wrong reasons. Think of all the artists who died prior to achieving that goal. In order to write continually, you have to love the process, writer's block and all. You have to love finding an idea and developing it into a story. You have to love pounding away at a computer all day, even when you hate it. You have to love words and images and action.

More importantly, you have to redefine success. Know what you're trying to achieve in each script and push yourself to accomplish that task. If your purpose is to write a piece that sells, so be it. Do the research, watch the market, and sell the script. If your purpose is to ask a question, ask it in every scene. If you write because you love the process, you'll be far better off when you approach the West Coast. Your scripts aren't always going to sell; those that sell won't always be commercially successful. If you love the process more than the product, you'll write regardless of how your last script fared.

I'm not talented enough to be a writer.

This myth is so common that it borders on an affliction. Every writer harbors an internal critic, otherwise known as the "little voice," and this is the voice's favorite quip. It is, of course, a false notion. You have talent. Anyone who's made it through adolescence has a story to tell and the experience with which to tell it. The real issue here is whether you have something to say. Do you have a story waiting in the wings? Do you have a question that you want to explore on the page? Has something made you angry, confused, exhilarated, or curious? If you answer yes to any or all of these questions, you should be writing.

Fear is a funny thing. It can be your best friend; it can force you to do research and prepare for a project in ways that you wouldn't have attempted in a more relaxed state. It can also completely shut you down. If you're worried about your own talent, remember this: If you choose to honor the fear, it will weaken your work. If you choose to honor the work, it will weaken your fear.

Index

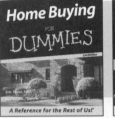

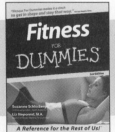

FOR DUMMIES®

A world of resources to help you grow

TRAVEL

0-7645-5453-0

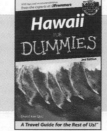

0-7645-5438-7

0-7645-5444-1

Also available:

America's National Parks For Dummies
(0-7645-6204-5)

Caribbean For Dummies
(0-7645-5445-X)

Cruise Vacations For Dummies 2003
(0-7645-5459-X)

Europe For Dummies
(0-7645-5456-5)

Ireland For Dummies
(0-7645-6199-5)

France For Dummies
(0-7645-6292-4)

Las Vegas For Dummies
(0-7645-5448-4)

London For Dummies
(0-7645-5416-6)

Mexico's Beach Resorts For Dummies
(0-7645-6262-2)

Paris For Dummies
(0-7645-5494-8)

RV Vacations For Dummies
(0-7645-5443-3)

EDUCATION & TEST PREPARATION

0-7645-5194-9

0-7645-5325-9

0-7645-5249-X

Also available:

The ACT For Dummies
(0-7645-5210-4)

Chemistry For Dummies
(0-7645-5430-1)

English Grammar For Dummies
(0-7645-5322-4)

French For Dummies
(0-7645-5193-0)

GMAT For Dummies
(0-7645-5251-1)

Inglés Para Dummies
(0-7645-5427-1)

Italian For Dummies
(0-7645-5196-5)

Research Papers For Dummies
(0-7645-5426-3)

SAT I For Dummies
(0-7645-5472-7)

U.S. History For Dummies
(0-7645-5249-X)

World History For Dummies
(0-7645-5242-2)

HEALTH, SELF-HELP & SPIRITUALITY

0-7645-5154-X

0-7645-5302-X

0-7645-5418-2

Also available:

The Bible For Dummies
(0-7645-5296-1)

Controlling Cholesterol For Dummies
(0-7645-5440-9)

Dating For Dummies
(0-7645-5072-1)

Dieting For Dummies
(0-7645-5126-4)

High Blood Pressure For Dummies
(0-7645-5424-7)

Judaism For Dummies
(0-7645-5299-6)

Menopause For Dummies
(0-7645-5458-1)

Nutrition For Dummies
(0-7645-5180-9)

Potty Training For Dummies
(0-7645-5417-4)

Pregnancy For Dummies
(0-7645-5074-8)

Rekindling Romance For Dummies
(0-7645-5303-8)

Religion For Dummies
(0-7645-5264-3)

Available wherever books are sold. Go to www.dummies.com or call 1-877-762-2974 to order direct

NOW AVAILABLE!

FOR DUMMIES™ Videos & DVDs

Basic Yoga Workout FOR DUMMIES

"The best video I have ever seen to introduce brand new students to yoga." —YogaBasics.com

with Sara Ivanhoe

An Easy-to-Follow Yoga Practice

Instructor Sara Ivanhoe offers step-by-step instruction of the 12 essential yoga postures. This workout shows you proper technique, as well as tips on modifying postures for your fitness level. Today, many people use yoga to help alleviate back pain, reduce stress, and increase flexibility.

VHS - 45 Mins. $9.99
DVD - 70 Mins. $14.98

Beyond Basic Yoga FOR DUMMIES

"Sara Ivanhoe makes yoga enjoyable and accessible for people at all levels... you'll love every minute." —Fitness Magazine

with Sara Ivanhoe

An Easy-to-Follow Workout

The *Beyond Basic Yoga Workout For Dummies* is the next step for anyone who has enjoyed *Basic Yoga Workout For Dummies* and is ready to enhance their practice with 12 more postures. This workout is a little more advanced than the basic yoga program but still features the *For Dummies* format.

VHS - 45 Mins. $9.99
DVD - 55 Mins. $14.98

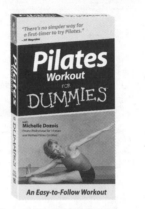

Pilates Workout FOR DUMMIES

"There's no simpler way for a first-timer to try Pilates." —FIT Magazine

Michelle Dozois

An Easy-to-Follow Workout

Instructor Michelle Dozois offers step-by-step instruction of 18 popular Pilates mat exercises to help you strengthen and lengthen your muscles, improve your posture, and tone and tighten your midsection.

VHS - 40 Mins. $9.99
DVD - 60 Mins. $14.98

Shaping Up with Weights FOR DUMMIES

"Tracy York has a flair for turning exercise into a 'Can't-wait-to-do-it' pleasure!" —College Video's Guide to Exercise Videos

Tracy York

An Easy-to-Follow Workout

Instructor Tracy York offers step-by-step instruction of 12 key strength-training exercises and makes it easy to work out at any level. This workout incorporates both upper- and lower-body exercises to help tone muscles and burn more calories per day, which leads to fat loss.

VHS - 51 Mins. $9.99

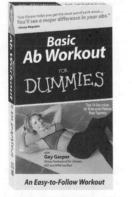

Basic Ab Workout FOR DUMMIES

"Gay Gasper helps you get the most out of each move... You'll see a major difference in your abs." —Fitness Magazine

with Gay Gasper

An Easy-to-Follow Workout

Instructor Gay Gasper demonstrates her top 10 exercises to tone and flatten your tummy. Throughout this workout, she gives you more advanced options for the exercises so you can start at any level and then advance as you become more fit.

VHS - 45 Mins. $9.99
DVD - 55 Mins. $14.98

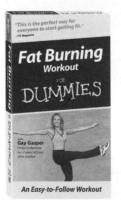

Fat Burning Workout FOR DUMMIES

"This is the perfect way for everyone to start getting fit." —FIT Magazine

with Gay Gasper

An Easy-to-Follow Workout

In this workout, instructor Gay Gasper offers step-by-step instructions of the 10 basic exercises that make up any aerobic routine. She incorporates both high- and low-impact choices in an effective workout to help you burn more fat, use more calories every day, and meet your fitness goals.

VHS - 45 Mins. $9.99

Learning Guitar FOR DUMMIES

"With Jon Chappell's teaching methods, you will have a blast learning the guitar!" —Michael Molenda, Editor-in-Chief, Guitar Player Magazine

with Jon Chappell

An Easy-to-Follow Guide to Techniques and Styles

Instructor Jon Chappell provides step-by-step instruction of all of the skills you need to become an accomplished guitar player! By simply watching the instructor onscreen and following along, you can learn to play songs — without reading music.

VHS - 75 Mins. $12.98
DVD - 75 Mins. $16.98

To Order Call: 1-800-546-1949

ANCHOR BAY ENTERTAINMENT

Distributed By
Anchor Bay Entertainment, Inc.
1699 Stutz Dr., Troy, MI 48084
© 2002 Anchor Bay Entertainment, Inc.